The First EASY-TO-SEE Needlepoint Workbook

OTHER BOOKS BY JOAN SCOBEY

Decorating with Needlepoint (with Marjorie Sablow)
Rugs and Wall Hangings (with Marjorie Sablow)
Needlepoint From Start to Finish (with Marjorie Sablow)
Rugmaking From Start to Finish (with Marjorie Sablow)
Celebrity Needlepoint (with Lee P. McGrath)
Do-It-All-Yourself Needlepoint (with Lee P. McGrath and Marjorie Sablow)
Creative Careers for Women (with Lee P. McGrath)
Gifts From Your Garden (with Norma Myers)
Gifts From Your Kitchen (with Norma Myers)

ALSO BY MARJORIE SABLOW

Making Silver Jewelry

The First EASY-TO-SEE Needlepoint Workbook

Joan Scobey and Marjorie Sablow

Rawson Associates Publishers, Inc.
New York

PHOTOGRAPHY CREDIT:

COLOR PLATES by Stephen T. Anderson, except for Roman Shade, Side Chairs, Headboard Panels, Child's Growth Chart, Christmas Stocking

Library of Congress Cataloging in Publication Data

Scobey, Joan.
The first easy-to-see needlepoint workbook.
Includes index.
1. Canvas embroidery. I. Sablow, Marjorie, joint author. II. Title.
TT778.C3S37 1977 746.4'4 76-43425 ISBN 0-89256-005-3

Published simultaneously in Canada by McClelland and Stewart, Ltd.
Manufactured in the United States of America

Designed by Evelyn O'Connor
First Edition

To Frieda and Sig

Acknowledgments

Whenever our call went out for volunteers to lend a hand with the stitching of projects, the hand that always appeared first with needle at the ready was Lillian Tucker's. With our thanks go our affection and gratitude.

We also want to acknowledge the help of other friends and colleagues, among them Judy Coulter, Joyce Helman, Evelyn O'Connor, Lenore Rosenbaum, Marilyn Schoenberger, and Debbie Slesinger, and not least, the enthusiastic support of Eleanor S. Rawson.

Contents

Before You Begin This Book

There is as much pleasure in the process of creating a piece of needlepoint as there is in the enjoyment of the completed work. The glorious colors of the wool, the comforting relaxation of rhythmically laying stitch on canvas, the texture of the growing needlework all delight during the creative process every bit as much as does the decorative impact and rewarding sense of permanence of the finished work.

For most people these pleasures carry no greater occupational hazard than perhaps an overabundance of pillows, but for some enthusiastic stitchers, small canvas mesh and fine needlework are uncomfortable to handle and may even cause eyestrain—reason enough to offer *The First Easy-To-See Needlepoint Workbook.*

This workbook brings together a number of concepts designed to make needlepointing as easy on the eyes as it is on the hands:

• A large-type, large-page, easy-reading format.

• The use of large-mesh canvas of five, seven, and ten holes to the inch.

• A wide variety of needlepoint projects, each with an original design on one of the large-mesh canvases, plus complete instructions for stitching and finishing.

• Many prefinished projects—photo album, picture frame, address book, tennis racquet cover, tote bag among them—that eliminate tedious sewing and finishing chores and display handcraft in professionally mounted items at reasonable cost.

• A workbook of designs, all of them "project-size" and scaled for large-mesh canvas. Some are complete compositions, others are design components to be arranged and assembled into new and entirely personal patterns. *All are meant to be traced right off the book page and used with any of the projects in the book.*

Whether or not you are quick of eye or nimble of finger, we hope *The First Easy-To-See Needlepoint Workbook* extends the creative fun of stitchery for needle enthusiasts and that its special appeal will commend it to a wider audience of men and children, athletes and gift givers, who may not yet know the pleasures of needlepoint.

PART I
Supplies and Techniques

Working in needlepoint requires very little special equipment in addition to the obvious canvas, yarn, and needles, which are described in detail below. These modest needs include two pairs of scissors—a small pointed pair for snipping yarn and a larger pair for cutting the canvas; inch-wide masking tape for binding the cut edges of the canvas; and an indelible marker for tracing the designs onto the canvas.

Blocking the finished needlepoint calls for a large sheet of paper, such as brown wrapping paper, on which to outline the project; a wooden or composition blocking board; and stainless steel T-pins or push pins for holding the canvas in shape on the board during blocking.

Finishing needlepoint projects occasionally requires all-purpose sewing needles and thread, plus white resin glue such as Elmer's Glue-All, Slomon's Sobo Glue, or Amco White Glue for protecting the edges of cut needlepoint and canvas, and for bonding the finished stitchery to porous materials. When special finishing supplies are called for, they are listed with the particular project under "Other Materials Needed."

CANVAS

There are three general types of needlepoint canvas—mono, penelope, and interlocking—which share many characteristics and differ primarily in their weaves. The horizontal and vertical threads of all three are usually made of cotton and are stiffened with sizing; they are fairly regularly spaced to form a grid on which the stitches are secured.

The size of each canvas is designated by the number of stitches that can be made on a linear inch; that is, on No. 10 canvas of each type ten stitches can be formed per linear inch (and one hundred stitches per square inch), on No. 5 canvas five stitches can be made per linear inch (and twenty-five stitches per square inch).

Mono canvas is formed by the intersections of single threads (see Figure 1) that are rigid enough to support the newly formed stitches as you lay them down on the canvas and that soften as you work, becoming nicely supple by the time you want to sew or mount the completed project. The canvas is usually white, which is easy on the eye and excellent for painting a design on. However, the single-thread canvas ravels easily when cut, making it unsuitable for certain projects.

Penelope canvas is formed by the intersections of two pairs of double threads (see Figure 2). Because these form a somewhat confusing grid on which to stitch and count threads and because the best penelope canvas is ecru or beige, penelope canvas is harder on the eye than other canvas weaves and is not recommended for this big-canvas needlepoint workbook.

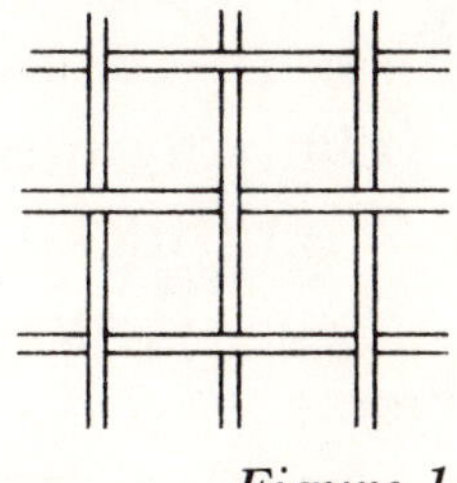

Figure 1

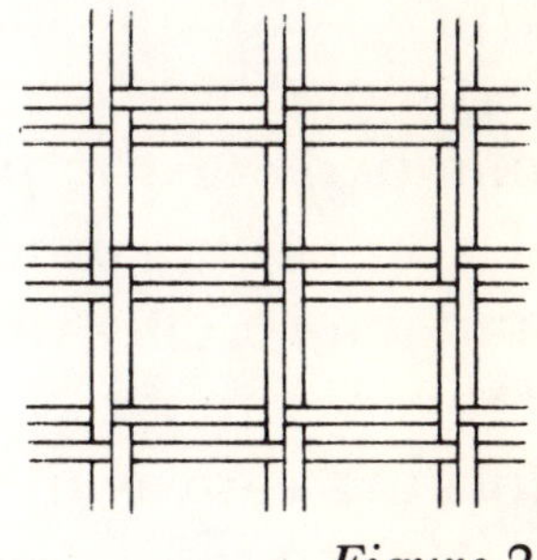

Figure 2

Interlocking canvas is formed when pairs of vertical threads are twisted around one or two horizontal threads to form a grid (see Figures 3 and 4).

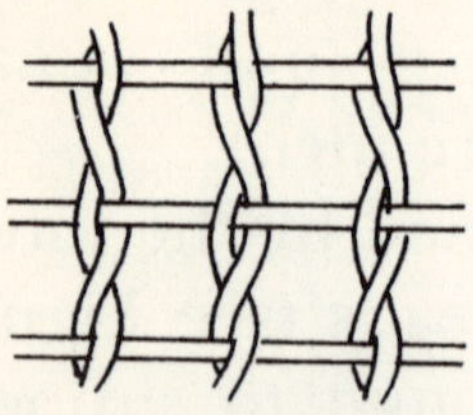

Figure 3

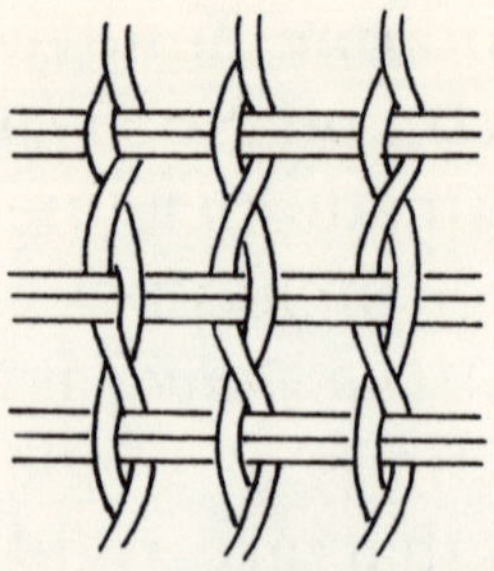

Figure 4

The resulting intersections of white threads are clearly defined and easy on the eye, and the interlocked double intersections resist raveling when cut, making the canvas invaluable for certain projects in which it is desirable to slit the canvas close to the needlepoint stitching. However, the interlocking canvas retains its stiffness even after having been worked, making it difficult to use in projects that require suppleness or hemmed edges.

All types of canvas are available in a variety of sizes, but the most appropriate sizes for big-canvas, easy-on-the-eye stitching are Nos. 5, 7, and 10 mono or interlocking canvas. (Note: No. 7 canvas is widely available in the penelope weave, which is not recommended for the projects in this book; if you cannot find the relatively new, and more elusive, No. 7 interlocking canvas, choose No. 5 or No. 10 interlocking canvas in its place.)

No. 10 canvas, with its one hundred stitches per square inch, can reproduce finer design details than No. 5 canvas, with only twenty-five stitches per square inch, but it will obviously take longer to work. For large projects such as rugs you may prefer the quickly-stitched larger-mesh canvas.

Designated for each of the projects in Part II are the type and size canvas that are most appropriate for the needlepoint design and for the finishing techniques used.

Note: You can stitch a design on a smaller-mesh canvas than the one suggested, but you cannot stitch it on a larger mesh without risking the loss of some of the design details.

YARNS

The best needlepoint yarn is made of wool with long smooth fibers and is mothproof and colorfast. Knitting worsted, although made of wool, has short fibers and lacks the durability necessary for most needlepoint projects.

Persian wool is made of three two-ply strands loosely twisted together which can be used as one thread or separated into its component strands, making it the most versatile of the needlepoint yarns. It is widely available from many companies and comes in hundreds of colors—often in five or six shades of the same color family. Because the Persian wool distributed by Paternayan Bros., Inc., is available at most needlepoint shops and comes in an extraordinary range of colors, it is used as the basis for the yarn estimates given with each project in the book.

Persian wool is sold in bulk by the skein, the ounce, and sometimes by the ½-ounce or by the thread, as well as in packages of 40 yards and 8 yards.

With the basketweave or continental stitch one thread (full triple strand) of Persian wool covers No. 10 canvas nicely; with the edging stitch one additional strand should be added to the regular three-strand thread for a total of four strands. On No. 7 canvas, use a double thread (six strands) of Persian wool with the basketweave or continental stitch, and add a strand or two (a total of seven or eight strands) for the edging stitch.

Tapestry wool is made of one tightly twisted four-ply thread that cannot be separated into strands. It is sold in 40- and 100-yard skeins in matched dye lots in over fifty colors. With the basketweave or continental stitch tapestry wool covers No. 10 canvas nicely and can be doubled for use on No. 7 canvas.

Rug wool is recommended for all projects stitched on No. 5 canvas. Pat-Rug wool, distributed by Paternayan Bros., Inc., is widely available at needlework shops and comes in a generous range of colors and color families, many of them coordinating with Paternayan Persian yarn. For these reasons Pat-Rug yarn is used as the basis for the yarn estimates given with each project stitched on No. 5 canvas.

YARN ESTIMATES

An estimate of yarn needs is given with each project based on Paternayan Persian or Pat-Rug yarns. These estimates are only general guides because your needs may vary with the wools of other manufacturers, with the tightness or looseness of individual stitching, and even with the color of the yarn because the plumpness (and thus the coverage) often varies with the yarn dye.

A test swatch, using a length of yarn stitched in the margin of your canvas, is the most reliable estimate of your yarn needs. Tabulate the number of stitches or the area covered by the length of yarn, then figure your total yarn needs from this swatch. Buy all your wool at the same time to ensure uniform yarn color; slight variations in color sometimes occur in different dye lots.

For your specific yarn calculations here is a miscellany of statistics.

- A common length—and a good working length—of both Paternayan Persian and Pat-Rug yarns is 32 inches. You will get this length by cutting a hank of yarn twice, once at each end.
- There are between forty-five and fifty 32-inch lengths of yarn in 1 ounce of Persian wool.
- On No. 10 canvas one 32-inch length of Persian yarn forms about eighty-five stitches, which will cover about ¾ square inch of canvas. One ounce of the yarn will cover about 32 square inches of No. 10 canvas.
- On No. 7 canvas a pair of 32-inch lengths of Persian yarn (the yarn is used double for proper coverage of the canvas mesh) forms about forty-five stitches, which will cover almost 1 square inch of canvas. One ounce of yarn will cover about 23 square inches of No. 7 canvas.
- There are about sixteen 32-inch lengths of yarn in 1 ounce of Pat-Rug wool.
- On No. 5 canvas one 32-inch length of rug yarn forms about thirty-eight stitches, which will cover approximately 1½ square inches of canvas. One ounce of the yarn will cover

about 24 square inches of No. 5 canvas.

NEEDLES

Tapestry needles are used for needlepoint. Their large eyes accommodate the yarn with a minimum of abrasion, and their blunt points pass easily through the canvas mesh without danger of piercing canvas thread or fingers.

On No. 10 canvas use No. 17, 18, or 19 needle; on No. 7 canvas use No. 15 needle; on No. 5 canvas use No. 13 needle.

PREPARING CANVAS FOR WORK

Each project specifies the mesh and the dimensions of the canvas needed. You will notice that, in general, canvas is cut about 2 inches larger all around than the finished project (except, of course, in prefinished items, where the canvas is already cut to size).

Always cut the canvas in a square or rectangle—no matter if the finished project is a circle, triangle, or odd shape—because you will need the straight opposing sides of a rectangle when you come to block the finished needlepoint. And try to plan the canvas layout so that the selvage runs up and down.

Protect the cut edges of the canvas by binding them with inch-wide masking tape. Many instructions call for a row of machine stitching or a line of glue to protect the canvas edges during subsequent finishing procedures, but these do not take the place of the tape binding, which protects the canvas during stitching.

After you have bound the edges of the canvas, prepare a "template" for subsequent blocking of the finished needlepoint: Lay the canvas on a large sheet of paper and outline the canvas—not just the design area—with an indelible marker; draw register lines at the four corners of the canvas and at the center of each side from the tape to the paper template (see Figure 5) so that during blocking

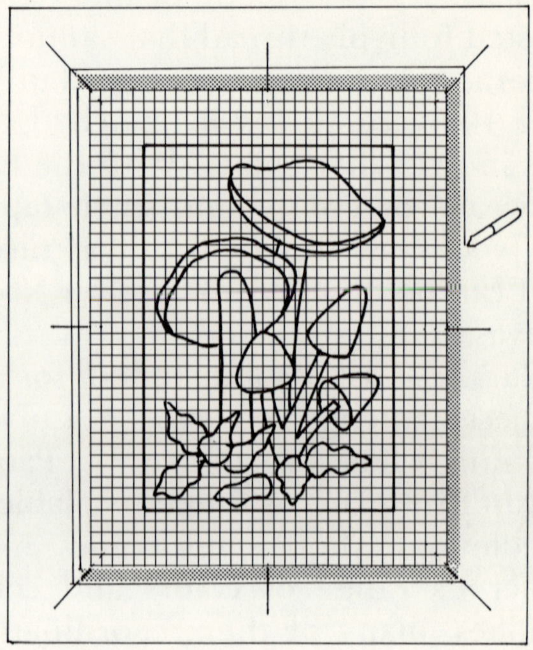

Figure 5

you can return the canvas to its original shape. If you are stitching a prefinished canvas, before you start to work outline the object on a piece of paper to use as the blocking guide (see Figure 6).

Set aside your paper template until you are ready to block the needlework.

USING THE DESIGNS

Many of the designs in this book are presented in their "project size," that is, they need no further enlarging or extending before they can be traced

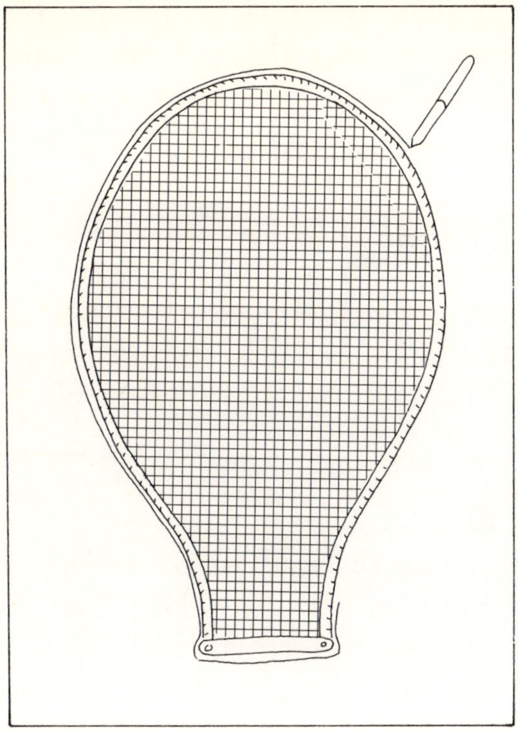

Figure 6

straight from the pages of the book and stitched (see instructions for tracing designs).

A few of the designs need to be repeated or extended—although not enlarged—during the tracing (see instructions for extending designs). And a few others must be enlarged before use with such large-scale projects as the rug and the wastebasket (see instructions for enlarging designs).

All the designs are presented in the same way: Black outlines delineate different areas of color; the colors themselves are designated by number or by a repeated pattern of lines or figures and are coordinated with a color key on the design page or in the text accompanying the design. Moreover, every design—even those that are now project-size—has an underlying gray grid that can be used to enlarge the design; if you are simply tracing the design and not enlarging it, ignore the grid.

Tracing designs. The majority of designs will be used straight from the pages of the book without further enlarging or extending. The easiest way to transfer them to canvas is to trace them directly from the book. Center the cut and taped canvas over the design in the book and simply trace the design onto the canvas with an indelible marker (see Figure 7). Go over all the dark lines that delineate separate areas of color, ignoring the gray grid; the design will show through the canvas clearly. Use a light touch so that the ink from the marker doesn't flood the design page; however, a little ink on the tracing lines won't harm the book.

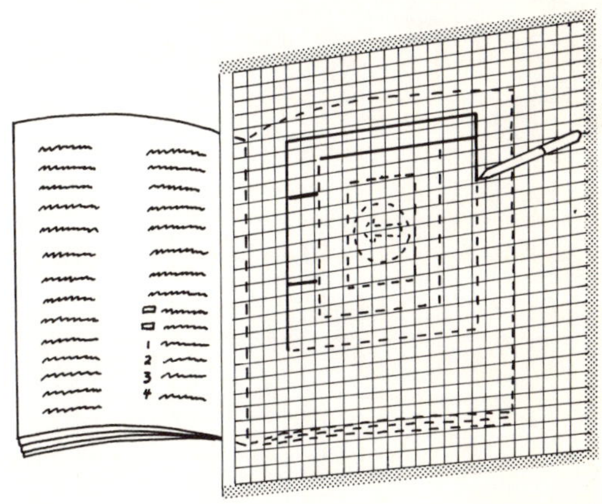

Figure 7

You may feel more comfortable transferring a project-size design from the book to a piece of tracing paper first (see Figure 8) and then laying the cut and taped canvas over the tracing paper for the final tracing onto canvas with an indelible marker (see Figure 9).

Extending designs. Sometimes a design needs to be repeated but not enlarged, and there are various ways to do this. You can move the same tracing to a contiguous spot under the

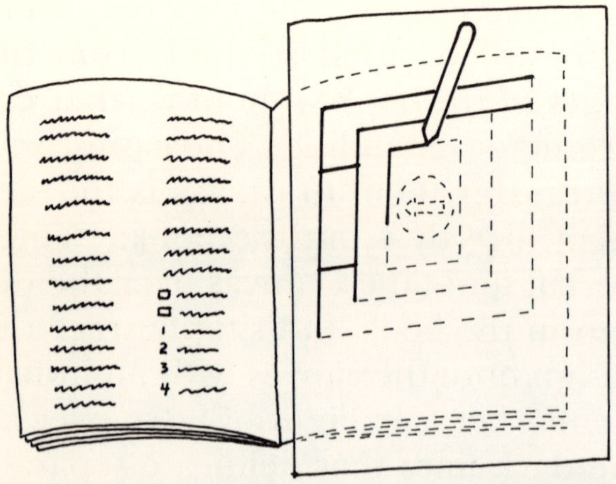

Figure 8

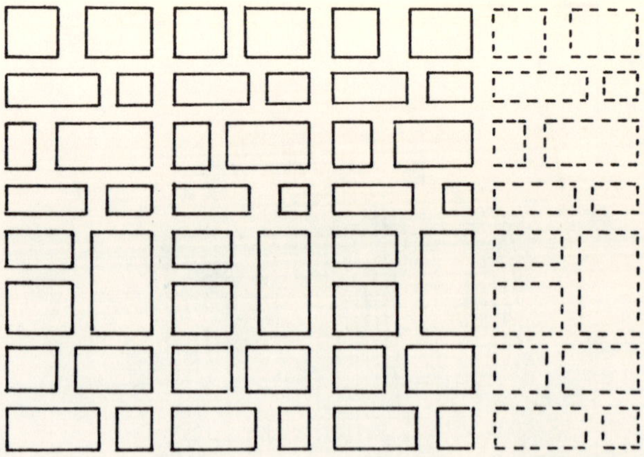

Figure 11

canvas and trace all or part of it again (see Figures 10 and 11). This is the way you would trace a small repeat pattern (see Figure 12) or a repeat-background design (see Figure 13).

Or you might want to select specific elements from a design and repeat

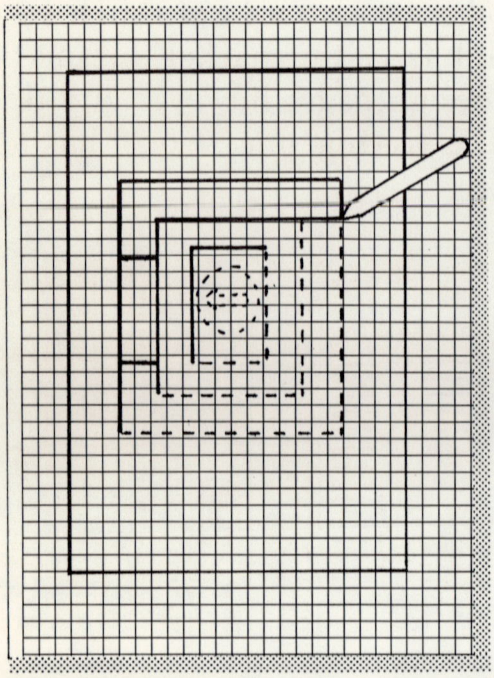

Figure 9

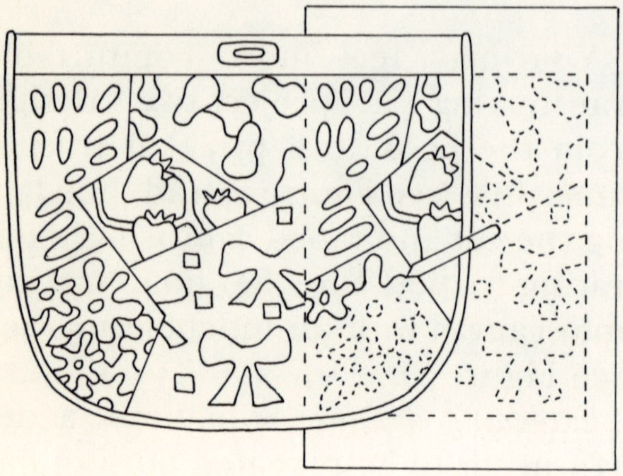

Figure 10

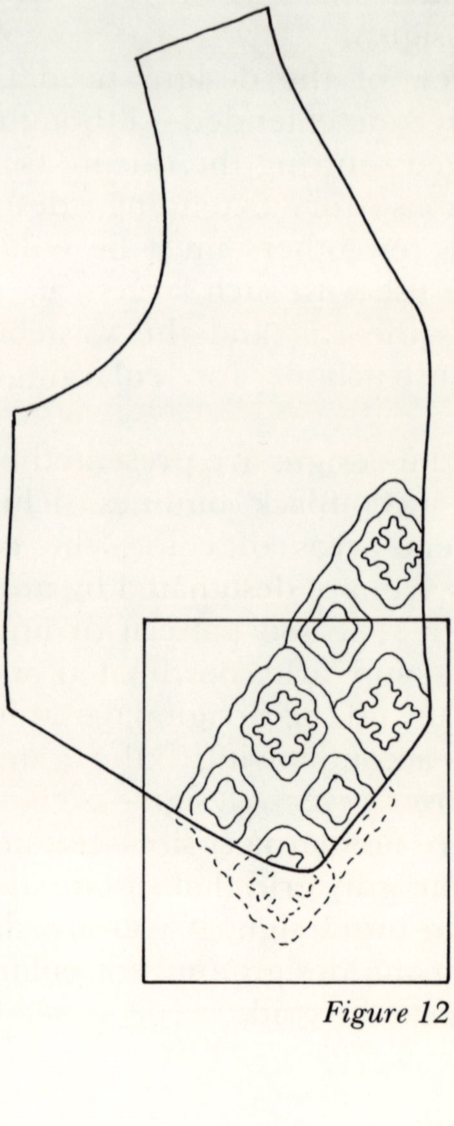

Figure 12

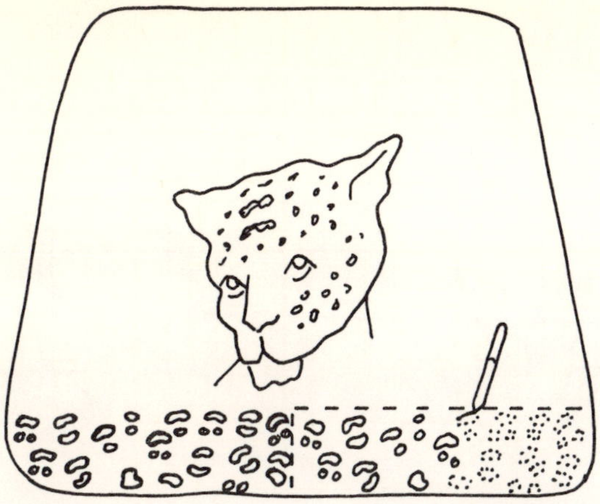

Figure 13

them in a different arrangement to extend the design area (see Figure 14).

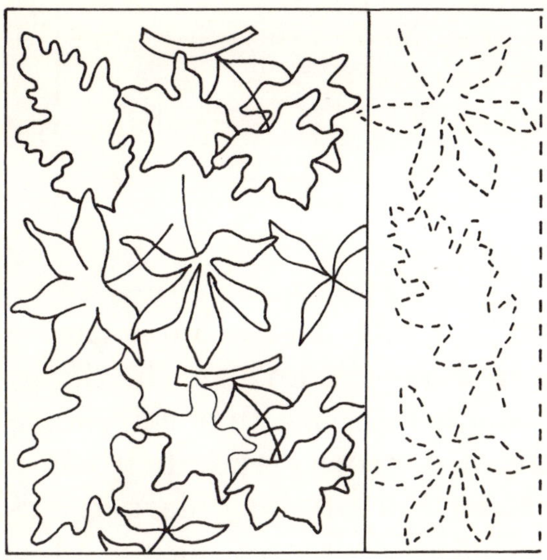

Figure 14

Or you may want to extend the pattern by "flopping" the entire design on the tracing paper (see Figure 15). You can flop a design any number of times to cover any size area you wish. This is an effective way of reversing designs and of creating continuous patterns (see Figure 16).

Enlarging designs. For a few big projects the designs themselves must be enlarged. To do this you will use the gray grid that appears on each design page. First mark the outline of your finished project on a separate

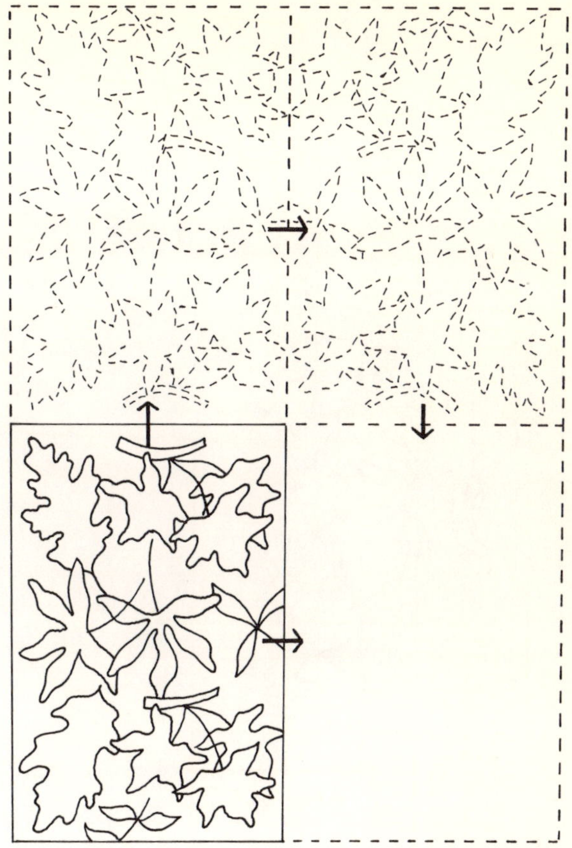

Figure 15

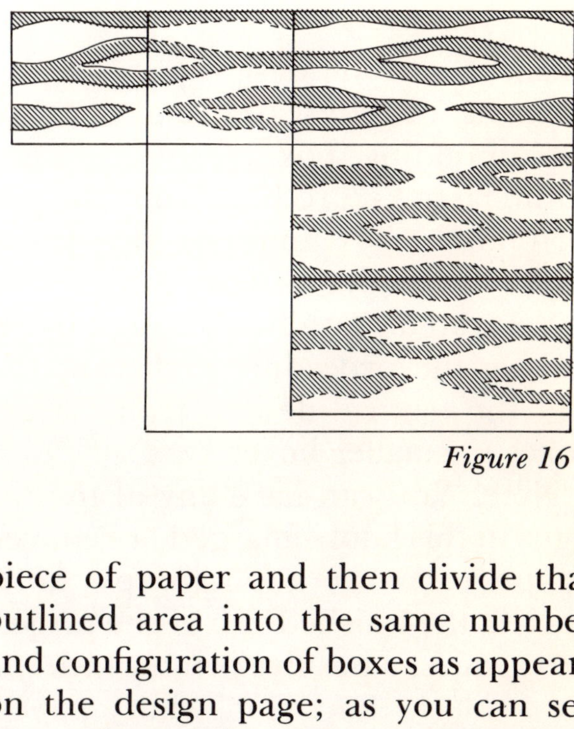

Figure 16

piece of paper and then divide that outlined area into the same number and configuration of boxes as appears on the design page; as you can see from Figure 17a, that design page is divided into seven horizontal and nine vertical squares, so the enlarged outline is divided into the same number of squares laid out in the same configuration. Working from each

Figure 17a

Figure 17b

small box of the design page, reproduce its contents freehand in each corresponding box of the enlarged outline (see Figure 17b). Copy the pattern box by box until you have transcribed the entire design.

You can also reduce a design by reversing the procedure and transcribing the entire design from larger boxes to smaller boxes.

Note: You can have any of the designs in this book enlarged or reduced by photostat at a photocopy store. Specify the finished size of the project and request a positive print, which will have black lines on white paper; otherwise you will receive a negative print.

Cropping designs. Sometimes you will want to use a design that doesn't fit the special size of your own custom project; this is likely to happen with a chair, for instance. In most cases you will first have to enlarge the design in the book to a size that will *encompass* your own project and then use only that portion of the enlarged design that falls within the outline of your special project (see Figure 18).

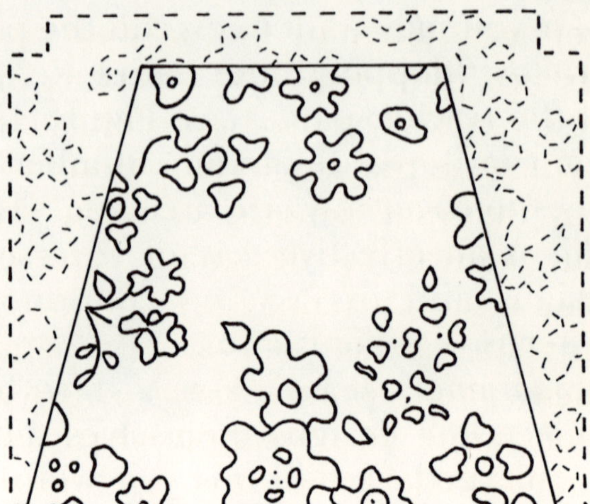

Figure 18

FROM DESIGN TO CANVAS

When you put the design on canvas—whether you trace it directly from the book or trace it first onto paper or enlarge it on paper—you should center the canvas over the design and then trace that design onto the canvas with an indelible marker. Use a neutral color; a dark marker will show through light-colored yarn. And test the colorfastness of all markers to both water and dry-cleaning solutions—even those that claim to be indelible.

Graphed designs. A few of the geometric designs, as well as the alphabets and numbers, are presented on graphs so that they can be worked with accuracy. Each box on a graph represents one stitch.

When you are planning a monogram or a date or are working with letters or numbers, plan that part of your design on graph paper, including the spaces as well as the figures.

COLOR KEY

As you can see, a color key accompanies every project design. Moreover, a number of the finished projects are photographed in color, and these can also be used as color guides. If you want to carry a color guide with you, tie small lengths of yarn onto your canvas to designate different color areas. Or paint the whole design on your canvas with acrylic paints. These paints are available in a wide color range at art supply shops, are water-soluble when wet and water-resistant when they have dried, and their use doesn't require any special skill.

STITCHING

All the projects in the book call for the basketweave stitch, which is recommended for its superior characteristics: It can be worked on any type of canvas; it forms a tightly woven surface on the canvas that is durable enough to withstand heavy wear, pliant enough for easy finishing; and it will not distort the canvas too much.

The continental stitch looks like the basketweave and is an acceptable substitute, even though it pulls the canvas severely out of shape, requiring careful and often repeated blocking. It is most useful for outlining odd-shaped areas of design.

The edging stitch is used for finishing projects on interlocking canvas.

Basketweave. The excellent qualities of this stitch stem from the diagonal sequence in which the stitches are laid down on the canvas (see Figure 19); this creates the crisscross interlocking pattern on the back that gives the stitch its name (and also the false impression that the stitch is difficult to master).

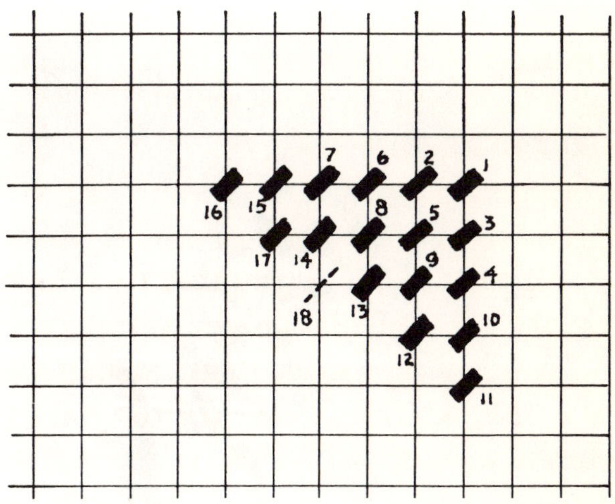

Figure 19

Start the sequence of stitches in the upper-right corner of the work area with your needle behind the canvas. Bring the needle up through the mesh marked *1* and down through the mesh marked *2;* follow the numbering in Figures 20 and 21, always bringing the needle up from the back of the canvas through the odd-numbered mesh and pushing it down through the even-numbered mesh. After a few rows you will see the logic and rhythm of the diagonal sequence of stitches.

Note: If you are left-handed, start stitching at the lower-left corner of the work area and turn the diagram upside down for the correct fingering.

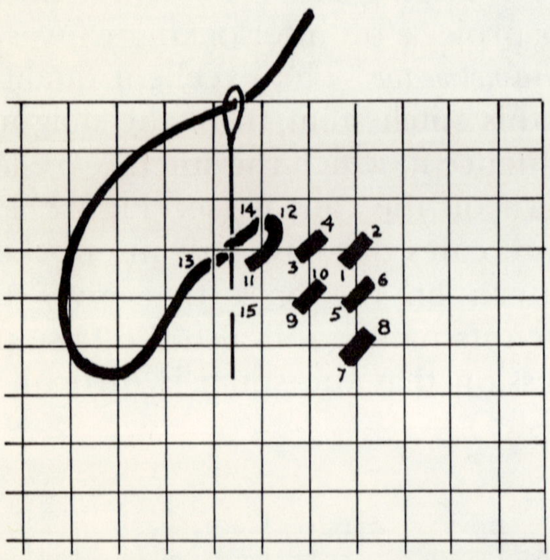

Figure 20

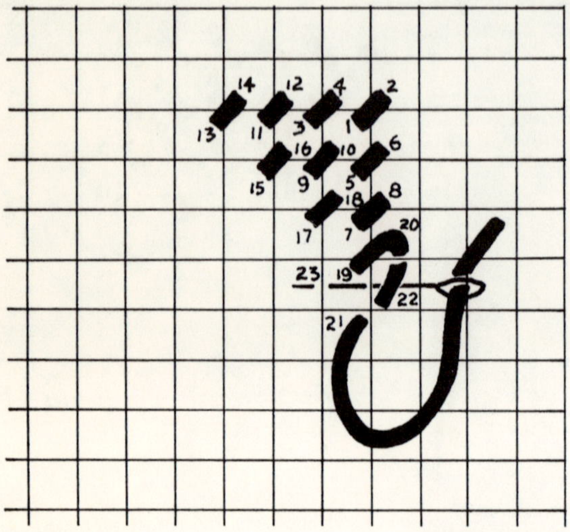

Figure 21

Continental. The popularity of this stitch derives from the ease of forming the stitches in horizontal rows (see Figure 22).

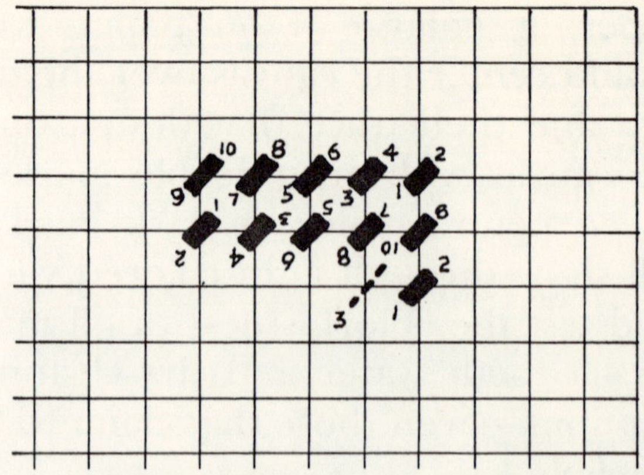

Figure 22

Start the sequence of stitches in the upper-right corner of the work area with your needle behind the canvas. Bring the needle up through the mesh marked *1* and down through the mesh marked *2;* follow the fingering in Figure 22, always bringing the needle up from the back of the canvas through the odd-numbered mesh and pushing it down through the even-numbered mesh. When you have worked the stitch across one row, turn the canvas upside down and stitch the next row from right to left. Try to keep all your stitches somewhat loose to reduce the tension of the yarn on the canvas that, in turn, causes the distortion.

Note: If you are left-handed, start stitching at the lower-left corner of the work area; work the first row from left to right, then turn the canvas upside down and work the return row from left to right as well.

Edging. The cut edges of interlocking canvas are nicely finished with the edging stitch. Because it includes the outermost row of stitching in the design area, the edging stitch must be anticipated during work.

After the design has been stitched and blocked (see page 14), carefully cut the canvas one row outside the existing needlepoint along all edges, leaving one thread all around. Work the edging stitch over the cut canvas, including in each stitch the outer unstitched canvas thread and the last actual needlepoint stitch (see Figure 23). When you come to a corner, make three or more edging stitches in the corner mesh in order to cover it adequately (see Figure 23).

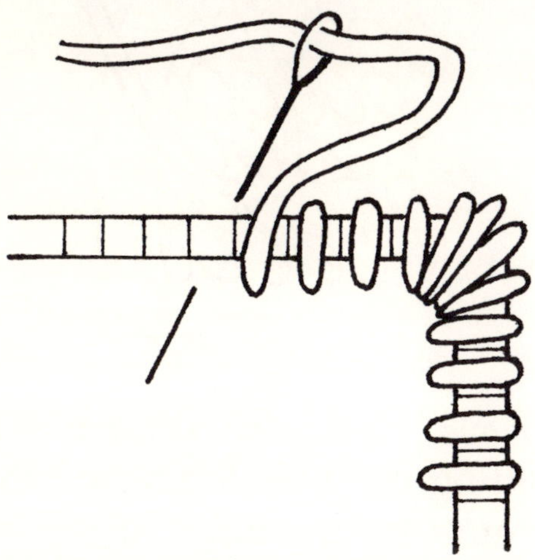

Figure 23

Note: Work the edging stitch in the same weight yarn you used for the project; however, if, as you work, you find that the canvas edge is showing through the edging stitches, add another strand (not a full thread) to your needle.

STITCHING REMINDERS

A working length of yarn should be about 1 yard; cut a skein of Paternayan Persian or Pat-Rug yarn twice and you'll have handy 32-inch lengths.

Thread the needle by doubling one end of yarn over the point of the needle, withdrawing the needle, and inserting the tightly doubled yarn through the needle's eye.

Start stitching a length of yarn by leaving a 1-inch-long tail at the back of the canvas, which you should catch in the back of the next several stitches.

End a length of yarn by running the last inch or two through the backs of the contiguous stitches.

Correct any overtwisted yarn (threads tend to become tightly twisted as you work) by periodically letting the needle dangle freely from the canvas. This will ensure plump stitches and proper coverage of the canvas.

Stitch major design areas first; tight stitching tends to draw in the canvas threads, contracting the overall dimensions, and you may have to add one or more rows to the background.

Outline complicated shapes with consecutive continental stitches worked horizontally, vertically, or diagonally from right to left and from top to bottom (see Figure 24). When you come to a shape that is above or to the right of your yarn, turn the canvas upside

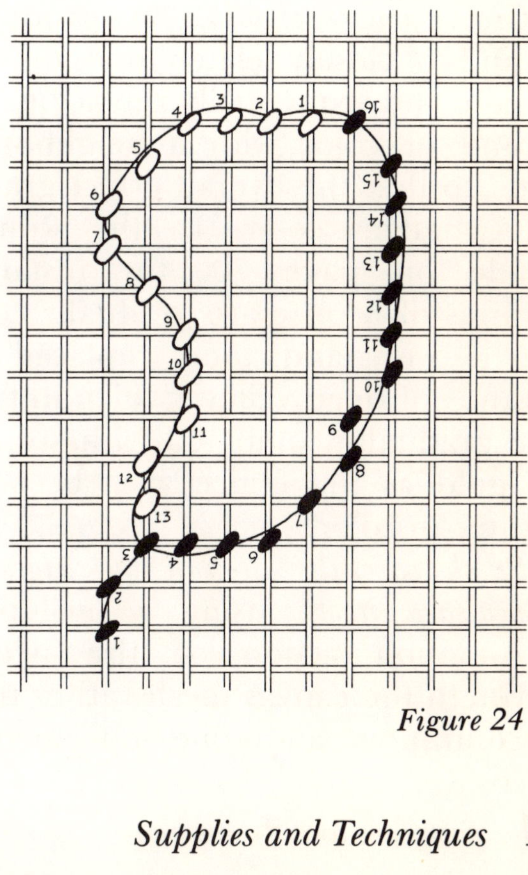

Figure 24

down so that the shape to be outlined will be to the left and below your needle (see dark stitches and upside-down numbers in Figure 24).

Tweed areas of color by combining strands of two different colored yarns in your needle (see Figure 25); two sharply different colors will create a "salt and pepper" look, colors closer in tone will appear more subtle and shaded.

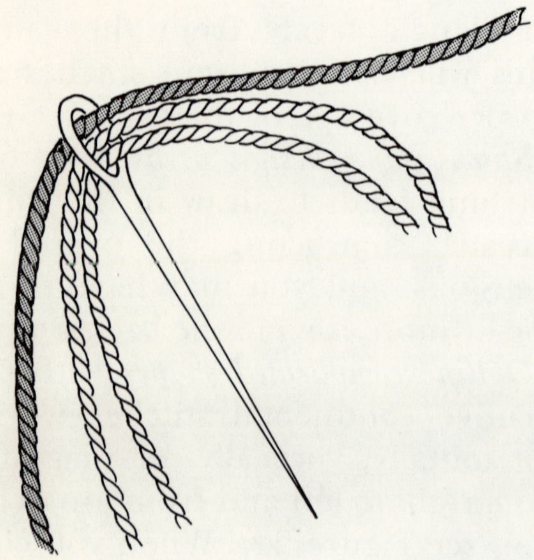

Figure 25

Create ombre shading by grouping strands of closely related tones in your needle and sequentially replacing one strand of color with a neighboring tone so that the overall effect gradually changes color. In the Roman shade on page 76, for instance, strands of bronze are gradually combined with and then replaced by strands of deep yellow, which in turn are gradually combined with strands of gold as the entire area becomes lighter in color.

Stitch carefully around the edges of prefinished items, using a push/pull, two-motion action of the needle through the canvas mesh rather than a continuous all-in-one movement—especially with the stitches that you tuck under the binding (see Figure 26). This will avoid excess strain on the canvas where it is sewn into the binding.

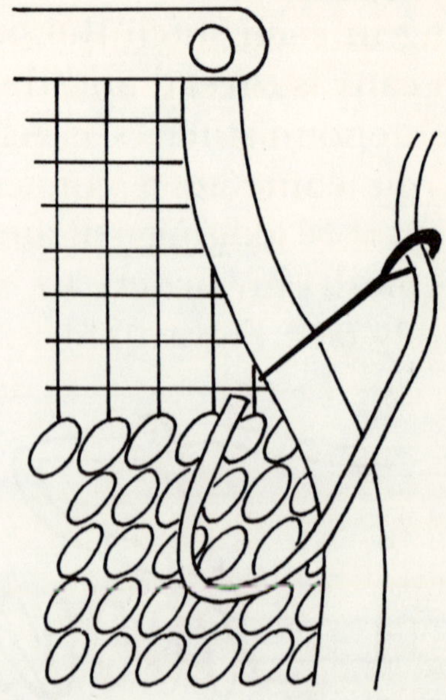

Figure 26

Remove unwanted stitches by unthreading the needle and pulling the yarn out with the point of the needle; never retrace the path of the yarn with the threaded needle.

BLOCKING

Every piece of needlepoint should be blocked after stitching. Even in the unlikely circumstance that the canvas itself has not been pulled out of shape during work, blocking gives the surface stitching a nicely smooth finish.

Use a blocking board made of a soft wood such as pine or a dense composition board like wallboard, into which you can push the blocking tacks or pins with relative ease.

The first step in blocking is to pin or tape to the board the large paper with its canvas outline that you set aside at the beginning of work.

Now roll the needlepoint with its taped canvas edges in a damp towel until the canvas is pliant but still retains some body; however, don't soak the needlework because overwatering will turn the canvas threads limp, thus making it more difficult to handle the canvas on the blocking board.

Lay the dampened needlepoint face down on the canvas outline now tacked to the blocking board, and match the register marks at the two top corners and in the middle of the top edge (see Figure 27). Through the

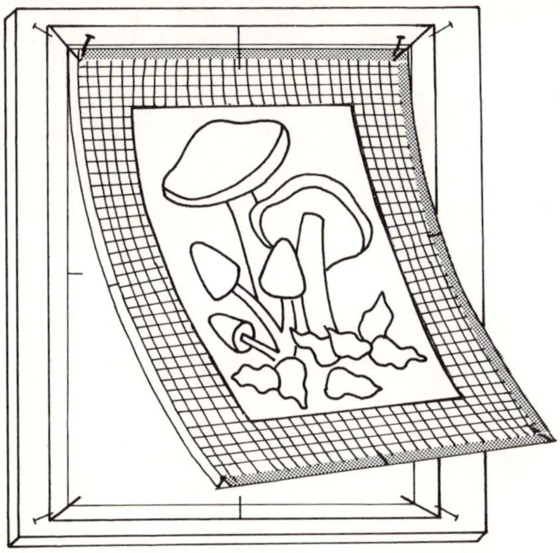

Figure 27

taped canvas edge secure the top corners with any rustproof tacks, such as stainless steel T-pins. Draw the bottom two corners of the now pliant needlepoint toward their corresponding corners on the outlined paper. When all the register marks on the tape match the register marks on the outline, tack the taped edges and selvage of the canvas at 1-inch intervals (see Figure 28).

If you have to redampen the needlepoint during blocking, spray it with warm water or with a steam iron. If a severely distorted canvas resists blocking, you may have to tack the two bot-

Figure 28

tom corners several times as you gradually pull it into conformity with the outline on the blocking board.

Once the needlepoint has been tacked in position, let it dry flat for a few days. Even when it has completely dried, leave it tacked on the board until you are ready to finish the project.

Blocking a prefinished needlepoint project calls for a slightly different technique since there are no taped canvas edges to hold the tacks:

Roll the needlepoint in a damp towel if you can, but if the backing fabric or zippers make this difficult, spray the needlework well with warm water or with a steam iron.

Lay the dampened needlepoint face down on the blocking board over the outline of the finished item, matching the top of the project with the corresponding portion of the outline. Through the mesh at the edge of the canvas, right next to the binding, tack the needlepoint to the blocking board, taking care not to penetrate either the canvas threads or the needlepoint stitches (see Figure 29).

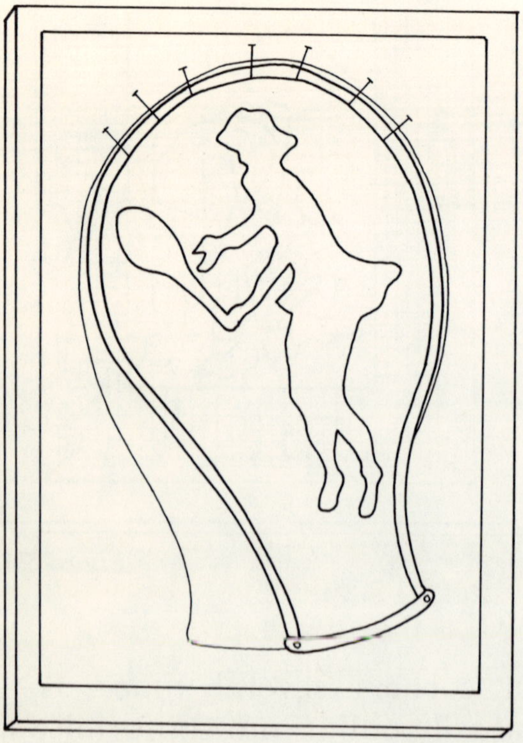

Figure 29

Following the instructions above, pull the needlepoint and its prefinished binding into conformity with the outline on the blocking board, then insert the blocking pins carefully through the canvas mesh every inch or so (see Figure 30). Leave the blocked piece in a horizontal position to dry for a few days.

MITERING CORNERS

Some projects call for mitered corners as part of the finishing. This procedure is always done in the same manner after the needlepoint has been blocked.

Sew a row of machine stitching on the excess canvas about ½ inch out from the needlepoint.

Cut the excess canvas away on all sides to within 1½ inches of the nee-

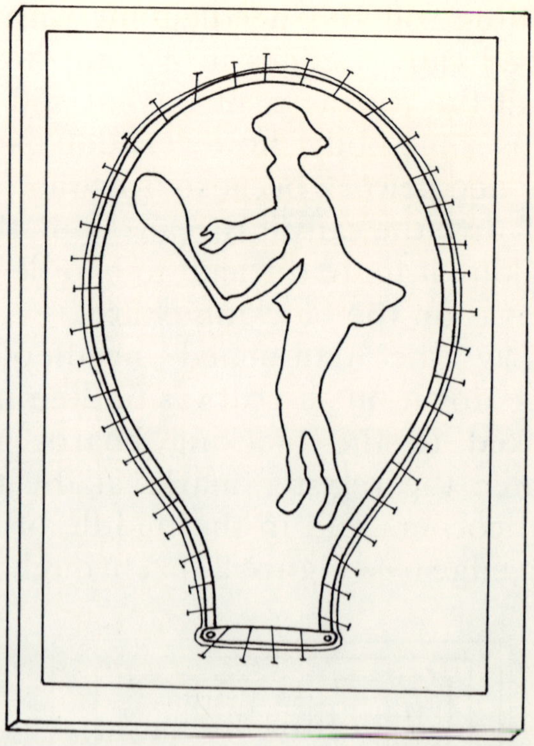

Figure 30

dlepoint, and cut the corners diagonally to within ½ inch of the stitching (see Figure 31).

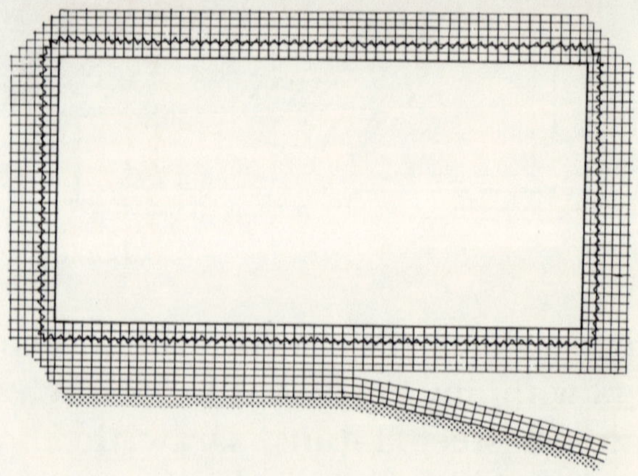

Figure 31

For each corner, follow these directions:

Place the needlepoint face down on your work surface. Turn back the diagonal edge to the corner stitch (see Figure 32). Then turn back one side adjoining the corner, pulling the canvas trimly over the back of the needlepoint (see Figure 33). Repeat for the other side adjoining the corner to complete the miter, and whip the abutting mitered edges together (see Figure 34).

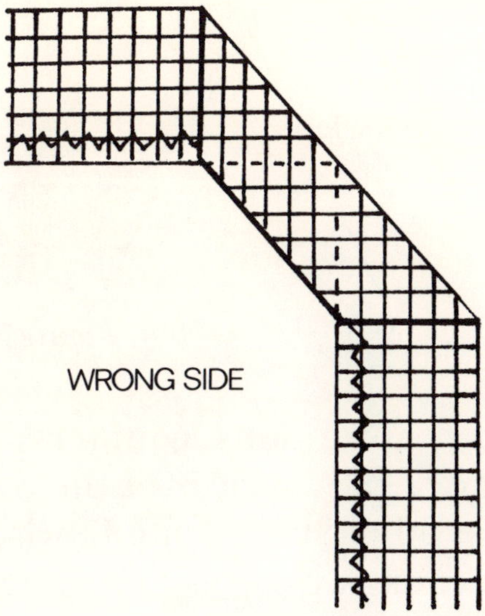

Figure 32

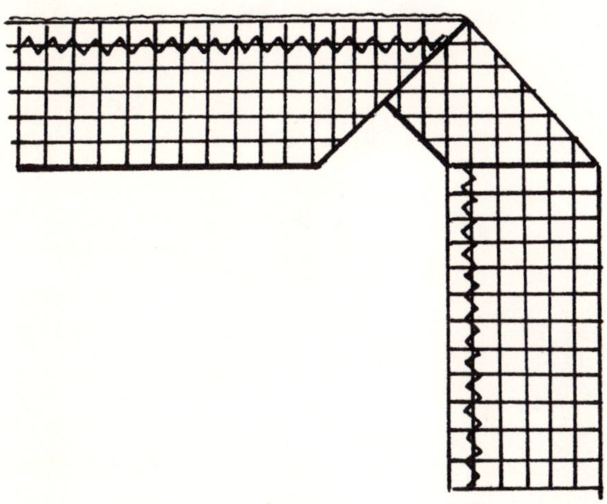

Figure 33

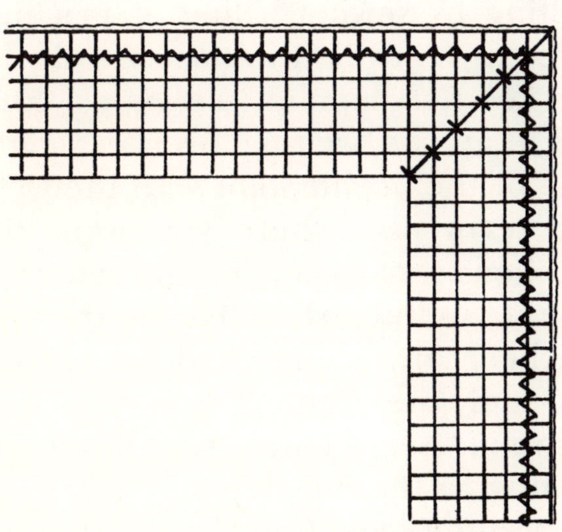

Figure 34

When all the corners have been mitered, sew the canvas "hem" to the back of the needlepoint with heavy-duty thread (see Figure 35).

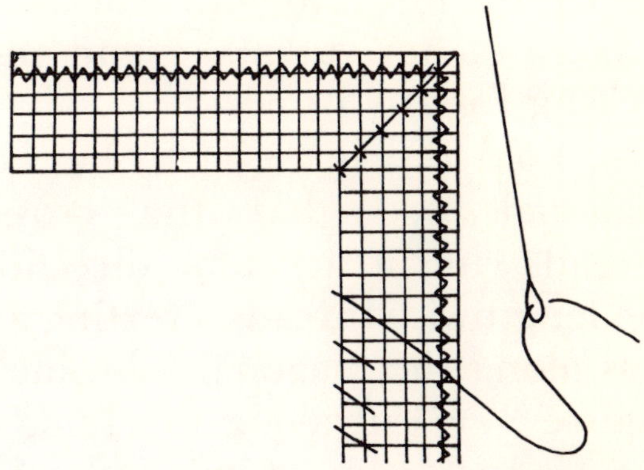

Figure 35

Note: If you want to miter over a stiff backing such as Masonite or a board, center the board over the back of the needlepoint and follow the instructions given above for each corner. As you whip the abutting corner edges together into the miter, you may want to hold the canvas in place temporarily with strips of masking tape (see Figure 36). As you can see, your needlepoint must be generous enough to cover the depth of the backing board as well as its face.

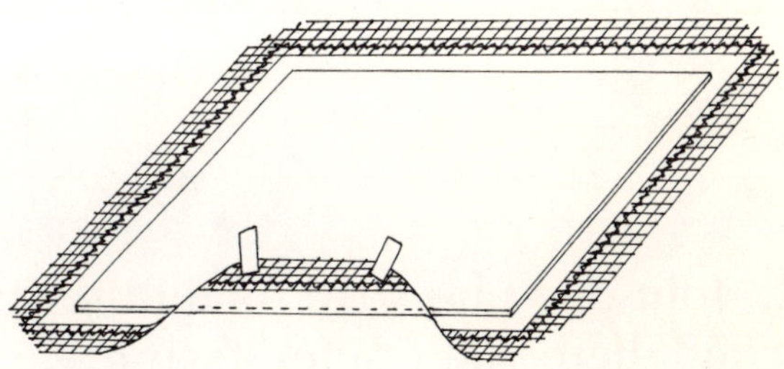

Figure 36

WELTING

Many projects call for welting to provide a finished edge to the needlepoint, and in each instance commercial welting is certainly acceptable. Sometimes, however, you may not be able to locate welting of just the right color or material, or you may prefer to make your own welting out of the fabric of the backing or the boxing strip in order to lend an incomparably handsome finish to your work.

Here is how to make and mount welting for any project:

1. Fold the material to be welted diagonally so that the crosswise threads run in the same direction as the lengthwise threads, creating a true bias along the diagonal fold line (see Figure 37). Cut along the fold, then cut 1½-inch-wide strips of the fabric parallel to the fold.

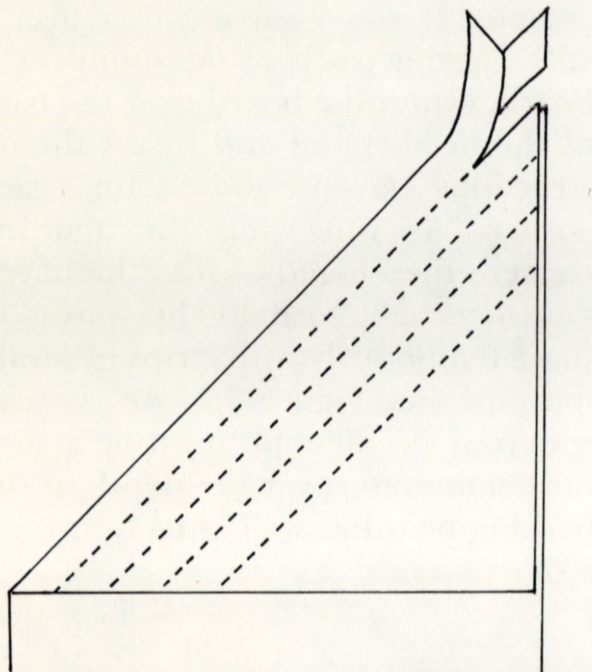

Figure 37

2. Join one bias strip to another by placing their right sides facing each other and seaming their short ends together (see Figure 38). Join the strips into one continuous piece the length of your required welting.

Note: One square yard of fabric produces about 24 yards of 1½-inch-wide bias strips.

3. Lay the pieced bias strip face down, and along the center place cotton cording (this is commonly

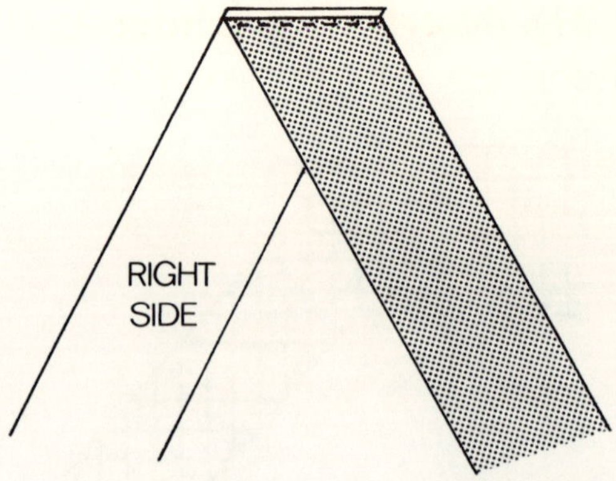

Figure 38

available at notions counters). Fold one side of the fabric over the cording and the other half of the fabric, then sew a seam as close as you can to the cording, using the zipper foot of the sewing machine (see Figure 39).

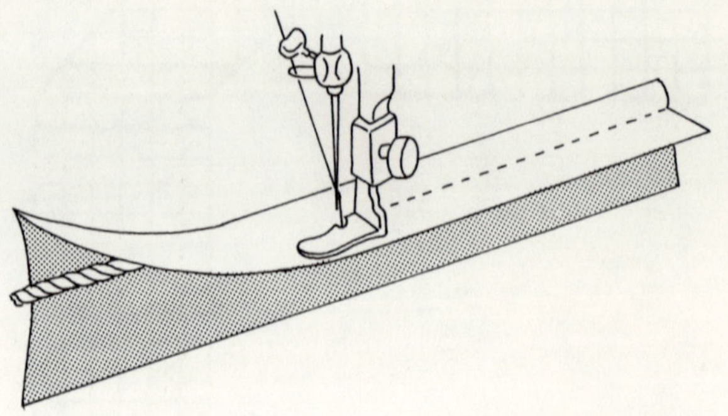

Figure 39

4. Prepare the needlepoint for welting by sewing a line of machine stitching on the canvas just outside the blocked needlepoint (see Figure 40).

5. Lay the welting over the right side of the needlepoint with the welting seam just where you want the finished seam to be, and the raw edge of the welting strip facing the unstitched canvas edge and the corded head of the welting over the needlepoint (see Figure 40). Baste the welting to the needlepoint right over the welting seam (see Figure 40), then seam over the basting with the zipper foot of the sewing machine (see Fig-

ure 41). Notch the welting at curves and corners (see Figure 41).

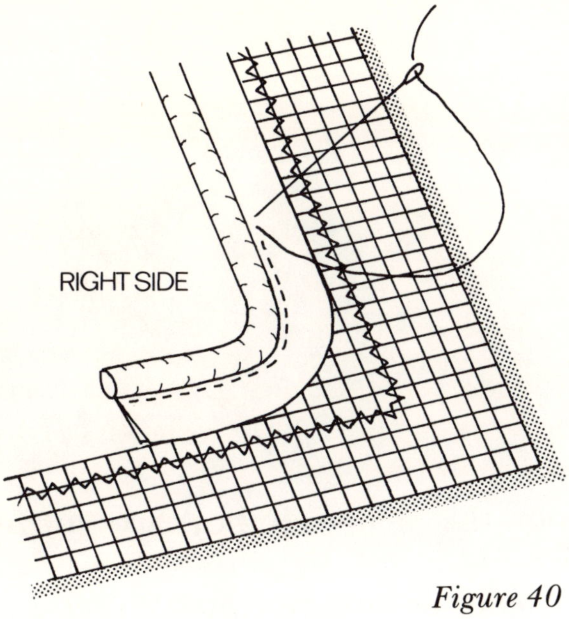

Figure 40

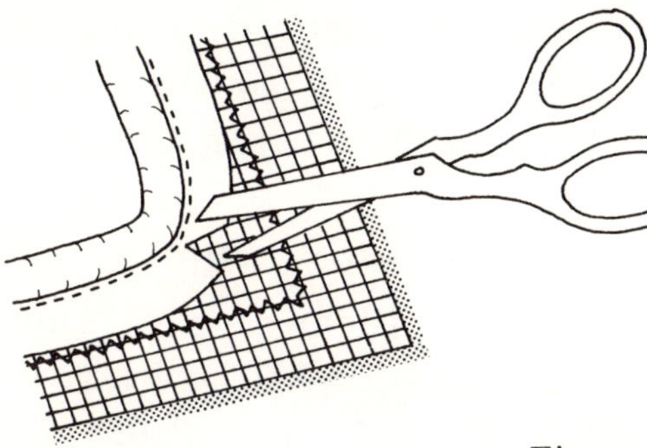

Figure 41

6. To join two ends of welting where they meet, stop basting and seaming the welting to the needlepoint 2 inches short of the planned join; snip the welting 1 inch past the intended join (see Figure 42). Open

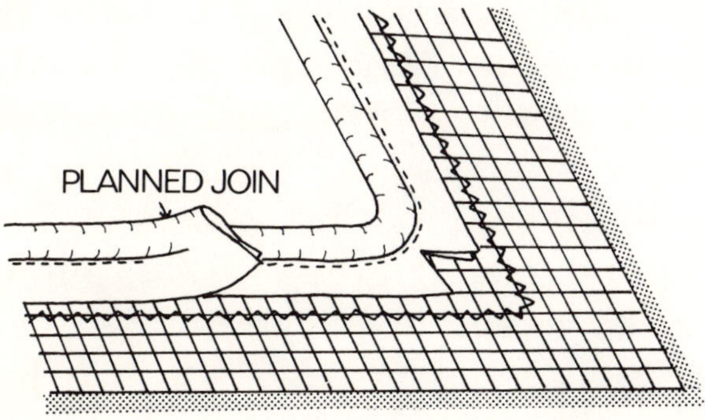

Figure 42

up the last inch of the welting seam on the end you just cut and cut 1 inch off the now exposed cording (see Figure 43). You can see that the cut cording will neatly abut the other end of the welting at the desired join.

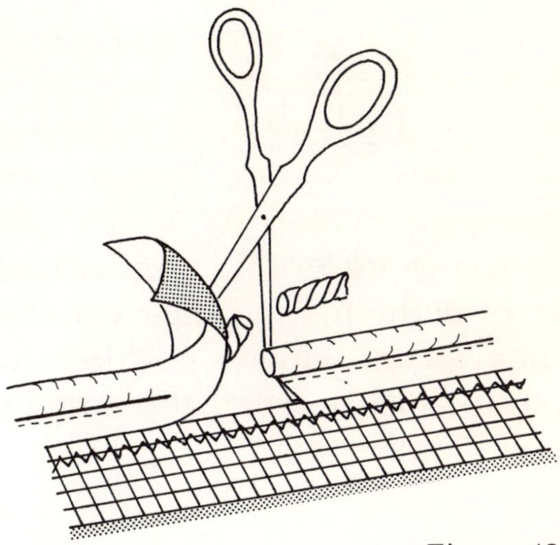

Figure 43

Make a ¼-inch "hem" at the short end of the open welting strip (see Figure 44). Tuck the open welting strip fabric around both the cording and the welting to complete the join.

Note: To keep the welting join as inconspicuous as possible, start the welting at the back or the bottom of your project.

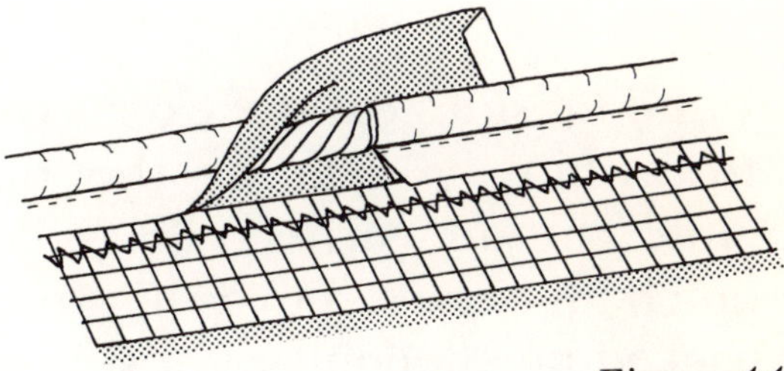

Figure 44

7. To turn the welted needlepoint into a pillow or cushion, lay the backing fabric face down over the needlepoint and welting; the right sides of both will be together (see Figure 45). Baste the backing fabric to the welted needlepoint along the welting

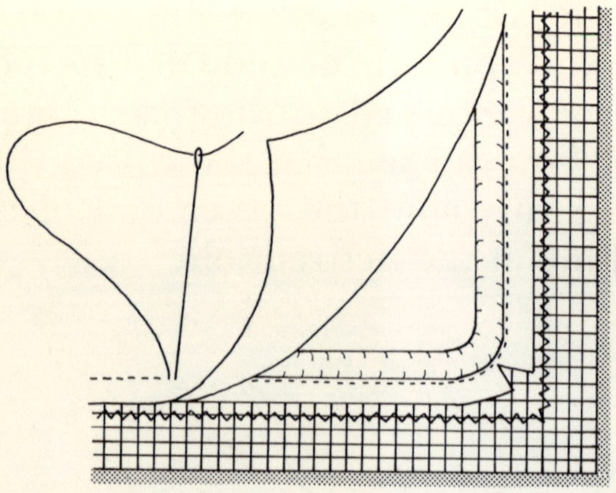

Figure 45

seam (see Figure 45), then machine stitch over the basting. Leave an 8-to-10-inch seam open in the back through which to stuff the inner pillow (see Figure 46).

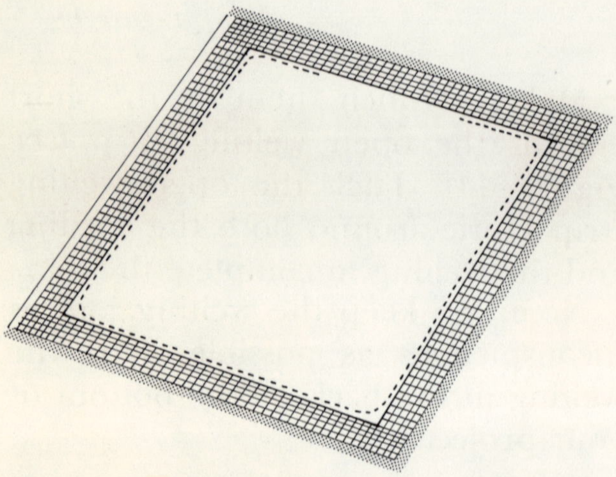

Figure 46

Around all sides cut the excess canvas to within ½ inch of the needlepoint; cut all corners diagonally and notch all curves. Turn the welted and backed needlepoint right side out through the open seam, insert the inner pillow, and blindstitch the opening (see Figure 47).

INNER PILLOWS

All pillows, cushions, bolsters, and pads derive at least some of their style

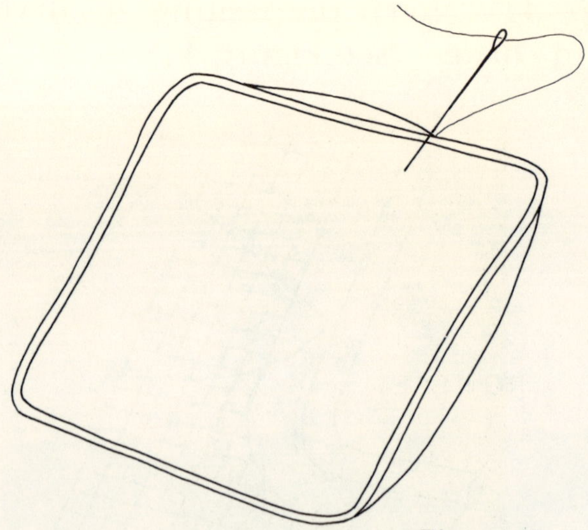

Figure 47

from the material they are stuffed with.

Clean, shipshape lines come with foam rubber cut to the full dimensions of your project in thicknesses ranging from 1 inch for slim pads to 12 or more inches for tailored hassocks.

Invitingly plump cushions come from soft and squashy inner pillows cut slightly smaller than your project and well filled with shredded foam rubber, polyester fiberfill, Dacron, or down. Make these inner pillows of muslin or similar fabric, stuff them well—especially in the corners—through a 6-inch opening in the seam, then blindstitch the seam opening; you need not turn the inner pillow right side out since it will not be seen (see Figure 48).

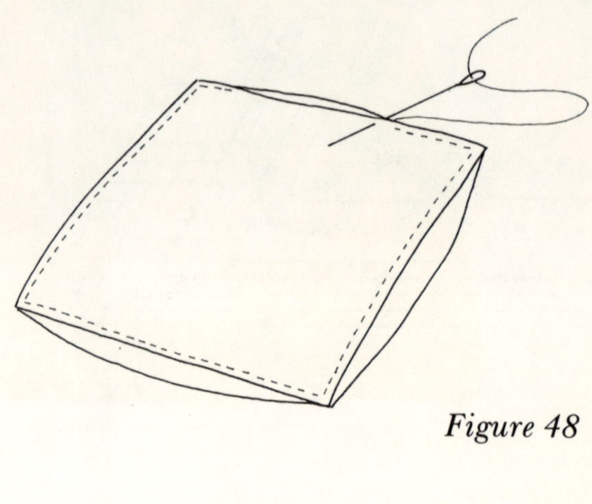

Figure 48

Shoulder Bag, page 110

Vest for a Man, page 117

Oriental Rug, page 94

Roman Shade, page 76

Side Chair, page 81

Side Chair, page 81

Address Book, page 47

Crib Gym, page 26

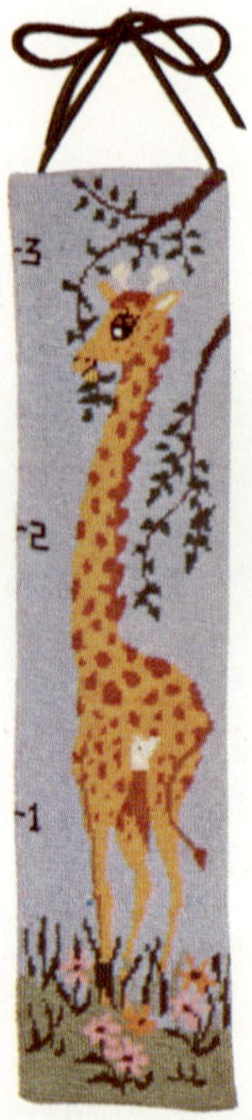

Child's Growth Chart, page 49

Christmas Stocking, page 144

Baby Carriage Cover, page 137

Headboard Panels, page 63

Christmas Tree Ornaments, page 149

PART II
Projects

Owl Puppet

A bird in the hand—in this case an owl in the guise of a puppet—is worth two on the wing, especially if you know a youngster who enjoys the make-believe world of pretending. This gaily colored owl could relay a bedtime story from parent to enthralled child or could happily become an alter ego for anyone who gives a hoot about playacting.

Stitch: Basketweave; edging.

Canvas: No. 10 interlocking canvas, 11 inches square.

Yarn: 1½ ounces of Persian wool.

Other Materials Needed:
- Piece of felt 1 inch larger all around than the finished needlepoint.

FROM DESIGN TO CANVAS

Bind the cut edges of the canvas with masking tape.

Center the canvas over the design on the book page. Following the instructions for tracing designs in Part I, trace the design from the book onto the canvas with an indelible marker. If you prefer, you can transfer the design to tracing paper first and then to the canvas.

STITCHING

Follow the color key for the design as you work. As you can see from the color key, the black lines you have traced onto the canvas should be stitched in black for outlining.

Around all edges extend the design for two additional rows.

FINISHING

Block the needlepoint.

Sew a row of machine stitching on the excess canvas just outside the needlepoint along all edges except across the bottom.

Lay the needlepoint face down over the felt. Baste, then sew them together just inside the two-row seam allowance; leave the bottom edge unstitched (see Figure 1).

Figure 1

Across the bottom edge carefully cut the canvas one row outside the existing needlepoint, leaving one thread. Finish the bottom with the edging stitch (see Figure 2).

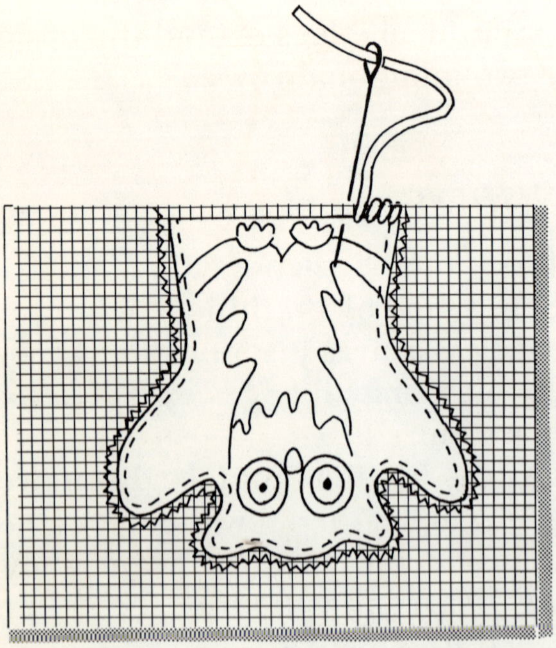

Figure 2

Around the rest of the puppet—that is, the wings and the head—cut the excess canvas and felt to within ½ inch of the needlepoint, notching all corners and curves (see Figure 3). Turn right side out.

Figure 3

COLOR KEY

The color key for the puppet appears on the design page.

yellow

white, center belly, outer eyes

1 green

2 orange

3 beige

black, eyeballs, all lines

Crib Gym

With the belief that it's never too early to begin a physical fitness program, we offer a crib gym for the tyke who wants to start out in shape. Since animals and children seem to have an affinity for each other, this benevolent lion, stuffed and suspended between the two sides of a crib, makes a good-natured punching bag. When your youngster outgrows his crib, this cat has other lives: As a shaped pillow tucked into the corner of an easy chair or as a hanging mobile suspended from ceiling or wall to show off both front and back designs.

Stitch: Basketweave.

Canvas: No. 10 interlocking canvas; two pieces, each 12 by 14 inches.

Yarn: 4 ounces of Persian wool for both sides of the design.

Other Materials Needed:
- Cotton or fiberfill for stuffing.

FROM DESIGN TO CANVAS

Bind the cut edges of each piece of canvas with masking tape.

Center one piece of canvas over the front of the lion on the book page. Following the instructions for tracing designs in Part I, trace the design from the book onto the canvas with an indelible marker. Trace the back of the lion onto the other piece of canvas in the same manner. If you prefer, you can transfer both lion designs to tracing paper first and then to each piece of canvas.

STITCHING

Follow the color key for the design and refer to the color photograph as you work. The black lines you have traced onto the canvas only delineate separate areas of color and should not be stitched, with this exception: The black lines around the eyes and the mouth as well as the black eyeballs, as indicated in the color key.

Around all edges extend the design for two additional rows.

FINISHING

Block the two pieces of needlepoint.

On each piece sew a row of machine stitching on the excess canvas just outside the needlepoint.

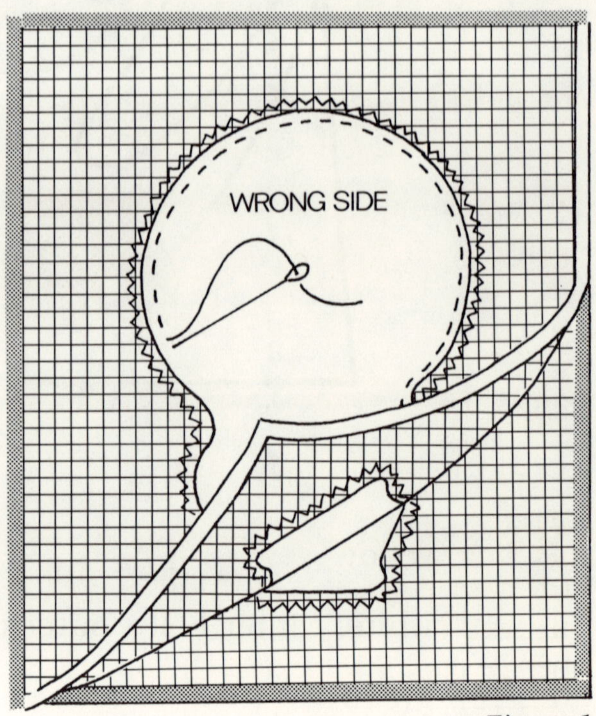

Figure 1

Place the two pieces of needlepoint right sides together. Baste, then sew them together just inside the two-row seam allowance, leaving the entire bottom open (see Figure 1).

Trim the excess canvas all around to within an inch of the needlepoint on both front and back, notching all corners and curves (see Figure 2).

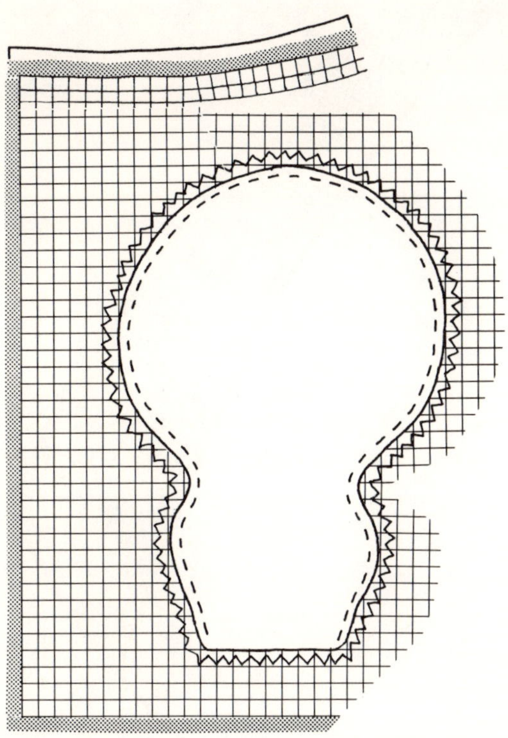

Figure 2

Turn right side out and stuff the lion with cotton or fiberfill, working it into the curves and edges. When the lion is well filled and nicely plump, turn the two canvas edges under at the bottom opening and blindstitch them together (see Figure 3).

Figure 3

To suspend the lion across the crib, braid three long lengths of matching yarn in the following manner: Anchor the center of each length of yarn at the back of the lion's head with simple tacking stitches (see Figure 4). On

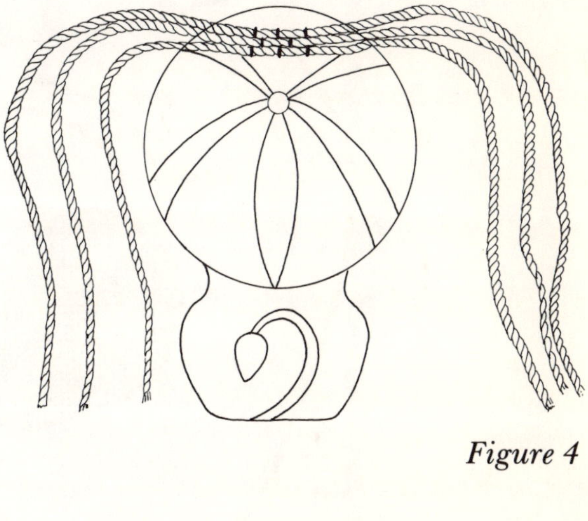

Figure 4

1
1
1
1
1
2
1

1
1
1
2
3
3
1
2
1
1
3
2
1
2
2
3
2

either side of the tacks braid the three pieces of yarn together and tie to the sides of the crib (see Figure 5).

Figure 5

COLOR KEY

- brown
- white
- 1 deep rust
- 2 gold
- 3 light rust line around legs and feet
- black line around eye and mouth, tail, eyeballs

A Game of Darts

In Britain the companionship of a spirited game of darts draws neighbors to their local pubs. To provide the same communal fun at home, we offer a dart game that combines the creative gamesmanship of the needlepointer with the absolute safety of a Velcro-dotted dart ball, that can grip the stitched game board tenaciously.

This particular game incorporates international road signs. You could turn "On the Road" into "Safari" by substituting the four animal heads —monkey, zebra, giraffe, elephant— on page 168 of the Design Workbook; they are scaled to fit into the four central rectangles of the board. (If you do so, stitch the game board on No. 10 interlocking canvas rather than on the No. 7 canvas suggested for the road signs in order to take advantage of the design details in the animal heads. The rest of the project instructions remains the same.)

Stitch: Basketweave; edging.

Canvas: No. 7 interlocking, 20 inches square.

Yarn: 11½ ounces of Persian wool.

Other Materials Needed:
- One piece of thin, rigid cardboard slightly smaller than the finished needlepoint (about 16 inches square).
- One piece of felt the size of the finished needlepoint.
- One small curtain ring for hanging.
- Three ping-pong balls.
- Small Velcro circles.

FROM DESIGN TO CANVAS

Bind the cut edges of the canvas with masking tape. Fold the canvas in half and then in half again to find the center point.

The design on page 35 is life-size, but shows only one quarter of the total game plan, so it must be copied onto the canvas four times. To do this, lay a piece of tracing paper over the book page and onto it trace the design in black ink.

Lay the tracing on a white table top or over a white piece of paper. Over it position the canvas with its center point over any one of the corners; it doesn't matter which corner since you will trace the line drawing four times to cover all four quadrants (see Figure 1). With an indelible marking pen transfer the design from tracing to canvas.

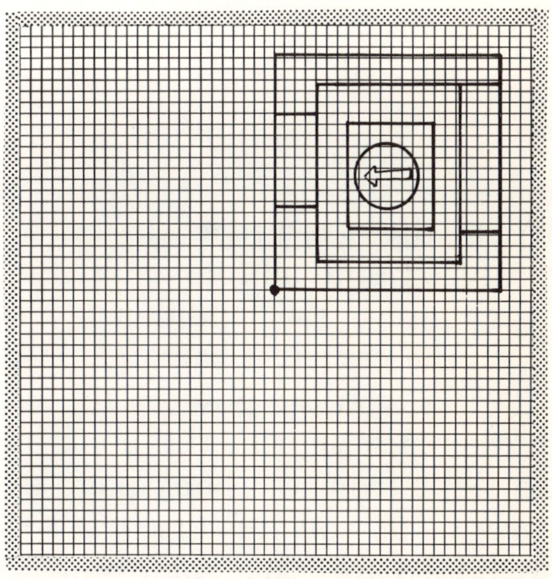

Figure 1

When you have completed the first transfer, move the tracing to another quadrant and repeat the process, transferring all the lines with this exception: Omit the road sign in the central rectangle because each quadrant has a different central motif (see Figure 2). In the same manner transfer the design to the remaining quadrants of the canvas.

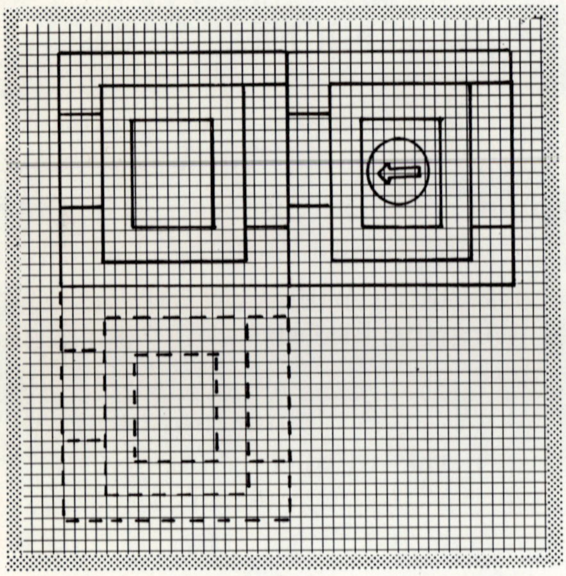

Figure 2

When the geometric design has been traced onto all four quarters of canvas, insert the additional road signs in the center of each quadrant. To do this, you can position the canvas over each sign in the book and trace right from the book page (see Figure 3), or you can first trace the signs onto paper and then onto the canvas, as described above. Arrange the four road signs in any pleasing order.

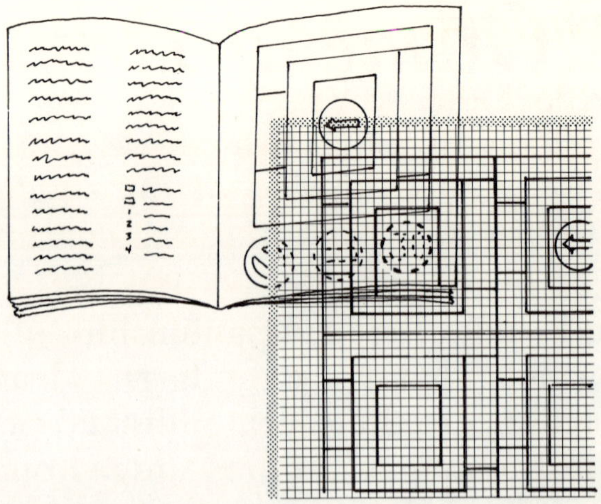

Figure 3

STITCHING

Follow the color key on page 34 as you stitch the canvas. The black lines you have traced onto the canvas only delineate separate areas of color and should not be stitched. As you work, you will see that the design has been planned so that the color areas on the borders join different-shaped areas of the same color on contiguous borders to form unusual geometric patterns (see Figure 4).

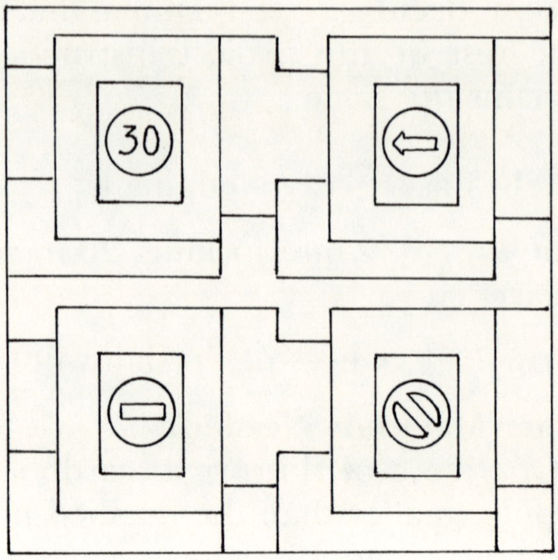

Figure 4

FINISHING

Block the canvas.

Along all four sides cut the canvas to within one thread of the stitched needlepoint. Work the edging stitch over this canvas thread and the outermost row of needlepoint (see Figure 5). Change yarn color to match the blocks of border colors. Remember to insert extra edging stitches in the corner meshes to cover them adequately.

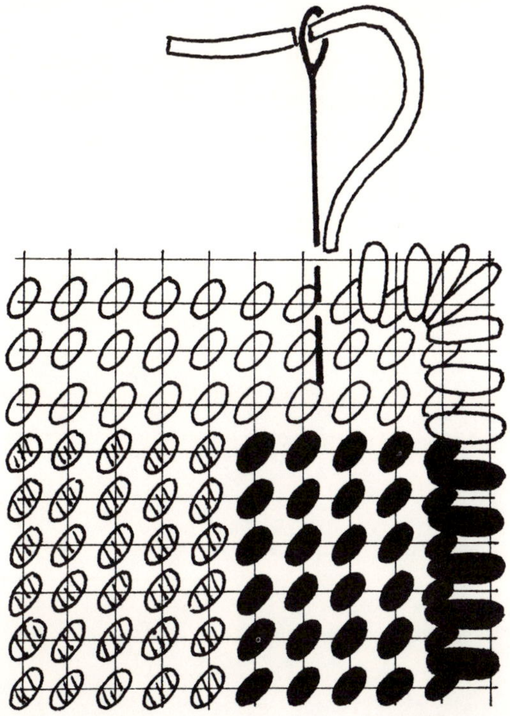

Figure 5

Glue the wrong side of the needlepoint to the cardboard backing with any white resin glue, such as Elmer's Glue-All.

To mount the game on a wall, sew the curtain ring to the felt backing in the middle of the top side, an inch or two in from the edge. Glue the felt to the cardboard.

THE DART BALLS

Ping-pong balls can be transformed speedily into dart balls by gluing small "dots" of Velcro to them with an epoxy cement. Use the smallest ready-made Velcro circles (available at sewing and notions counters) and dot them randomly around the surface of the three balls (see Figure 6). Of the

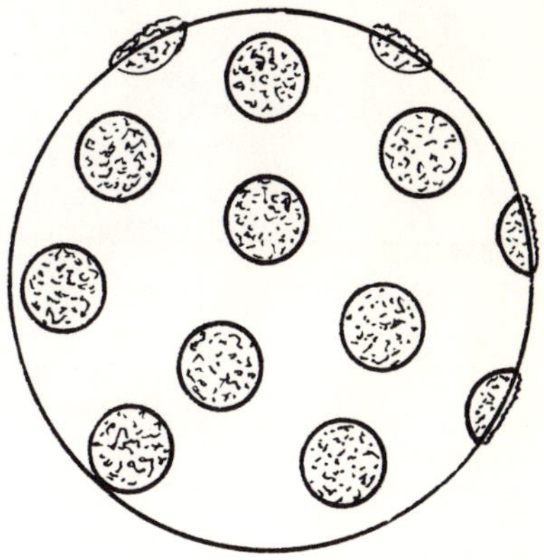

Figure 6

two-part nylon fastener, glue the stiffer "hook" half to the balls rather than the softer "loop" section. If you are in doubt, press each half of the fastener against a needlepoint surface and you will quickly see which part to use.

THE RULES OF THE GAME

The great fun of creating your own game is making up the rules that go with it. Here are our suggestions for one simple "On the Road" game in which the object is to have the highest score, or to be the first to accumulate a certain number of points, say 1,000.

Scoring: Any yellow areas, 50 points; orange, 40; green, 30; turquoise, 20. For hitting the No Parking sign, a 10-point fine; No Entry, lose a throw; One Way Only arrow, take an extra throw; "30," 30-point bonus. If a dart ball lands on more than one color, count the lower score.

Rules: Each player throws two balls per turn. If a ball hits the board and then falls off, take the throw over; if the ball misses the board entirely, no points accrue, and the throw is not taken over.

COLOR KEY

red

blue

white

1 turquoise

2 green

3 yellow

4 orange

black, number "30"

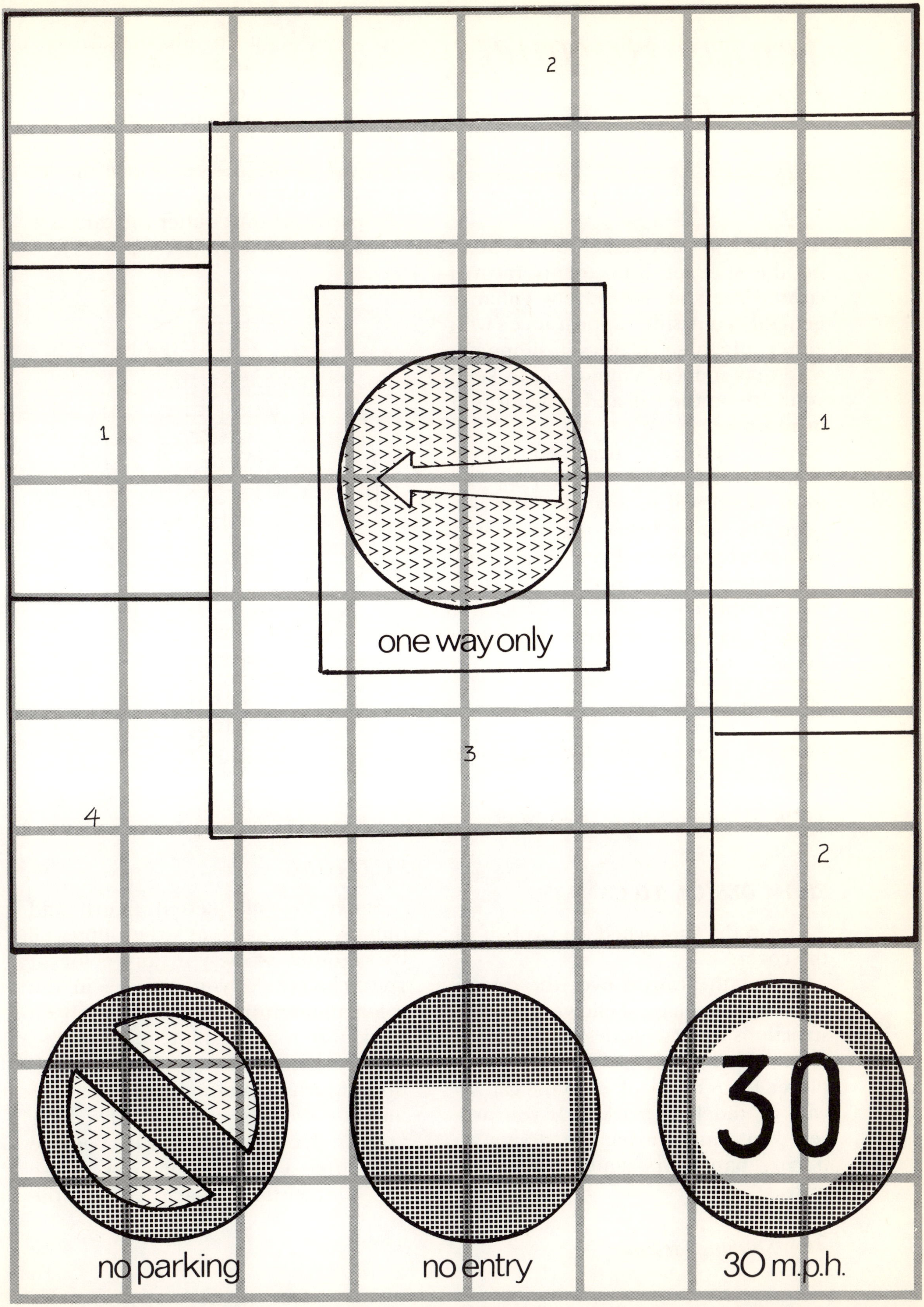
2
1
1
one way only
3
4
2
no parking
no entry
30
30 m.p.h.

Tennis Racquet Cover

The form of your game won't depend on the style of your tennis racquet cover, but you will surely enhance general courtside appearance with either of these players-in-silhouette who may indeed remind you to keep your eye on the ball and your racquet head up.

Each figure is designed for a prefinished cover (see "Source," below), which will fit any standard racquet; the space below the racquet is available for initials if you like. For actual stitching, the cover unzips into two completely separate halves, and beyond blocking, it needs absolutely no finishing.

Stitch: Basketweave.

Canvas: No. 7 interlocking, premounted.

Yarn: 5½ ounces of Persian wool.

FROM DESIGN TO CANVAS

Unzip the unstitched canvas half of the cover.

Center the canvas over the design on the book page. Following the instructions for tracing designs in Part I, trace either male or female tennis player from the book onto the canvas with an indelible marker. If you prefer, you can transfer the design to tracing paper first and then to the canvas.

If you want to add initials or a monogram, transfer the letters you need from one of the alphabets in the Design Workbook onto tracing paper. Plan the letters to fit under the tennis racquet in the design. Trace the letters onto the canvas, moving the tracing paper around under the canvas as needed for spacing (see Figure 1).

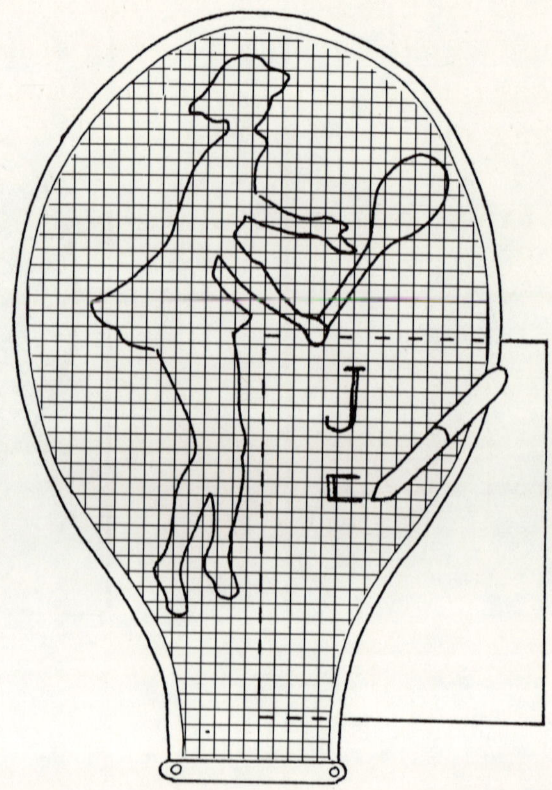

Figure 1

STITCHING

Stitch the silhouetted figure and initials, as well as the optional background stripes, in any color of your choice. As you can see in the color photograph, one cover has been worked in tones of blue and green.

The horizontal stripes are in random widths, ranging from ¾ to 5 inches wide; they can be in any order and, in fact, in any width. Because they offer a nice opportunity to use up oddments of yarn colors, the widths and colors of the stripes may very well be dictated by your yarn supply.

The black outline of the silhouette that you traced onto the canvas only delineates the separation of color and should not be stitched.

To keep distortion of the canvas as slight as possible, work the basketweave stitch by the "push/pull" method (see pages 11–12), that is, by forming each stitch with two separate strokes rather than in one continuous flowing motion. Tuck the outermost row of stitches under, or as close as you can to, the prefinished binding (see Figure 2).

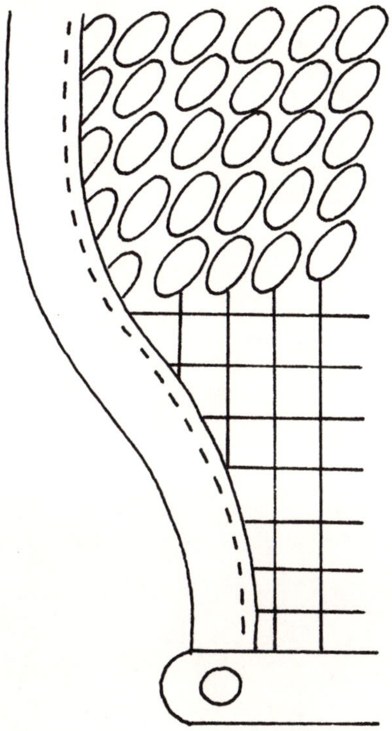

Figure 2

FINISHING

Block the needlepoint, if necessary, following the instructions given for blocking prefinished projects in Part I.

COLOR KEY

Choice of color is entirely optional.

SOURCE

This prefinished tennis racquet cover is available in navy, red, brown, and white; it retails for $19.00 at the time of publication. For a retail source near you, write the manufacturer, Markann Mfg. Corp., 69 Warren St., New Rochelle, N.Y. 10801.

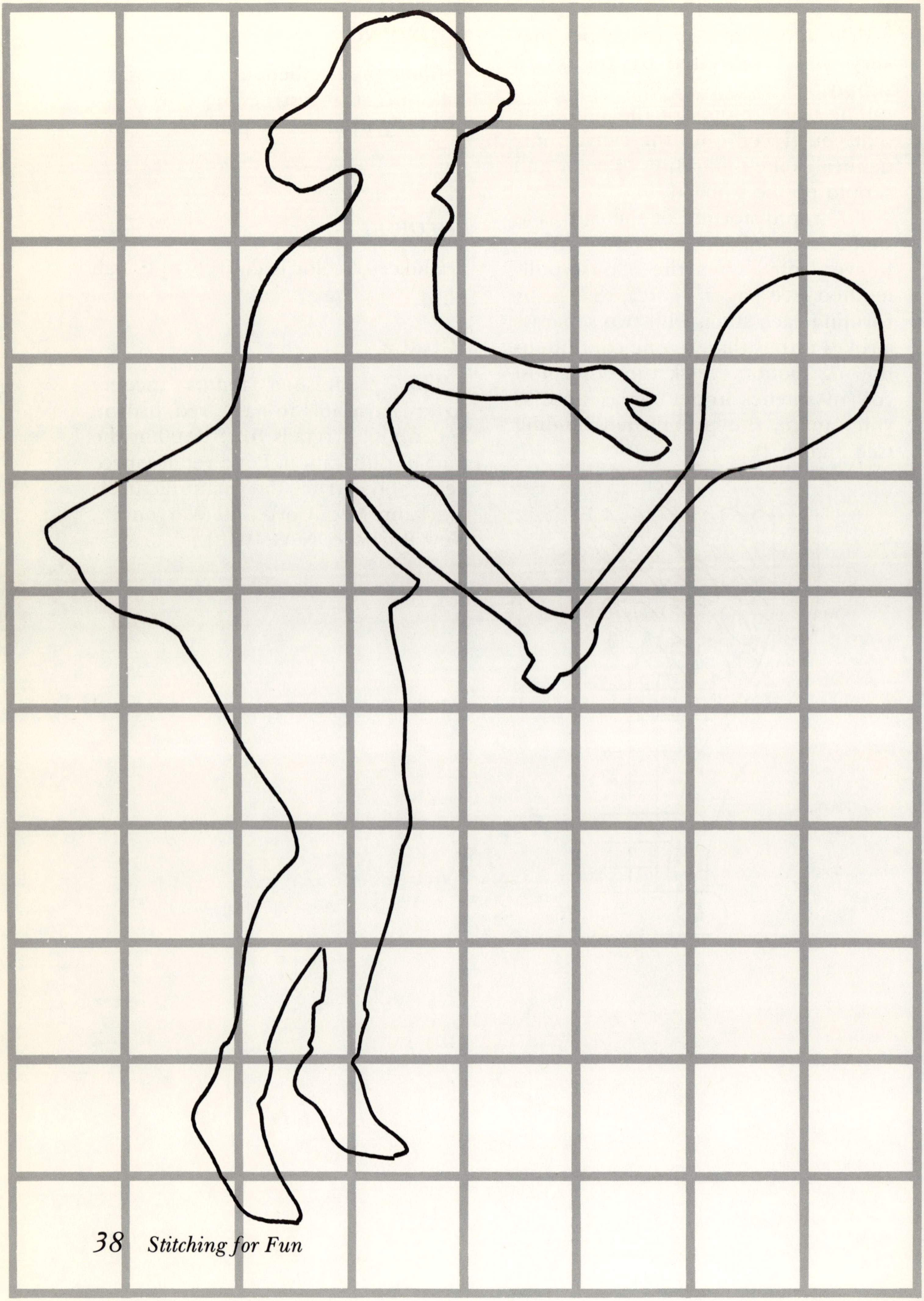

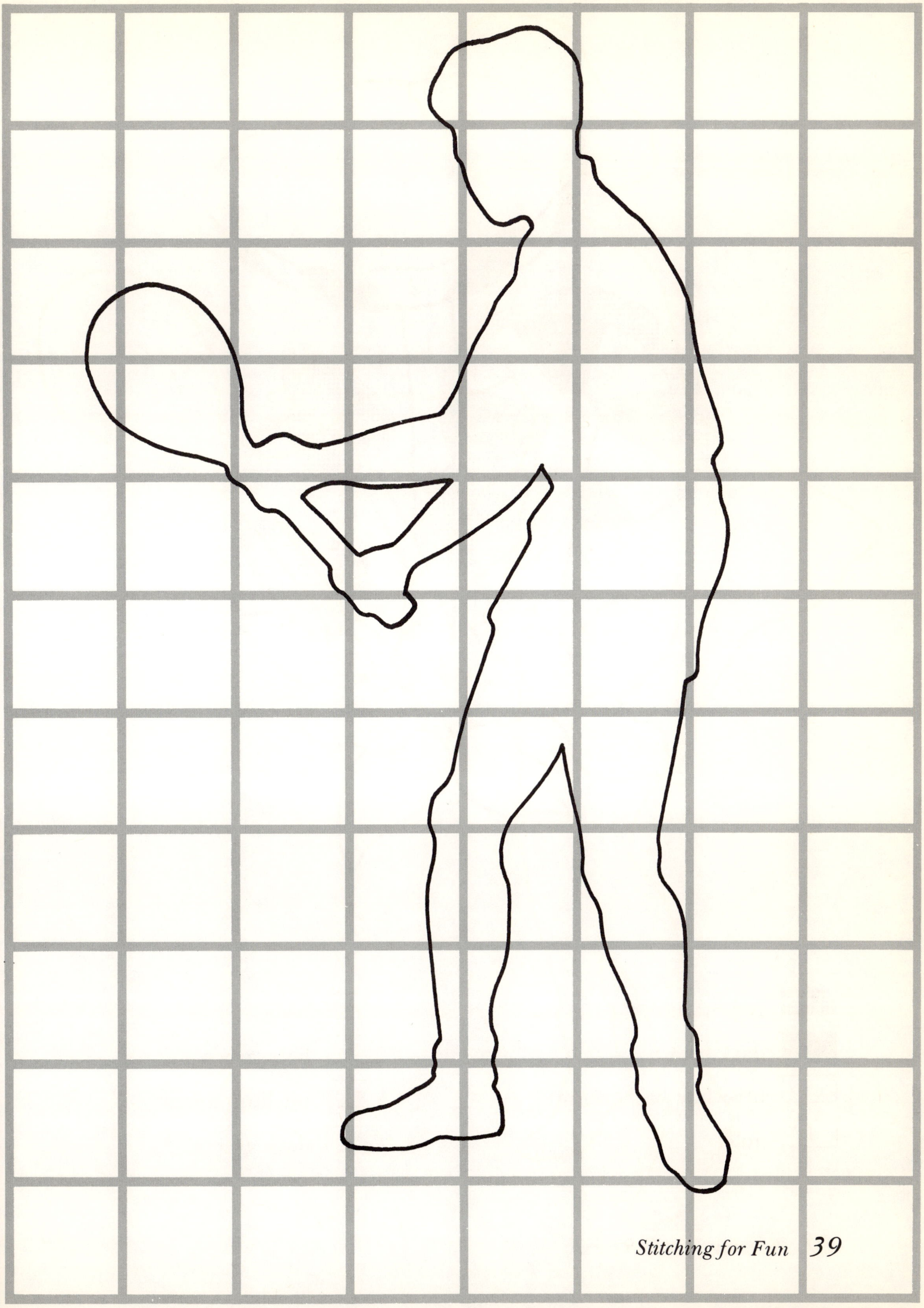

red-orange	2 beige
dark brown	3 light green
off-white background	4 medium green
1 gold	5 dark green

Picture Frame

A stand of mushrooms lends a pretty garden touch to this double folding picture frame that accommodates two 5-by-7-inch photographs inside (see "Source," below). The needlepoint panel locks into the 7-by-10-inch cover without additional mounting. The same motif is scaled to fit the address book cover on page 47, which utilizes the same simple mounting technique.

Stitch: Basketweave.

Canvas: No. 10 interlocking canvas, 9 by 11 inches.

Yarn: 1¼ ounces of Persian wool.

FROM DESIGN TO CANVAS

Bind the cut edges of the canvas with masking tape.

In the center of the canvas outline a rectangle exactly 5¼ by 7¼ inches with an indelible marker.

Center the canvas over the design on the book page. Following the instructions for tracing designs in Part I, trace the design from the book onto the canvas with an indelible marker. If you prefer, you can transfer the design to tracing paper first and then to the canvas.

STITCHING

Follow the color key for the design and refer to the color photograph as you work. The black lines you have traced only delineate separate areas of color and should not be stitched.

Work up to but not beyond the outline of the design so that the finished needlepoint measures exactly 5¼ by 7¼ inches.

FINISHING

Block the needlepoint.

Sew a row of machine stitching on the outermost row of needlepoint on all four sides (see Figure 1).

Figure 1

Along all sides carefully cut the canvas one row outside the existing needlepoint, leaving one thread all around (see Figure 2).

Set aside the white plastic mounting board, which you will find stored in

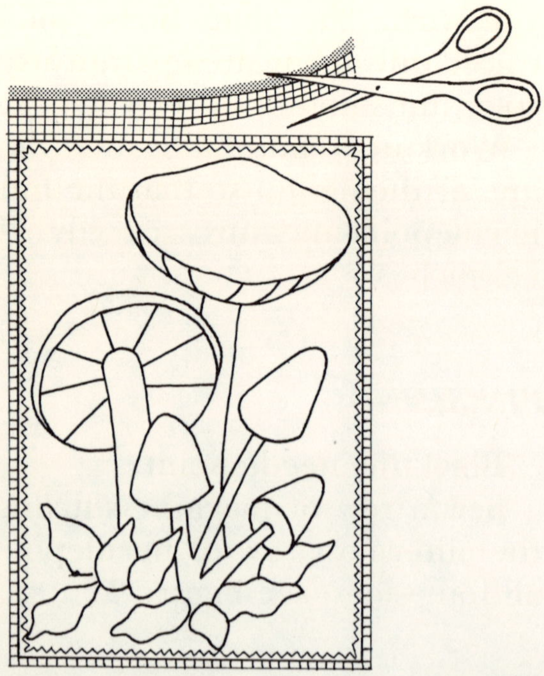

Figure 2

the recessed frame of the picture frame cover. Slip two adjacent sides of the needlepoint under the recessed frame and slide the white mounting board under the needlepoint (see Figure 3). Using any flat, dull tool, such as a spatula or a butter knife, wedge the other two sides of the needlepoint under the frame (see Figure 4).

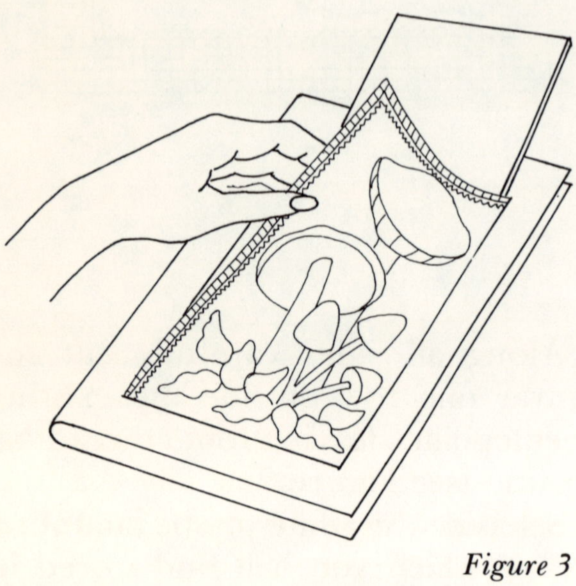

Figure 3

Figure 4

COLOR KEY

The color key for the picture frame appears on its design page. Use a color of your choice for the background.

SOURCE

The picture frame is made in simulated leather in ivory, white, black, brown, red, green, blue, lime, and lemon, and retails for $17.50 at the time of publication. You can order it by mail from Giftiques Unlimited, P.O. Box 412, Little Neck, N.Y. 11363; or your local needlework shop can probably order it for you from the manufacturer, Adolph Burkland, 28–18 Steinway St., Long Island City, New York, N.Y. 11103.

Photo Album

Organize your family photographs in a loose-leaf album that holds hundreds of 3½-by-5-inch pictures in flip-up acetate sleeves (see "Source," below). The album measures 7¼ by 10 inches and frames a 6-by-9-inch needlepoint insert, which simply locks in place in the album cover. The panel of needlepoint shells that here heralds your family pictures, perhaps even your seaside snapshots, also fits the jewel box cover on page 129, which uses the same mounting technique.

Stitch: Basketweave.

Canvas: No. 10 interlocking canvas, 10 by 13 inches.

Yarn: 1¾ ounces of Persian wool.

FROM DESIGN TO CANVAS

Bind the cut edges of the canvas with masking tape.

Center the canvas over the design on the book page. Following the instructions for tracing designs in Part I, trace the design from the book onto the canvas with an indelible marker. If you prefer, you can transfer the design to tracing paper first and then to the canvas.

STITCHING

Follow the color key for the design and refer to the color photograph as you work. The black lines you have traced only delineate separate areas of color and should not be stitched.

Work up to but not beyond the outline of the design so that the finished needlepoint measures exactly 6 by 9 inches.

FINISHING

Block the needlepoint.

Sew a row of machine stitching on the outermost row of needlepoint on all four sides (see Figure 1).

Figure 1

Along all sides carefully cut the canvas one row outside the existing needlepoint, leaving one thread all around (see Figure 2).

Figure 2

Set aside the white plastic mounting board, which you will find stored in the recessed frame of the album cover. Slip two adjacent sides of needlepoint under the recessed frame and slide the white mounting board under the needlepoint (see Figure 3). Using any flat, dull tool, such as a spatula or a butter knife, wedge the other two sides of the needlepoint under the frame (see Figure 4).

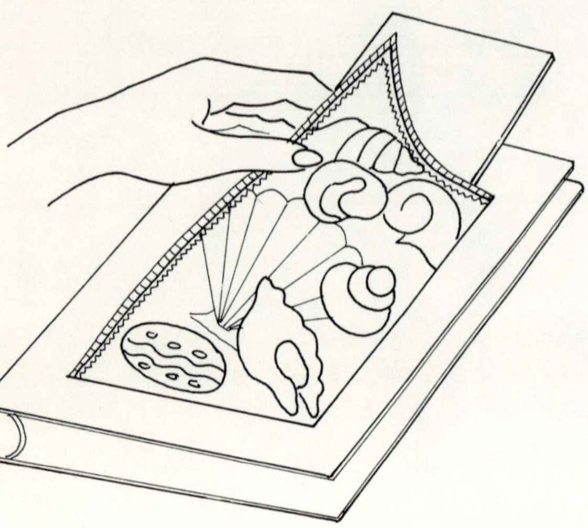

Figure 3

Figure 4

COLOR KEY

The color key for the photo album appears on its design page.

SOURCE

The photo album is made of simulated leather in ivory, white, black, brown, red, green, blue, lime, and lemon; it comes with three cards, each capable of holding twenty 3½-by-5-inch photographs and it retails for $17.50 at the time of publication. Additional photo cards are available for $4.00 per three cards. You can order the album by mail from Giftiques Unlimited, P.O. Box 412, Little Neck, N.Y. 11363; or your local needlework shop can probably order it from the manufacturer, Adolph Burkland, 28–18 Steinway St., Long Island City, New York, N.Y. 11103.

brown

orange

off-white areas and background

1 yellow

2 beige

3 pink

(checked)	red-orange
(solid)	dark brown
(blank)	white, eyes
1	gold
2	beige
3	light green
4	medium green
5	dark green

Address Book

Chinese dragons, unlike their Western counterparts, are benevolent creatures, even the five-clawed species, which represents the emperor. This particular imperial dragon rests on the cover of a loose-leaf address book (see "Source," below) and is locked into place by the ingenious construction of the lid, which requires no special mounting. The same design could be used happily on the double folding picture frame, which utilizes the same simple mounting.

Stitch: Basketweave.

Canvas: No. 10 interlocking canvas, 9 by 12 inches.

Yarn: 1¼ ounces of Persian wool.

FROM DESIGN TO CANVAS

Bind the cut edges of the canvas with masking tape.

In the center of the canvas outline a rectangle exactly 5¼ by 8 inches with an indelible marker.

Center the canvas over the design on the book page. Following the instructions for tracing designs in Part I, trace the design from the book onto the canvas with an indelible marker. If you prefer, you can transfer the design to tracing paper first and then to the canvas.

STITCHING

Follow the color key for the design and refer to the color photograph as you work. The black lines you have traced only delineate separate areas of color and should not be stitched.

Work up to but not beyond the outline of the design so that the finished needlepoint measures exactly 5¼ by 8 inches.

FINISHING

Block the needlepoint.

Sew a row of machine stitching on the outermost row of needlepoint on all four sides (see Figure 1).

Figure 1

Along all sides carefully cut the canvas one row outside the existing needlepoint, leaving one thread all around (see Figure 2).

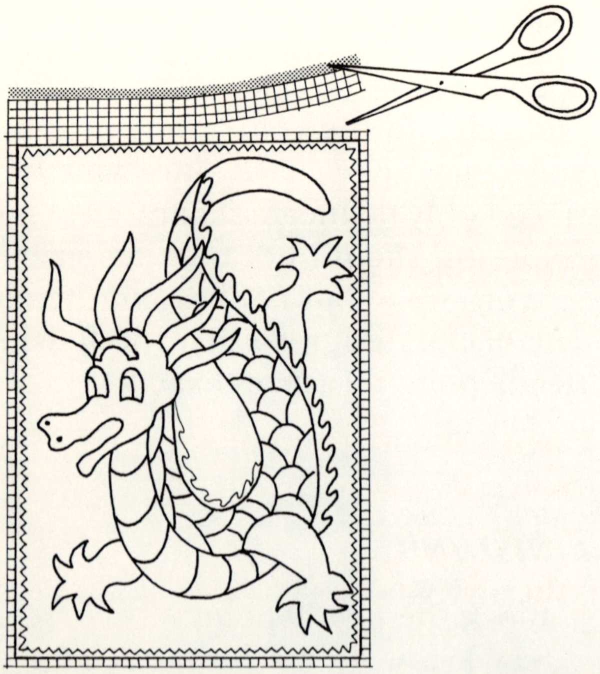

Figure 2

Set aside the white plastic mounting board, which you will find stored in the recessed frame of the address-book cover. Slip two adjacent sides of needlepoint under the recessed frame and slide the white mounting board under the needlepoint (see Figure 3).

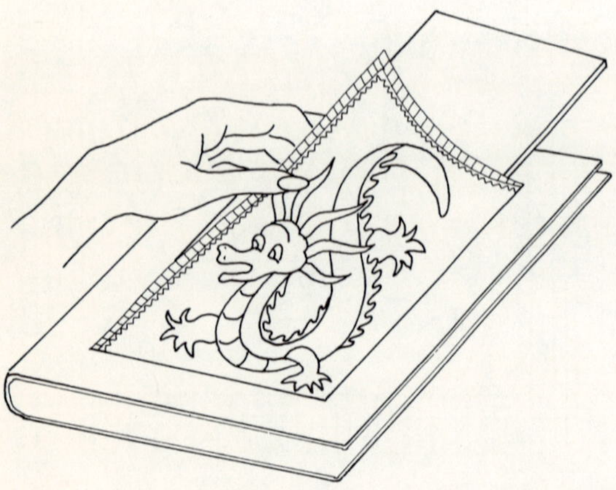

Figure 3

Using any flat, dull tool, such as a spatula or a butter knife, wedge the other two sides of the needlepoint under the frame (see Figure 4).

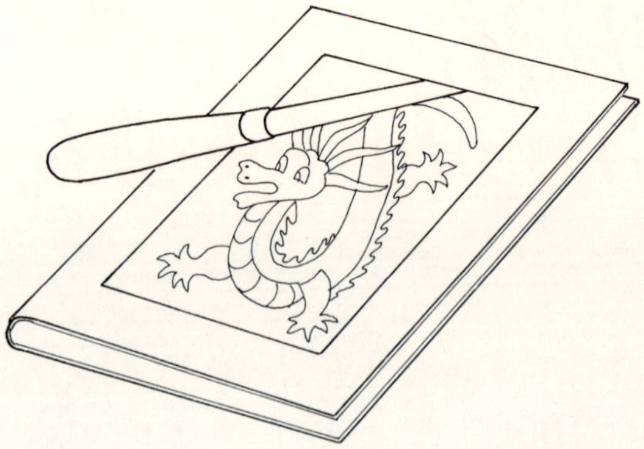

Figure 4

COLOR KEY

The color key for the address book appears on its design page. Use a background color of your choice.

SOURCE

The address book is available in simulated leather in ivory, white, black, red, brown, green, blue, lime, and lemon for $14.00 or in velvet in green, yellow, rose, or blue for $16.50 at the time of publication. You can order it by mail from Giftiques Unlimited, P.O. Box 412, Little Neck, N.Y. 11363; or your local needlework shop can probably order it for you from the manufacturer, Adolph Burkland, 28–18 Steinway St., Long Island City, New York, N.Y. 11103.

Child's Growth Chart

Family records are rarely a decorative asset, but keeping tabs on growing youngsters with this whimsical giraffe is a visual delight. You can use the hanging "yardstick" to record the upward movement of one child over the years or to mark the relative heights of all your youngsters at a given time (see Figure 1).

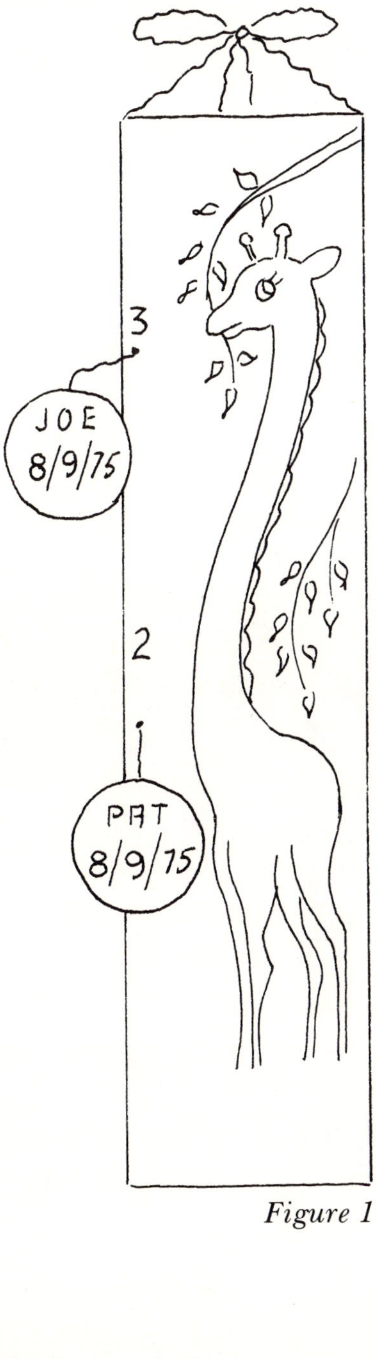

Figure 1

The growth chart is marked at 1-foot intervals and should be hung 2 feet off the floor. Remember to add the extra 2 feet when recording measurements.

Stitch: Basketweave.

Canvas: No. 10 mono canvas, 14 by 42 inches.

Yarn: About 15 ounces of Persian wool, 9 ounces of it for the background.

Other Materials Needed:
- Felt for lining.
- One piece of lattice stripping 8½ inches long (this is a thin strip of wood 1 inch high and ¼ inch deep).
- Two yards of ¼-inch cording.

FROM DESIGN TO CANVAS

Bind the cut edges of the canvas with masking tape.

Following the instructions for enlarging designs in Part I, enlarge the design on pages 52–53 so that the width measures 9½ inches; the height will be about 37½ inches.

Center the enlarged design face up under the canvas and trace it onto the canvas with an indelible marker.

STITCHING

As you stitch the canvas, follow the color key for the design and refer to the color photograph. The black lines you have traced onto the canvas only delineate separate areas of color and should not be outlined.

Around all four edges add one row of stitches to turn under when finishing.

FINISHING

Block the needlepoint.

Sew a row of machine stitching on the excess canvas about ½ inch out from the needlepoint.

Cut the excess canvas away on all four sides to within 1½ inches of the needlepoint, and cut the corners diagonally to within 1 inch of the stitching (see Figure 2).

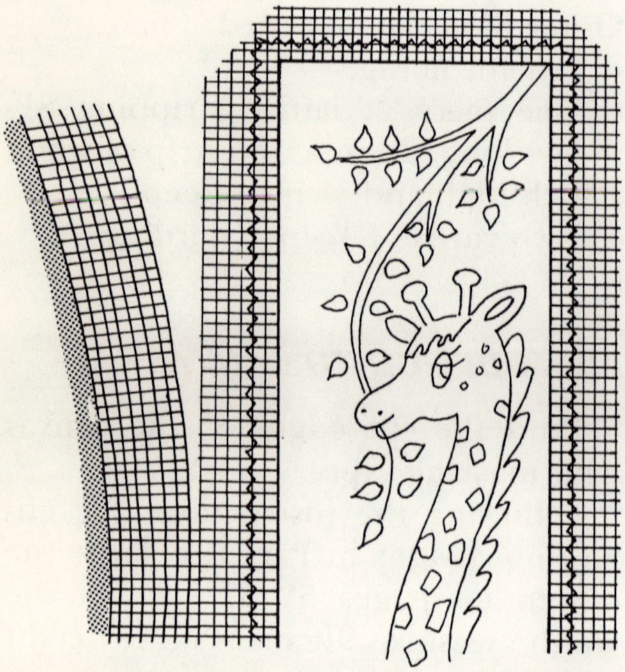

Figure 2

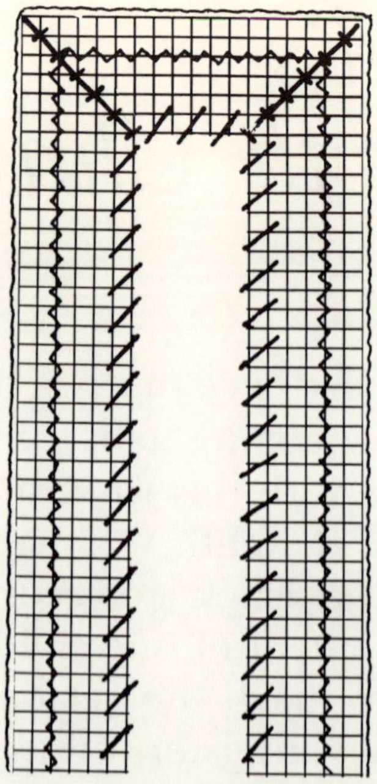

Figure 3

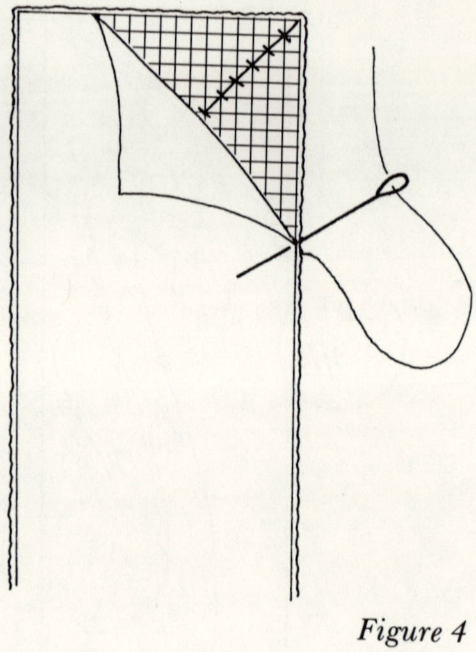

Figure 4

Miter the four corners of the needlepoint and tack the excess canvas to the back of the stitching, making sure the rows of stitching are straight and that no unstitched canvas shows along the edges (see Figure 3).

Cut the felt lining just smaller than the mitered needlepoint. Lay it over the back of the needlepoint and blindstitch it into place (see Figure 4).

Glue the lattice strip to the top of the lining, centering it about 1 inch down from the top (see Figure 5). Spread it with any white all-purpose glue and let dry.

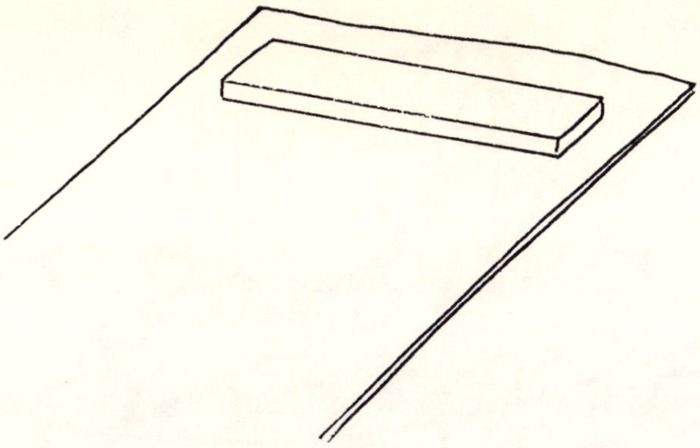

Figure 5

Glue the cording around the bottom and sides of the wooden strip so that two equal lengths hang free; tie them in a bow (see Fig. 6). Hang so that the bottom of the growth chart is 2 feet off the floor.

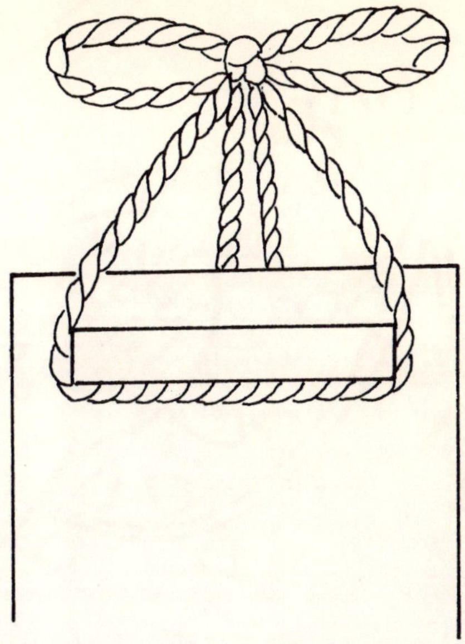

Figure 6

COLOR KEY

The color key appears with the design on page 52.

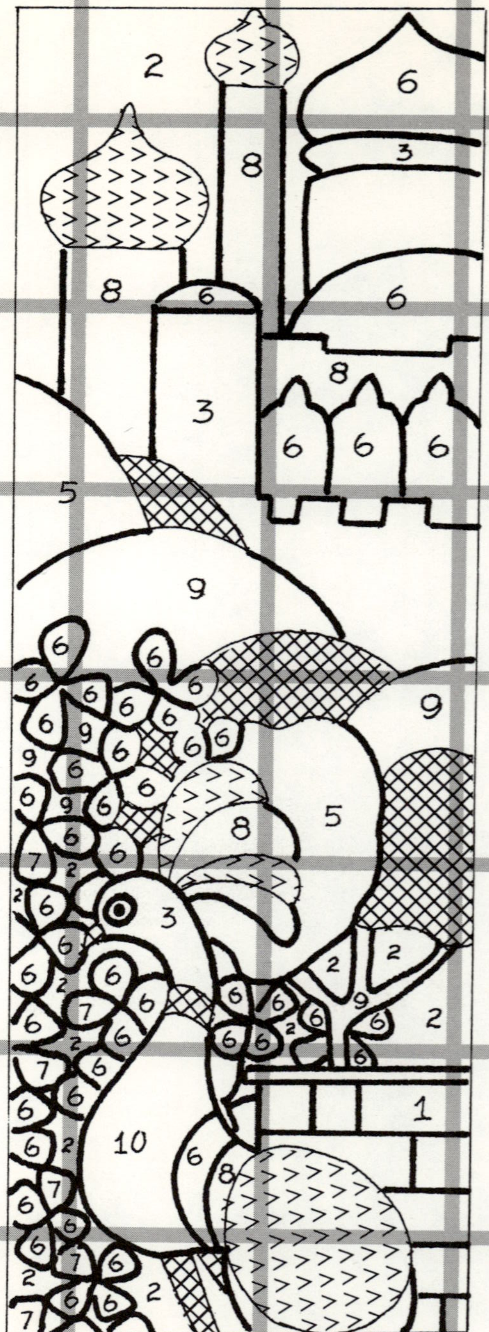

Child's Growth Chart ▶

(dotted pattern)	deep gold shadows, tail, eyelid
(wavy pattern)	pale yellow horns, ear, belly
1	light blue background
2	rust spots, mane, tip of tail
3	bright yellow body
4	brown branch
5	kelly-green leaves
6	olive-green grass
7	dark green stems and leaves of flowers, grass shoots
8	pink flowers
9	orange flowers
(blank)	white, eye
	black, eyelashes and eyeball

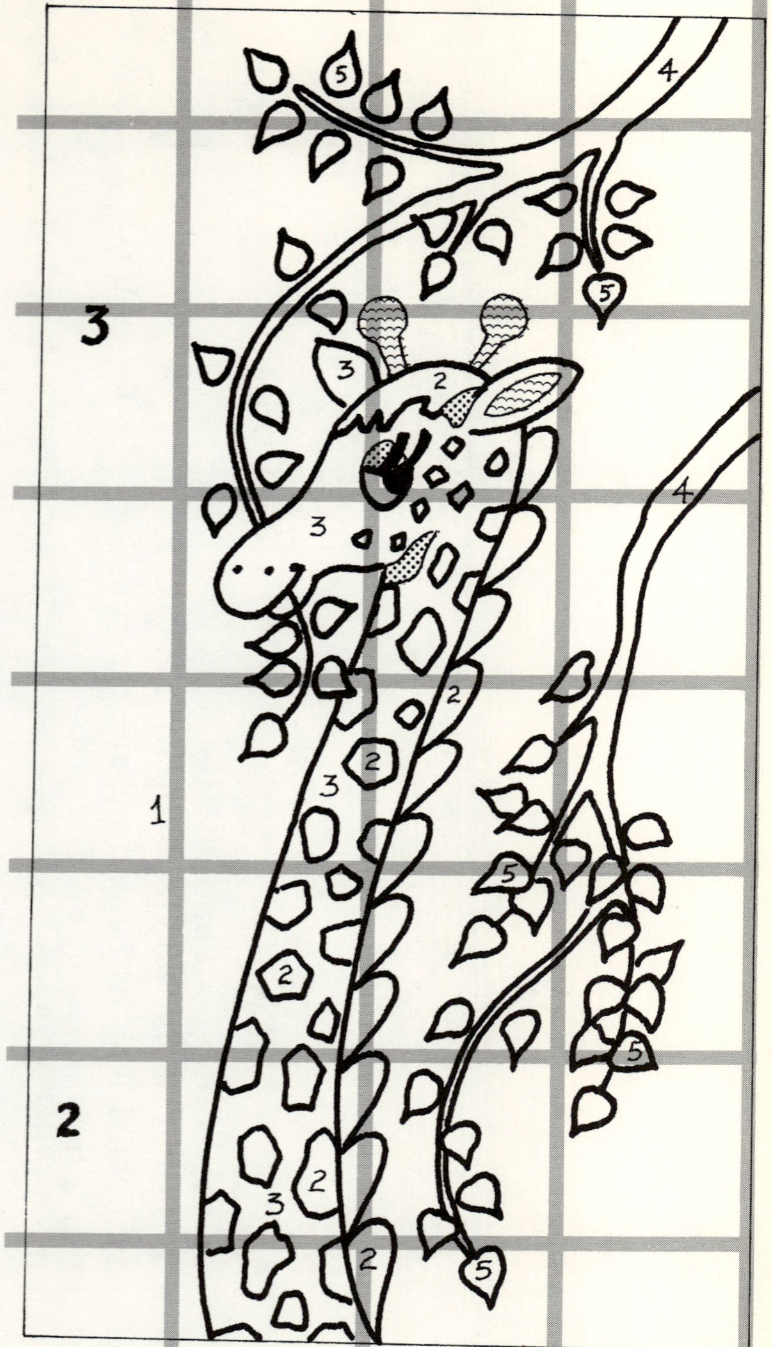

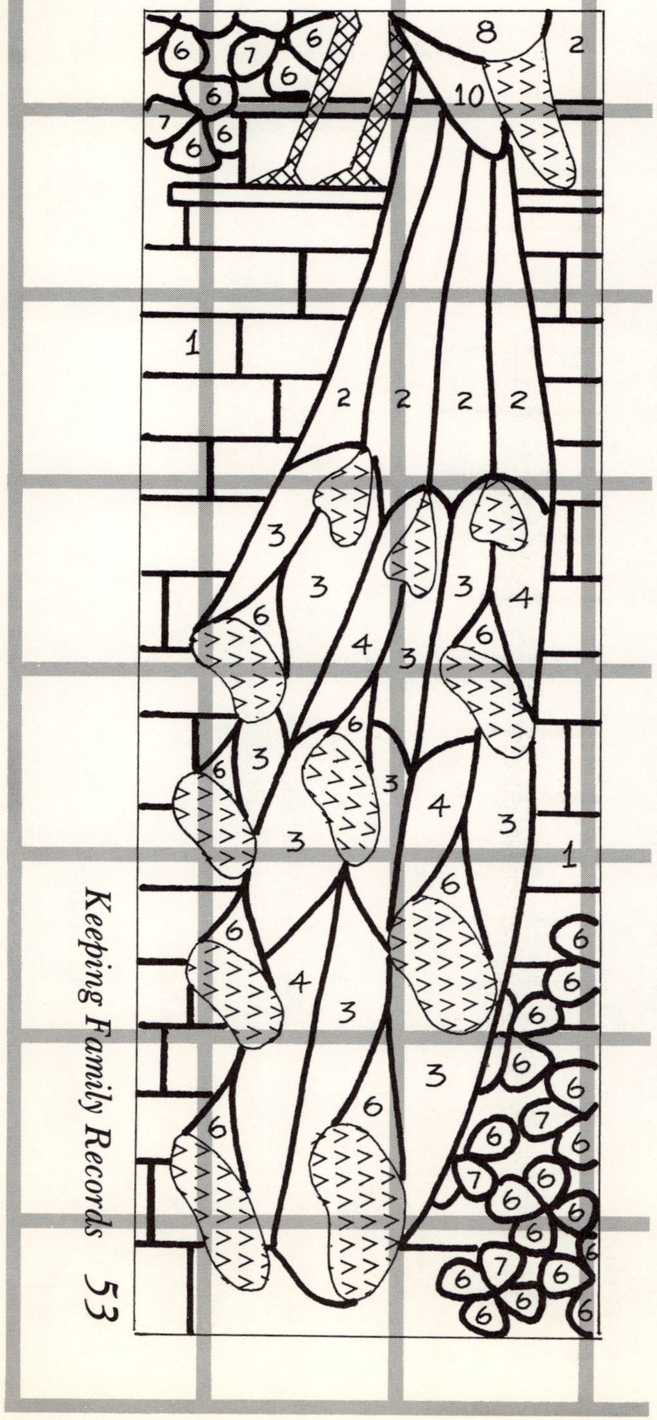

◀ **Peacock Bellpull**

- (crosshatch) light yellow-green trees,
- (>>>> pattern) red-orange beak, legs
- 1 pale yellow wall and steps
- 2 aqua sky and behind flowers (center)
- 3 turquoise
- 4 aqua and turquoise tweed
- 5 brass
- 6 gold
- 7 pale yellow and gold tweed
- 8 royal blue
- 9 deep olive-green
- 10 gold and red-orange tweed
- (black bar) black outline around

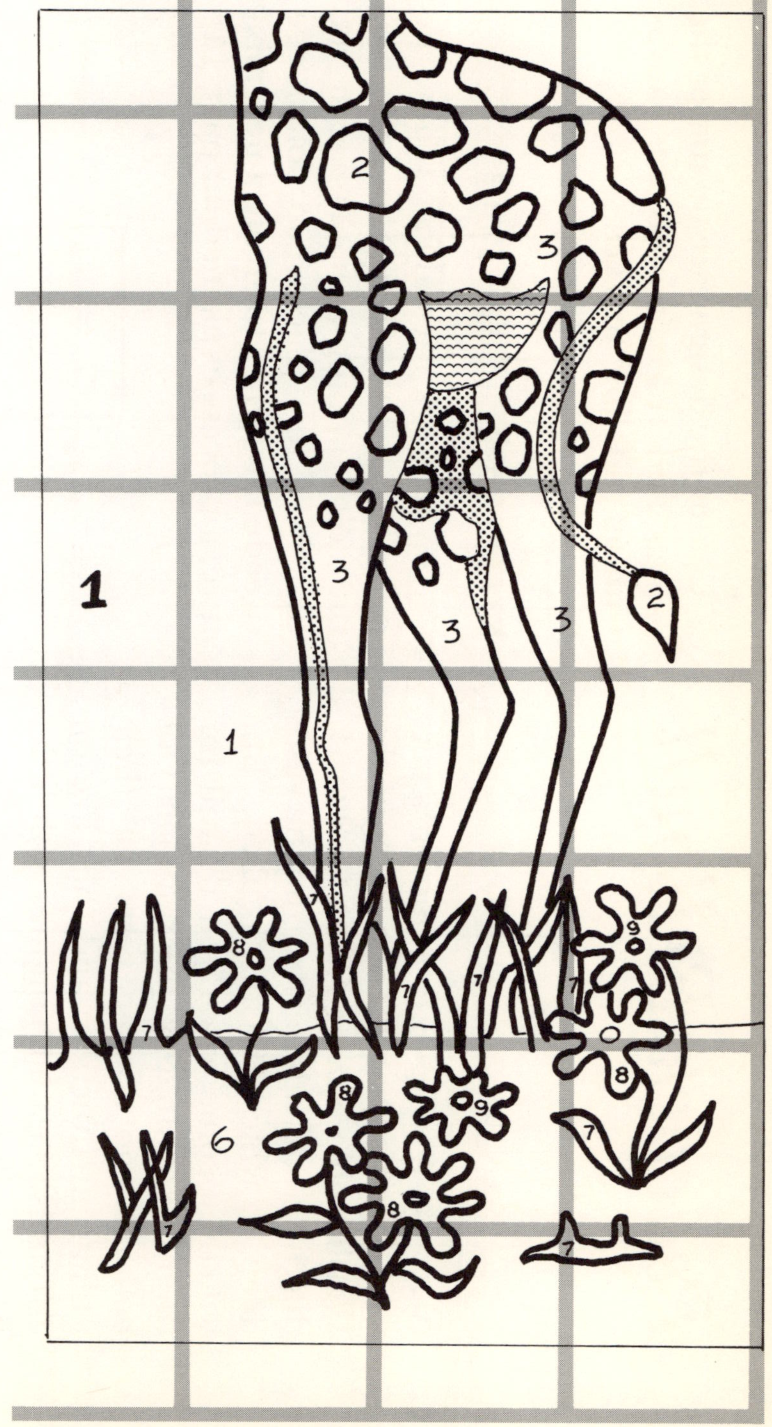

Peacock Bellpull

A tug on a bellpull to summon a servant is somewhat like the claim of the Welsh noble in *King Henry IV,* Part I, that he could call spirits from the vasty deep, to which Hotspur replied, "But will they come when you do call for them?" Fortunately, the popularity of bellpulls no longer rests on their utilitarian function, and they live on as handsome wall hangings with little, if any, calling power.

This particular bellpull is contemporary in feeling, although its design betrays the influence of heavily leaded stained glass as well as the colors and architectural shapes of Persian carpets.

Stitch: Basketweave.

Canvas: No. 10 mono canvas, 10 by 50 inches.

Yarn: 8 ounces of Persian wool.

Other Materials Needed:
- Felt for lining.
- Two clear plastic (Lucite, Plexiglas) dowels, each 8 inches long and 1 inch in diameter.

FROM DESIGN TO CANVAS

Bind the cut edges of the canvas with masking tape.

Following the instructions for enlarging designs in Part I, enlarge the design on pages 52–53 so that the width measures 6 inches; the length will be about 36 inches.

Center the design face up under the canvas and trace it onto the canvas with an indelible marker.

STITCHING

As you work the canvas, follow the color key for the design and refer to the color photograph. You can see that in a few places two colors are tweeded together to create a new mixture, a process explained on page 14.

Figure 1

The black lines you have traced onto the canvas should be outlined in black yarn to evoke the stained-glass leading.

Extend the top end 4½ inches in the background color (blue) and do the same at the bottom end (yellow). (See Figure 1.) These ends will be looped over the dowels.

Add one row of stitches all around to turn under when finishing.

FINISHING

Block the needlepoint.

Sew a row of machine stitching on the excess canvas about ½ inch out from the needlepoint.

Cut the excess canvas away on all four sides to within 1½ inches of the needlepoint, and cut the corners diagonally to within ½ inch of the stitching (see Figure 2).

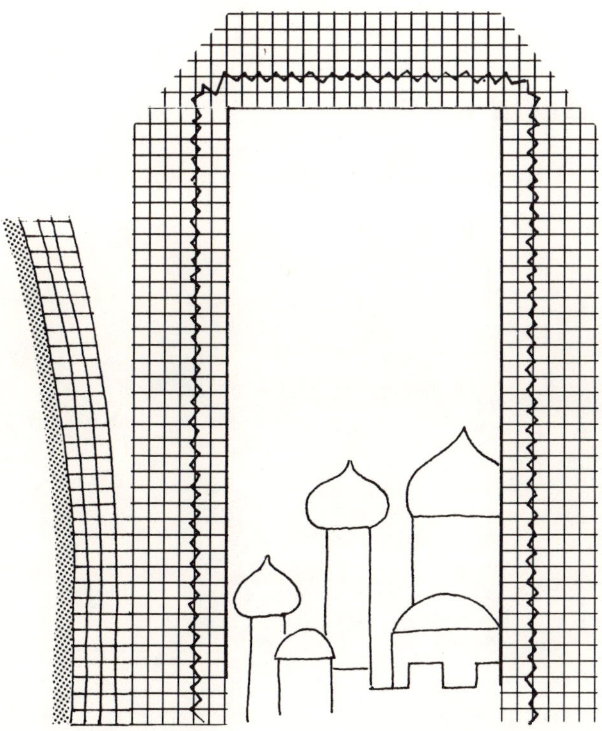

Figure 2

Miter the four corners of the needlepoint and tack the excess canvas to the back of the stitching, making sure the rows of stitching are straight and that no unstitched canvas shows along the edges (see Figure 3).

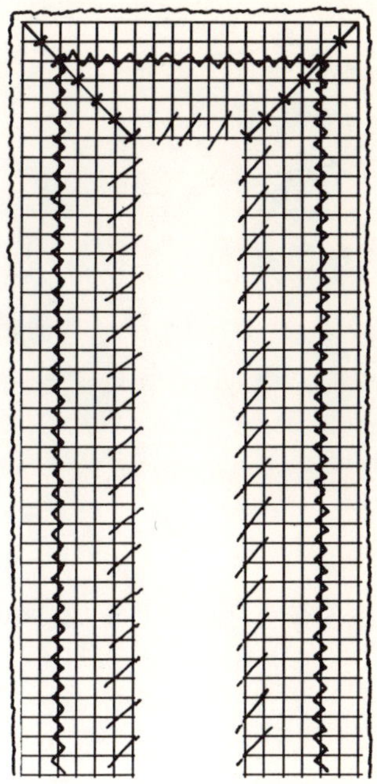

Figure 3

Cut the felt lining the same size as the design area, excluding the extended ends to be looped over the dowels. The lining will measure about 6 by 36 inches. Blindstitch it to the back of the needlepoint (see Figure 4).

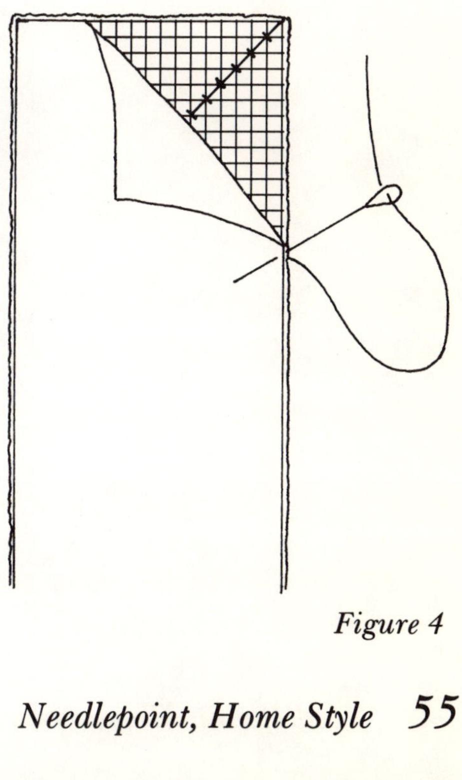

Figure 4

Loop each end around a dowel and tack securely to the lining (see Figure 5). Suspend the upper dowel from a length of cording or on two small hooks (see Figure 6).

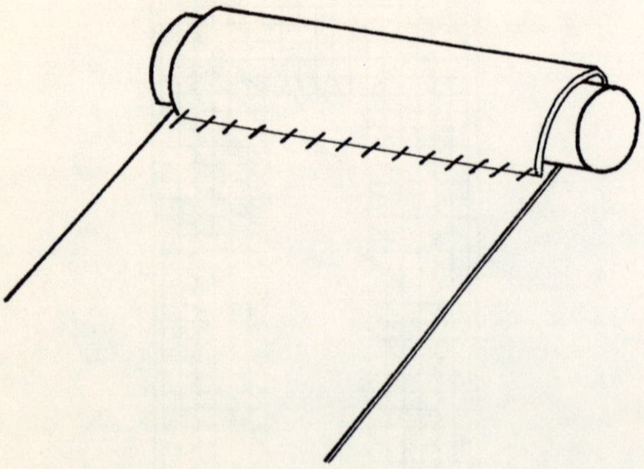

Figure 5

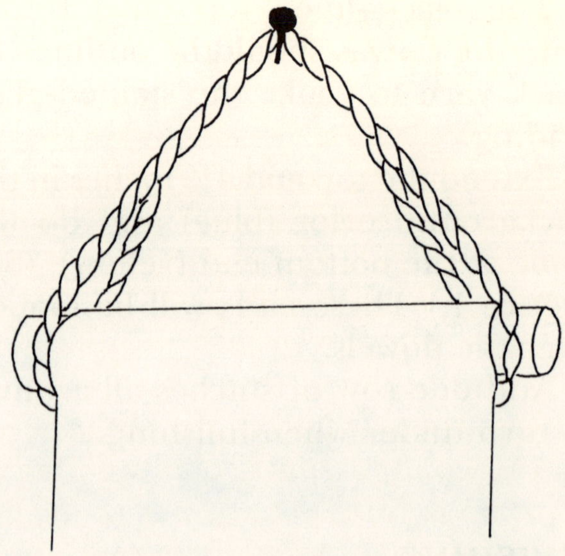

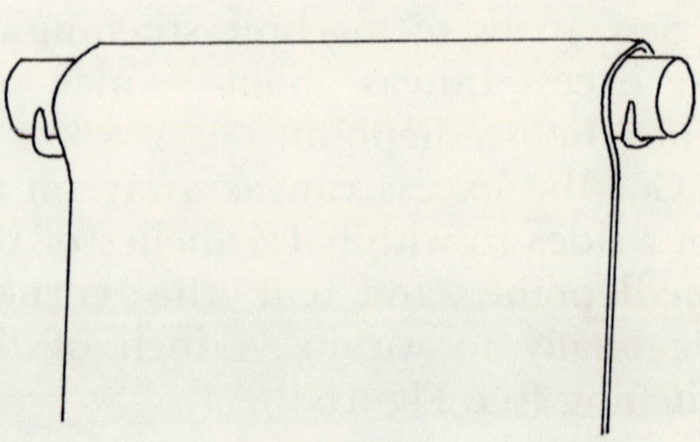

Figure 6

COLOR KEY

The color key appears with the design on page 53.

Wastebasket

Since wastebaskets are necessary fixtures, why not hide their utilitarian function under a decorative mantle? This particular basket assembles some of the components from the Design Workbook into a charming underwater scene that would fit happily into den, bedroom, or office.

Stitch: Basketweave.

Canvas: No. 5 interlocking canvas, 35 by 16 inches.

Yarn: About 19 ounces of Persian wool.

Other Materials Needed:
- Cardboard cylinder, 14 inches high and 10 inches across.
- Two strips of Leatherette or heavy decorative paper whose length is the circumference of the cylinder, one 2 inches wide, the other 1 inch wide.
- Self-adhesive lining of felt or decorative paper, 13½ inches high by the circumference of the cylinder.

FROM DESIGN TO CANVAS

Bind the cut edges of the canvas with masking tape.

Following the instructions for enlarging designs in Part I, enlarge the design on pages 60–61 so that the width is 31 inches; the height will be about 12 inches. The design on the double pages of the book is exactly half the width and length of the project size.

Center the design face up under the canvas and trace it onto the canvas with an indelible marker.

To make a smaller wastebasket, eliminate as much of the design from the right side as is necessary; it doesn't matter if only part of a shell or seaweed show or if a fish is cut off in midfin. To make a larger basket, repeat any of the shells, fish, or seaweed to fill the space (see Figure 1).

Figure 1

STITCHING

Follow the color key for the design as you work. The black lines you have traced onto the canvas only delineate separate areas of color and should not be stitched.

On the top and bottom (the long edges) work the design to the pattern outline, but on the sides (the short edges) stop the design one thread short of the design outline (see Figure 2).

Figure 2

FINISHING

Block the needlepoint.

On the two long sides sew a row of

machine stitching on the excess canvas just outside the needlepoint.

Cut the excess canvas away on all four sides to within an inch of the needlepoint.

Check the width of the needlepoint against the circumference of your cylinder. If they are the same size, finish the basket with the butt join, described below. If the needlepoint is narrower than the circumference of the cylinder, add a row or two of stitches vertically, but still stop the design one thread short of the width of the circumference so you can finish the wastebasket with the butt join. If the needlepoint is wider than the circumference of the cylinder, fit the needlepoint around the cylinder, mark that seam line with a pin, and use the seam join, described below.

Butt join. Turn the excess canvas to the back on each short edge, leaving just one row of canvas thread showing on each end (see Figure 3). Bring the

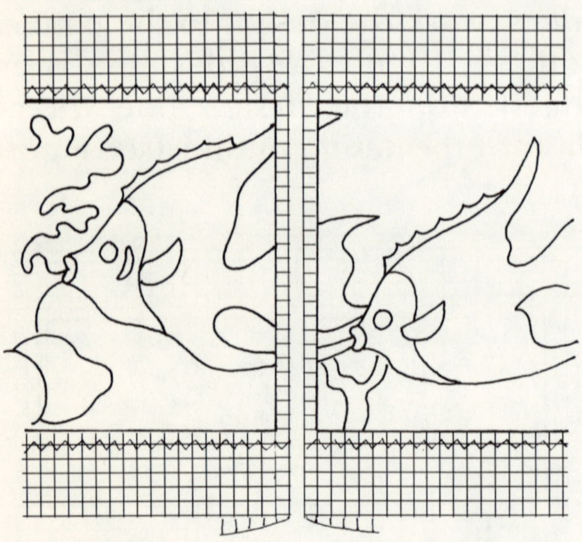

Figure 3

ends together and whip the two outermost vertical threads together, matching them for a butt join (see Figure 4). Using appropriate color yarn, work over the whipped row with

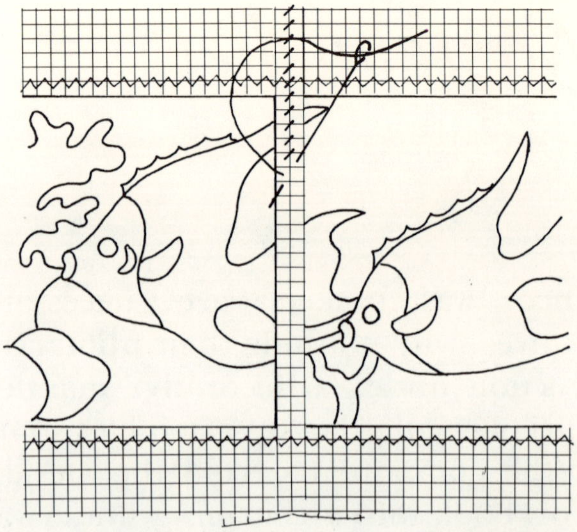

Figure 4

a vertical outline stitch to complete the design or fill in the background (see Figure 5).

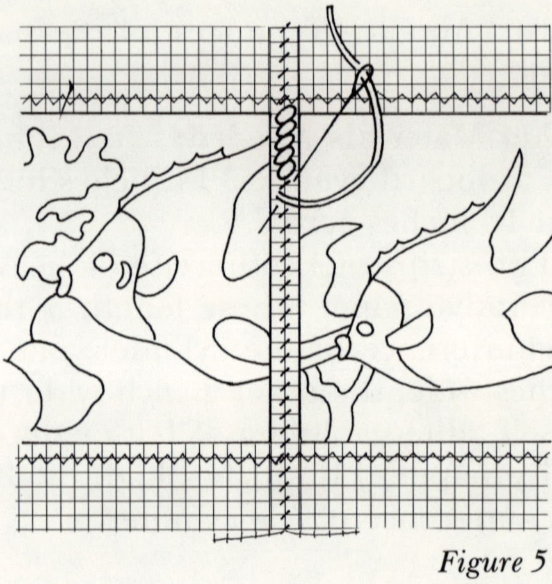

Figure 5

Seam join. Place the two ends with right sides together and baste along the fitted seam line, which you have marked with a pin; carefully match the rows (see Figure 6). Sew over the basting with a row of machine stitching. Turn each side of the "seam allowance" back and hem each to the back of the needlepoint (see Figure 7).

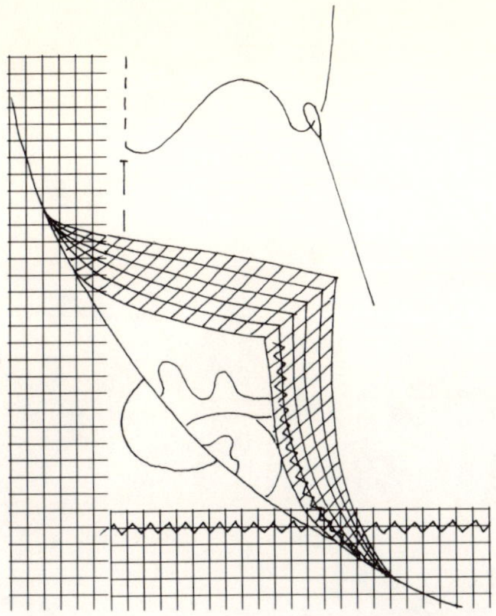

Figure 6

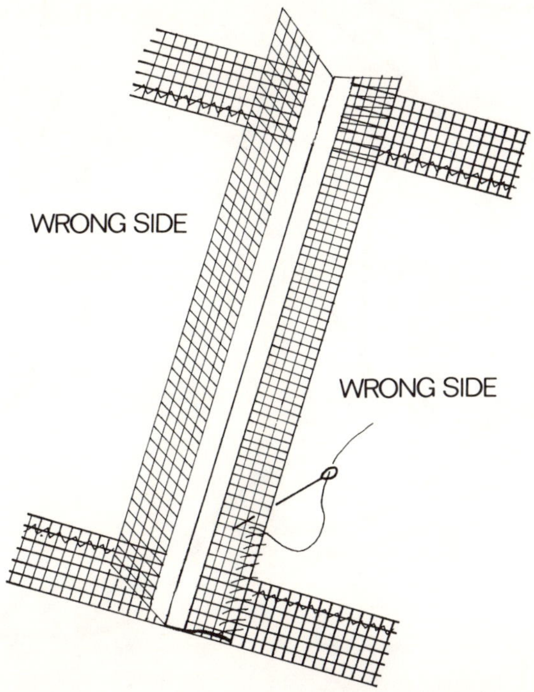

Figure 7

Turn the needlepoint right side out and pull the needlepoint sleeve over the cylinder. There will be about 1 inch of unstitched canvas around the top and the bottom.

Glue the 1-inch-wide decorative strip around the bottom edge; it should just meet the needlepoint stitching (see Figure 8). Glue the 2-inch-wide strip over the unstitched canvas at the top so that it just meets the needlepoint; about an inch or so of the strip will extend over the top edge (see Figure 8). Snip the extended

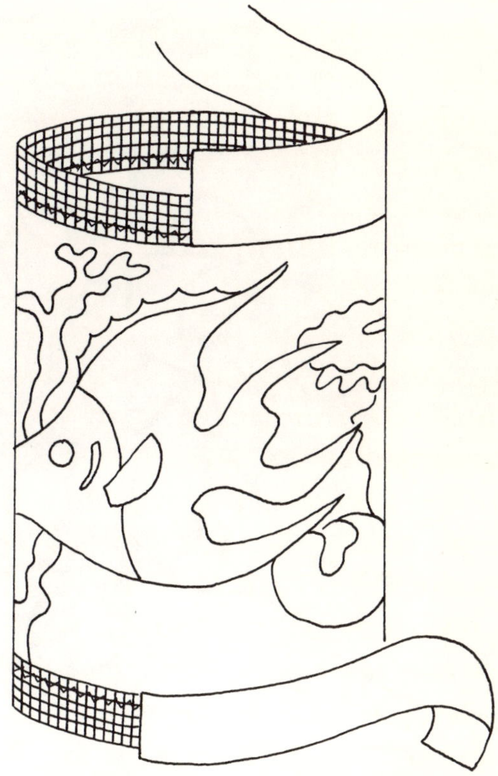

Figure 8

part of the strip every inch or so, then turn these tabs back and glue to the inside of the cylinder, where they will partially overlap each other (see Figure 9).

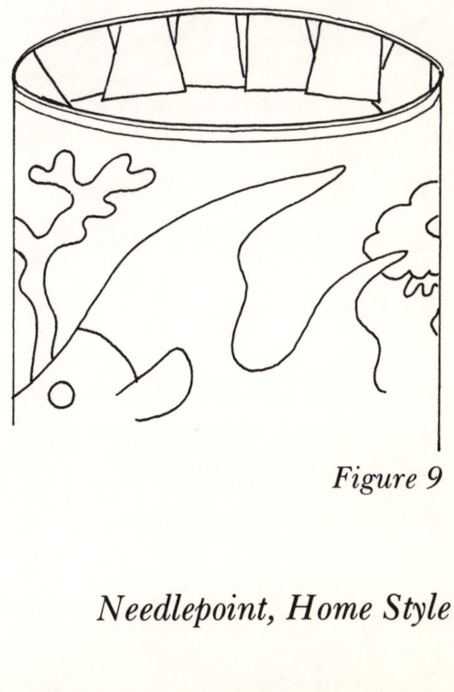

Figure 9

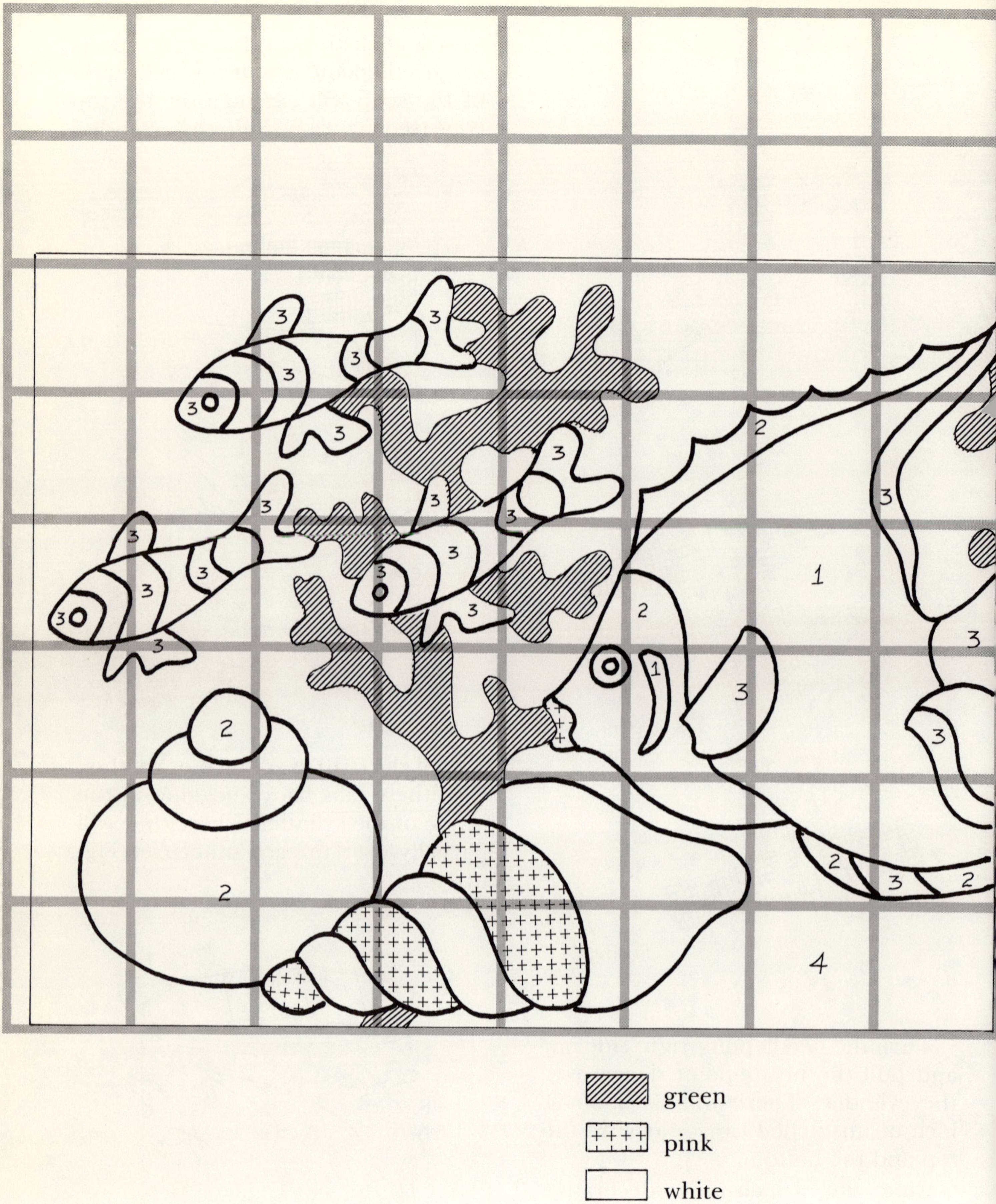
green
pink
white

1 yellow

2 brown

3 orange

4 beige

Line the inside of the wastebasket with self-adhesive felt or paper, which will hide the overlapping tabs. If the liner extends beyond the top edge, trim it carefully (see Figure 10).

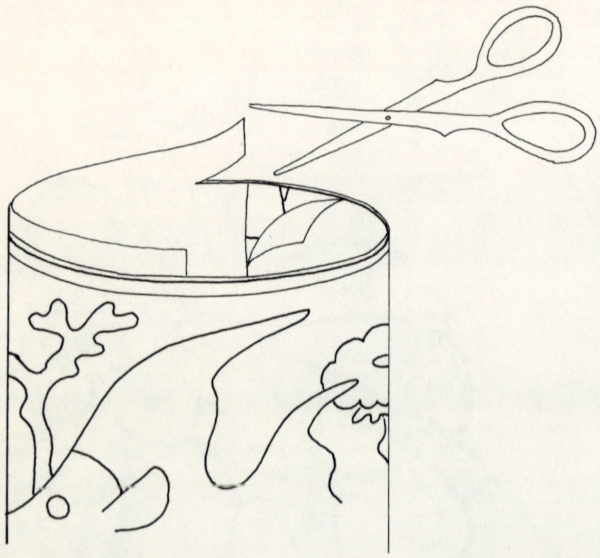

Figure 10

COLOR KEY

The color key for the wastebasket appears on the design pages.

Headboard Panels

A needlepoint panel set into a piece of wooden furniture has a decorating value far in excess of the effort required. In this particular project—a headboard—the five separate panels were mounted over existing caning, and the design derived from the striped bedspread. The plaid was repeated as many times as needed and the flowers scattered at random over the plaid field. Obviously, the plaid can be extended to fill any size or shape panel and, in fact, can be reproduced over an entire plywood headboard if you wanted to make one from scratch. The technique is just as useful for covering the panels of a dining room hutch, an armoire, or any kind of cupboard.

Making a custom pattern. To utilize this design, you must make a custom pattern for each panel to be covered. To do this, lay a piece of brown paper over each panel and on it outline the shape to be stitched with a dark marker (see Figure 1). Mark only the finished dimensions of the needlepoint. If the panel is removable, as is sometimes the case, you can use it as a pattern.

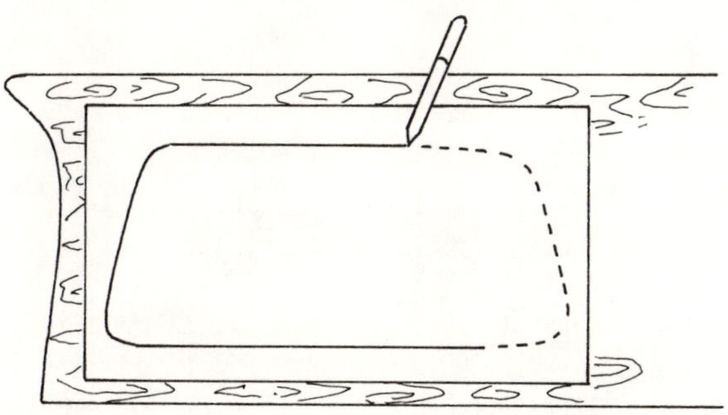

Figure 1

Stitch: Basketweave.

Canvas: No. 10 interlocking canvas. For each panel, cut a rectangular piece of canvas 4 inches larger than the widest and longest dimensions.

Yarn: 1¼ ounces of Persian wool for each full plaid repeat (including the flowers).

Other Materials Needed:
- Thin commercial cording twice the perimeter of each panel.

FROM DESIGN TO CANVAS

Bind the cut edges of each piece of canvas with masking tape.

Center the custom pattern for each panel face up under its canvas and trace the shape onto the canvas with an indelible marker.

On one piece of tracing paper transfer the plaid from the book page. On another piece of tracing paper transfer the four floral shapes. Both designs are project-size and will be traced repeatedly onto the needlepoint canvas to fill the design area.

Use the floral shapes first. Place the flower tracing face up under the canvas and trace the flowers individually onto the canvas wherever you want them to fall, moving the tracing around under the canvas to locate the flowers in a completely random pattern (see Figure 2).

Now place the tracing of the plaid under one corner of the canvas outline and transfer it to the canvas with

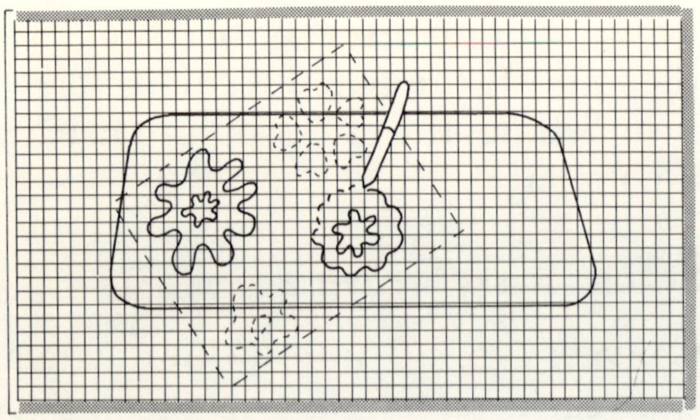

Figure 2

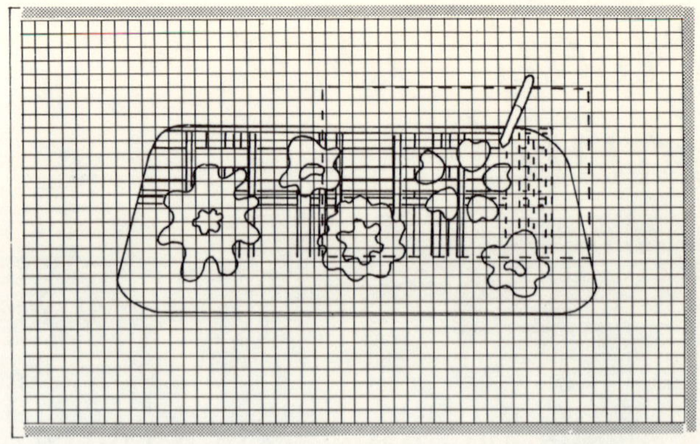

Figure 4

an indelible marker (see Figure 3). Move the tracing to a contiguous part of the canvas so that its lines abut and match the already traced plaid, and trace the same plaid a second time (see Figure 4). Continue to move the tracing of the plaid under the canvas, matching abutting lines, and to transfer the plaid to the canvas until you have filled the entire background area. Wherever the plaid falls on an already traced flower, do not trace that portion of the plaid onto the canvas; you want to create the illusion that the plaid pattern actually continues under the flowers. But do remember to resume the plaid wherever it should be seen—through the eyes and around the petals of the flowers (see Figures 3 and 4).

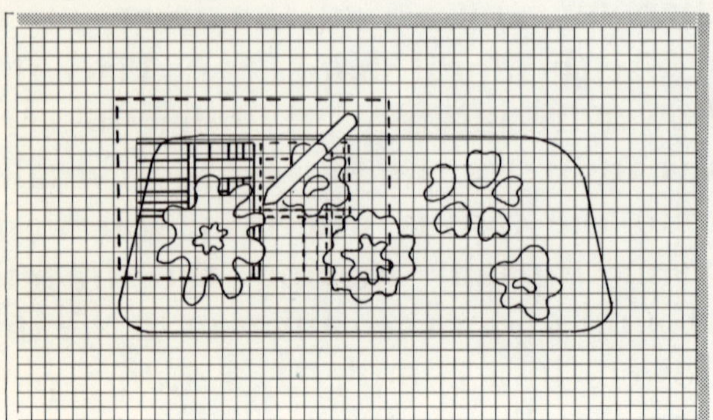

Figure 3

STITCHING

Follow the color key for the design and refer to the color photograph as you work. The black lines you have traced onto the canvas only delineate separate areas of color and should not be stitched.

Stitch all the flowers first, then work the background plaid. On all the edges stitch only to the outline of the panels.

FINISHING EACH PANEL

Block the needlepoint.

Sew a row of machine stitching on the excess canvas just outside the needlepoint.

Cut the excess canvas away on all sides to within 1 inch of the needlepoint. Cut the corners diagonally and notch the curves where necessary to reduce the bulk (see Figure 5).

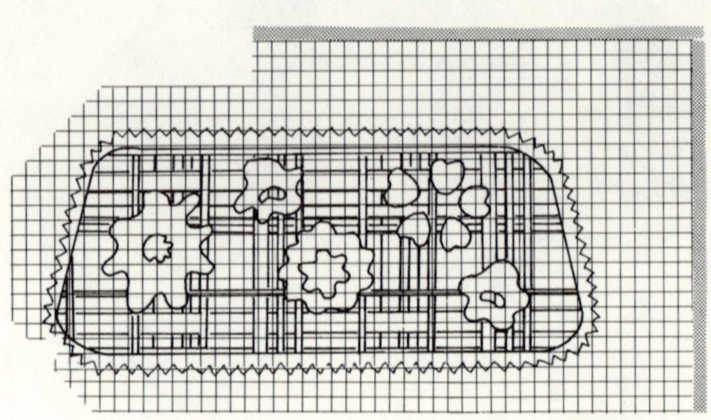

Figure 5

Turn the excess canvas under and hem to the back of the needlepoint.

Set the hemmed needlepoint into your panel and tack or glue it close to the edge (see Figure 6). The tacks will be covered with cording.

Figure 6

Figure 7

Glue the cording over the edge of the needlepoint, butting the ends where they meet (see Figure 7). You can glue a second row of cording inside the outer row if you like the look or need it for a neater finish.

COLOR KEY

- yellow
- 1 pale green
- 2 yellow-green
- 3 kelly green
- 4 dark green
- 5 gold
- 6 brown
- 7 orange
- 8 beige background

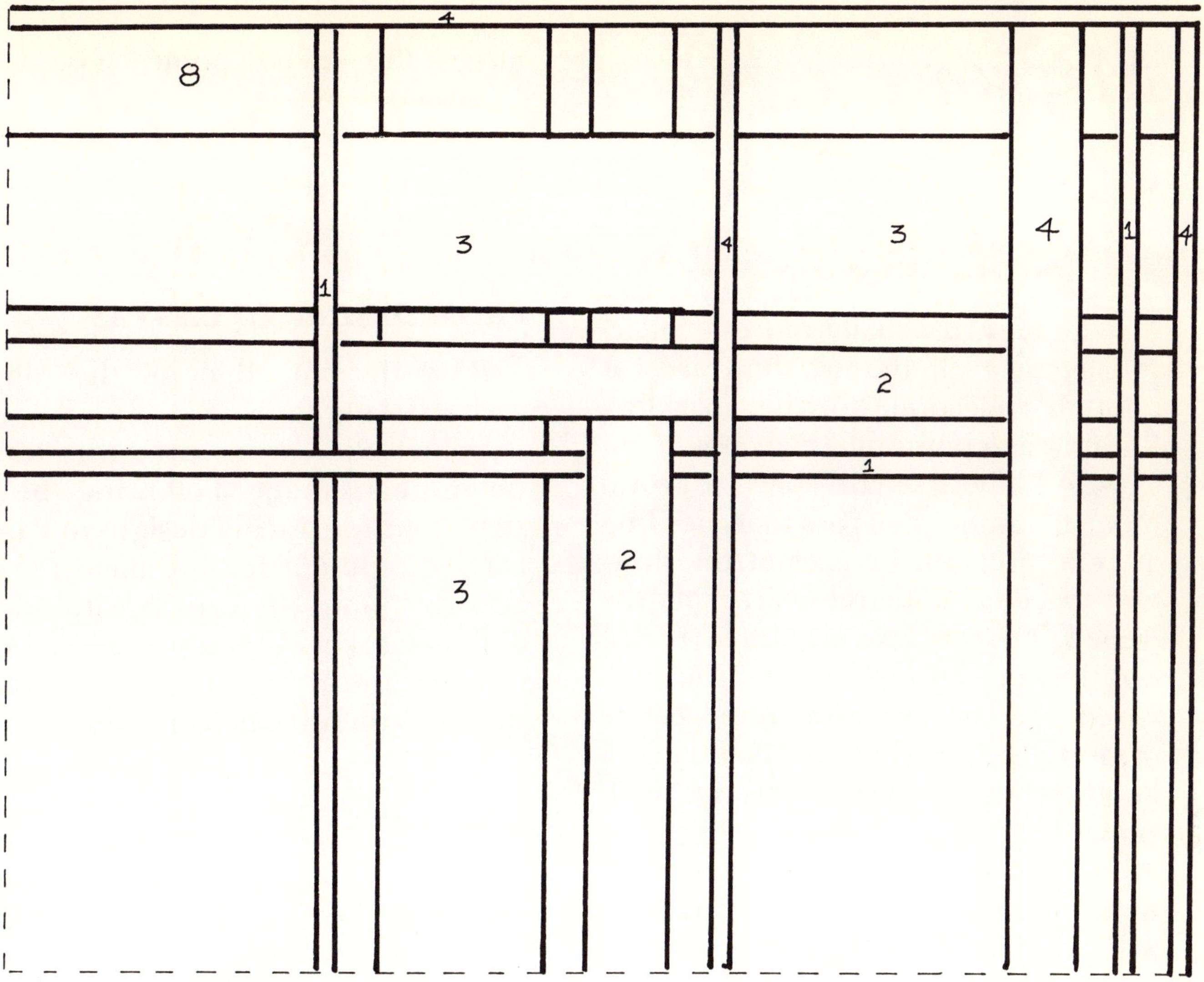
4
8
1
3
4
3
4
1
4
2
1
2
3

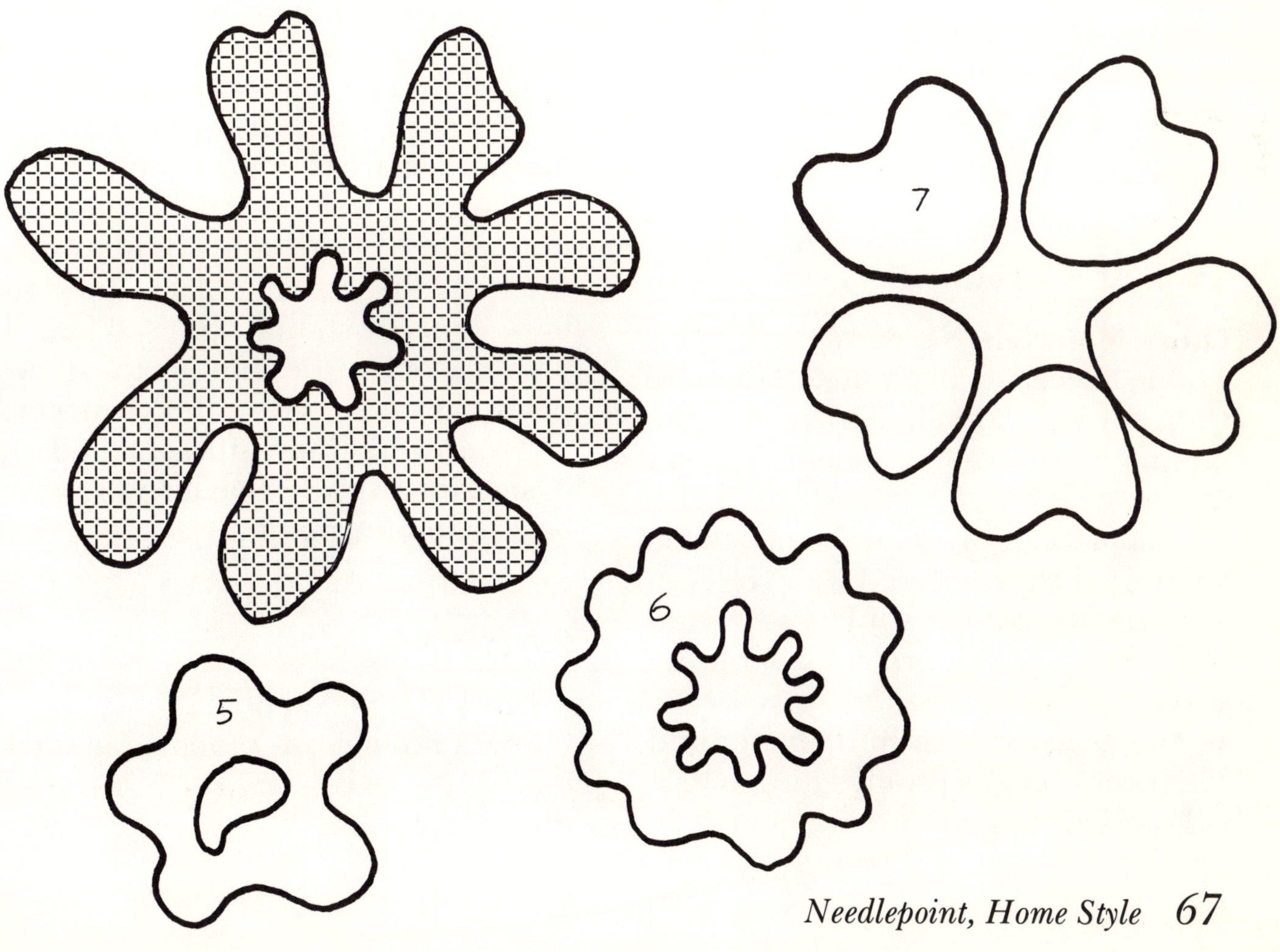
7
6
5

Mirror

Needlepoint is usually more a collector's item itself than a showcase for another collection, but this sparkling floral needlepoint mirror frame manages to be both as it displays a group of small antique mirrors that, nestling as reflections in the eyes of the flowers, become integral parts of the design. To set off the multimedia composition more emphatically, the mirrored needlepoint is mounted on its own backing and then "floated" on another, larger board covered with velvet.

The nicest part of this reflective flower garden is that you can start with the needlepoint and have the mirrors cut to size after you have completed the stitching.

Stitch: Basketweave.

Canvas: No. 10 interlocking canvas, 14 by 17 inches.

Yarn: About 3 ounces of Persian wool.

Other Materials Needed:

- One piece of perforated Masonite with corners rounded to match the outline of the design, about 8 by 11 inches.
- One piece of plywood, ¼ inch thick, 12 by 15 inches, covered with velvet in a color to match your decor and backed with felt or brown paper if desired.
- Two bolts, ⅛ inch in diameter and 1¼ inches long, with matching nuts.
- Four lightweight mirrors, cut to size after the needlepoint has been mounted.
- Two picture eyes for hanging.
- Heavy carpet thread and upholsterer's needle.

FROM DESIGN TO CANVAS

Bind the cut edges of the canvas with masking tape.

Center the canvas over the design on the book page. Following the instructions for tracing designs in Part I, trace the desigr for the mirror from the book onto the canvas with an indelible marker. If you prefer, you can transfer the design to tracing paper first and then to the canvas.

STITCHING

Follow the color key for the design and refer to the color photograph of the mirror as you work. As you can see, the centers of each flower are left unstitched where the mirrors will be mounted. The lighter black lines you have traced onto the canvas around the mirror areas and in the petals of the large flower only delineate separate areas of color and should not be stitched; the heavier black lines you have traced should be stitched in brown wool to outline all the flower petals, as described in the color key.

Around all four sides extend the design for five additional rows to turn back when finishing.

FINISHING

Block the needlepoint.

Sew a double row of machine stitching on the excess canvas just outside the needlepoint.

Cut the excess canvas away on all four sides to within 1½ inches of the needlepoint. Glue the cut edges lightly and let dry (see Figure 1).

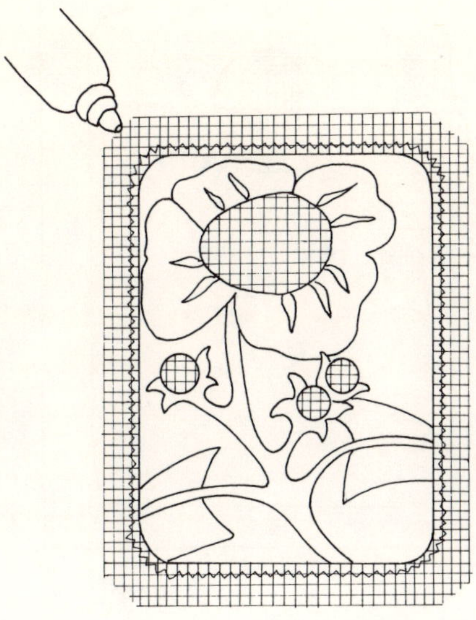

Figure 1

Insert the two bolts through the front of the Masonite, one in the center of the upper half and the other in the middle of the lower half. Thread the nuts onto each bolt to hold them in place temporarily (see Figure 2).

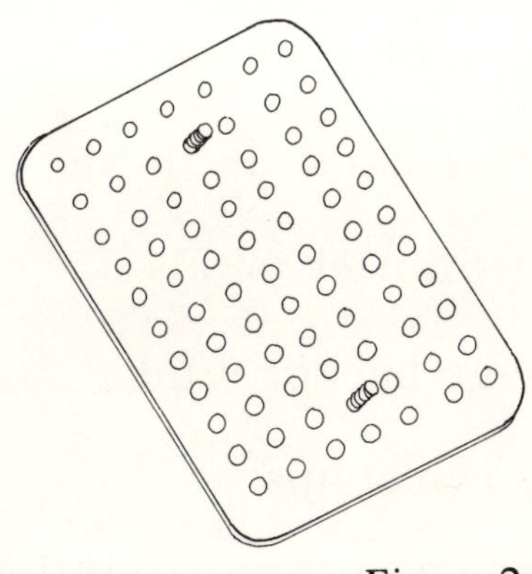

Figure 2

Center the Masonite over the plywood board. Drill holes through the plywood (and the covering fabric) where the ends of the two bolts touch the plywood (see Figure 3).

Figure 3

Set the plywood board aside while you mount the needlepoint on the Masonite.

Lay the needlepoint face down and center the Masonite over it. Temporarily anchor the needlepoint to the Masonite with short strips of tape, making sure that the rows of stitching are straight (see Figure 4).

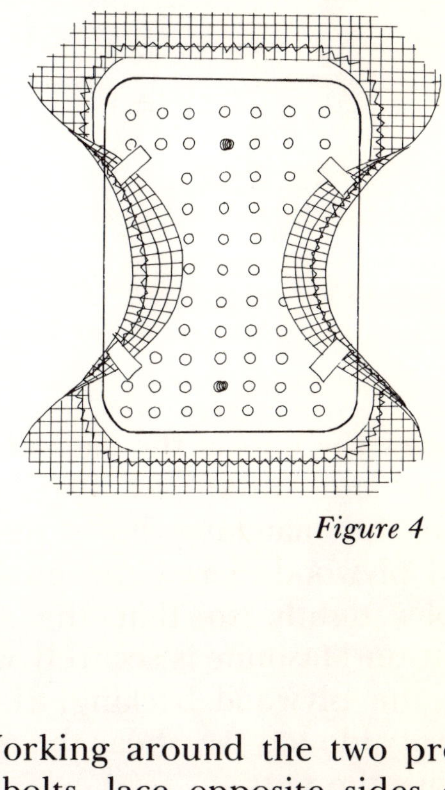

Figure 4

Working around the two protruding bolts, lace opposite sides of the canvas together with heavy carpet thread, starting in the center of the sides and working to within 2 inches of each corner (see Figure 5). Then lace opposite corners together, easing the canvas into neat folds around the curved corners of the Masonite (see Figure 6).

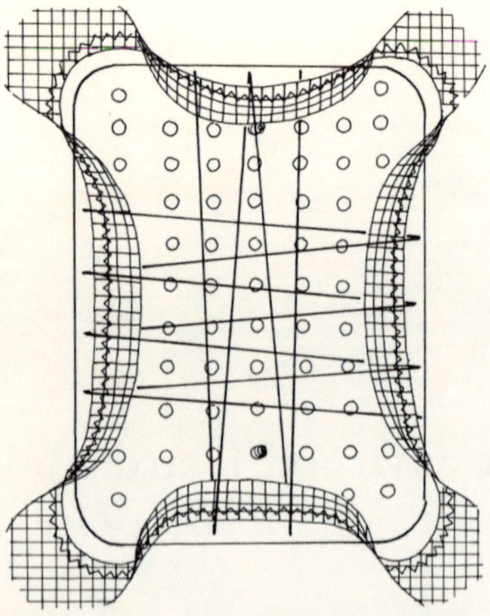

Figure 5

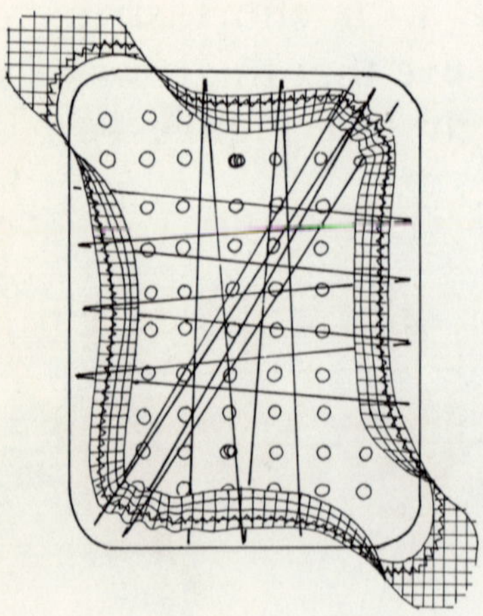

Figure 6

Unscrew the nuts at the back of the Masonite and insert the two bolts through the matching holes in the covered plywood. Screw the nuts on the bolts tightly so that the needlepoint-on-Masonite is securely wedded to the plywood backing. If the bolts protrude too far, shear them off flush with the nuts.

When the needlepoint frame has been assembled, take it to a glazier for four lightweight mirrors cut exactly to fit the four canvas areas. They need not have polished edges. Glue each mirror to its unstitched canvas "bed," using an adhesive, such as Black Magic Tough Glue, that will not harm the silver backing on the mirror (see Figure 7).

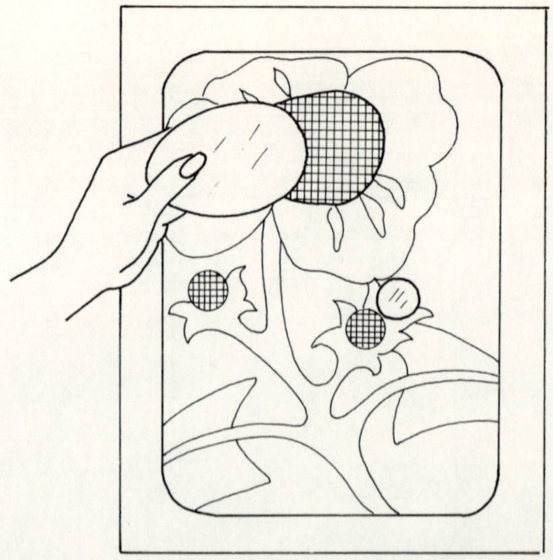

Figure 7

Screw two picture eyes into the back of the plywood frame toward the top of each side, string with picture wire, and hang on the wall.

COLOR KEY

- blank canvas under each mirror
- royal blue leaves
- 1 white bands in flower
- 2 rust flower petals
- 3 beige background
- 4 brown stems
- brown outline around all flower petals

3
1
1
2
1
1
2
1
1
2
1
1
1
1
2
2
3
3
2
2
2
4
2
2
2
3
4
4

Bulletin Board

A needlepoint bulletin board can add a welcome touch of color and texture to the kitchen, often the most used and least "decorated" room in the house. The density of the stitching is ideal for tacking up memos, shopping lists, and notes to the family, and this display of fresh vegetables is entirely appropriate to the setting.

Stitch: Basketweave.

Canvas: No. 10 interlocking canvas, 16 by 25 inches.

Yarn: 7½ ounces of Persian wool, including about 5 ounces for the background.

Other Materials Needed:
- Backing board of cork or cardboard covered with Dacron batting, 21 inches by about 11¾ inches.
- Felt for lining the backing board.
- Two fabric picture hooks.
- Heavy carpet thread and upholsterer's needle.

FROM DESIGN TO CANVAS

Bind the cut edges of the canvas with masking tape.

Following the instructions for enlarging designs in Part I, enlarge the design so that the width is 21 inches; the height will be about 11¾ inches. Center the design face up under the canvas and trace it onto the canvas with an indelible marker.

STITCHING

Follow the color key on the design and refer to the color photograph as you stitch the canvas. Around all four edges extend the design for three additional rows.

FINISHING

Block the needlepoint.

Sew a row of machine stitching on the excess canvas about ½ inch out from the needlepoint.

Cut the excess canvas away on all four sides to within 1½ inches of the needlepoint, and cut the corners diagonally to within an inch of the stitching. Glue the cut edges and let dry (see Figure 1).

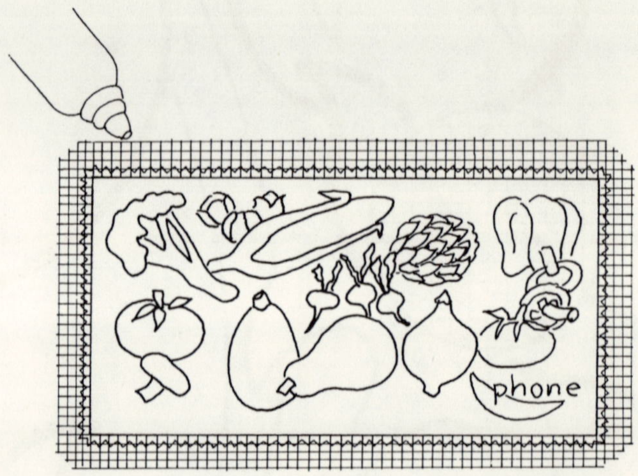

Figure 1

Lay the needlepoint facedown and center the cork or padded board over it. Temporarily anchor the needlepoint to the edge of the board with thin tacks, making sure that the rows of stitching are straight.

Lace opposite sides of the canvas to the backing board with heavy carpet thread and an upholsterer's needle, starting in the center of each side and working to within 2 inches of each corner (see Figure 2). Miter each corner and sew the mitered seams.

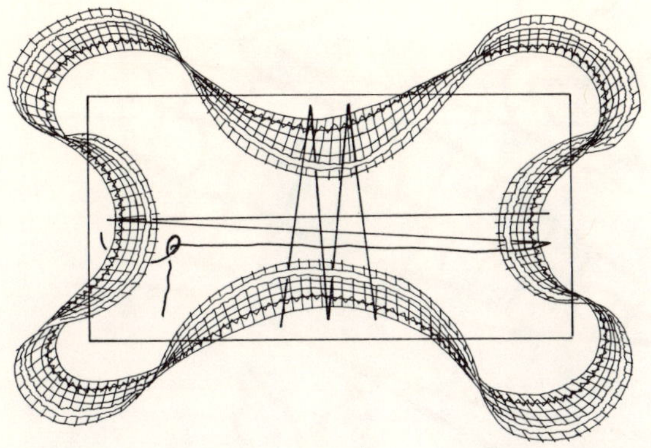

Figure 2

Finish lacing opposite sides together (see Figure 3).

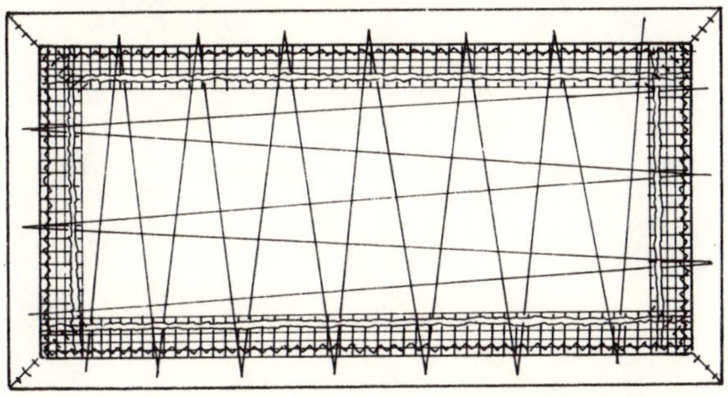

Figure 3

Cut felt to cover the back of the board and blindstitch in place.

To hang on a wall, glue a pair of fabric picture hooks to the felt. To attach to a refrigerator or metal wall cabinet, press strips of double-stick tape to the back.

COLOR KEY

The color key appears on the design page.

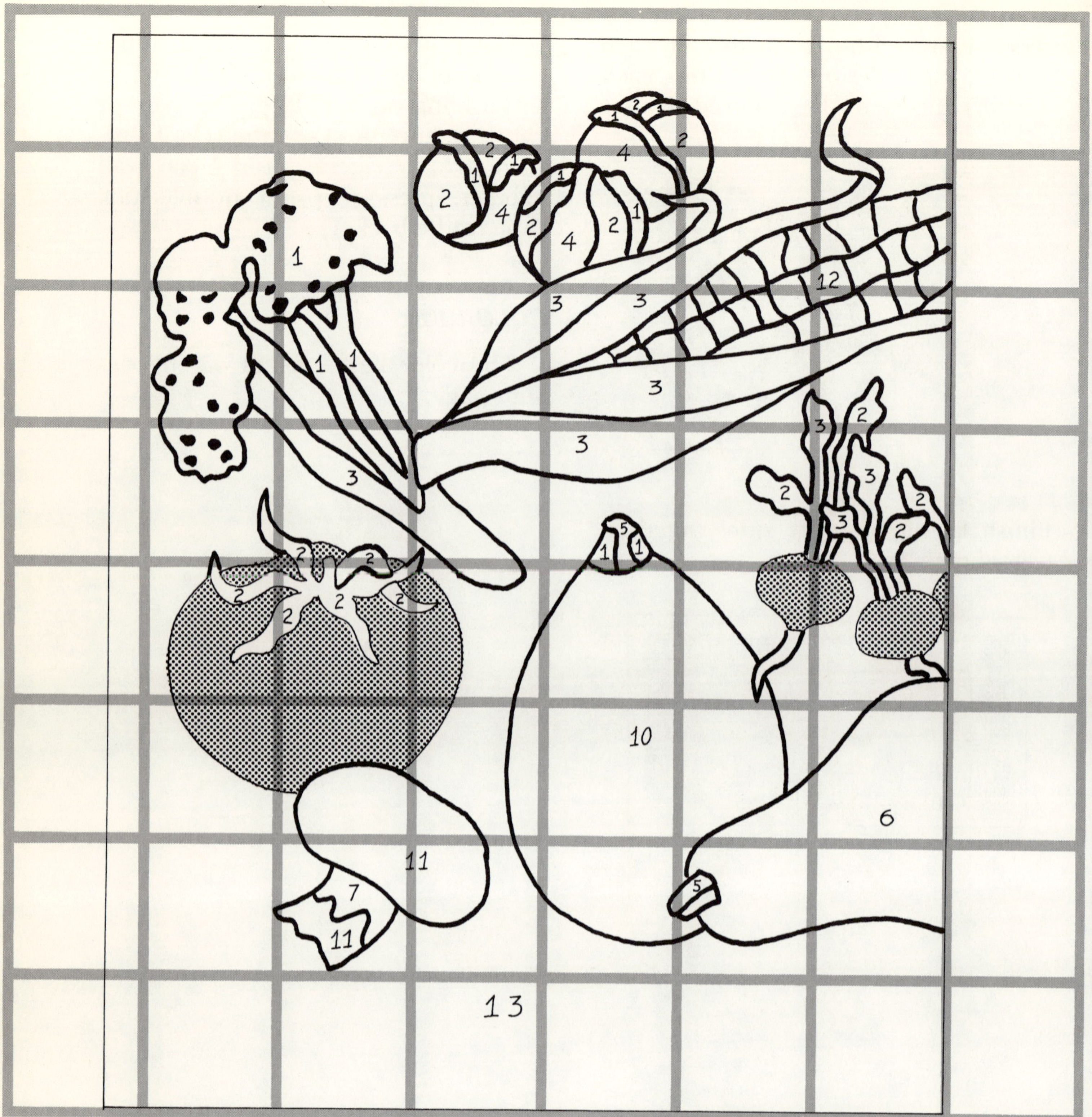

(shaded)	red	5	dark green
1	yellow-green	6	cream
2	kelly green	7	medium brown
3	medium green	8	white
4	gray-green	9	light yellow-beige

10	purple
11	beige
12	bright yellow
13	medium blue background
—	navy letters; orange and yellow lines in onion; dark green lines in cornhusk, artichoke, broccoli, and bottom of pea pod; orange lines in corn; medium-brown lines around squash

Roman Shade

A wall hanging that pulls up like a shade combines the best of artistic and utilitarian worlds. In its guise as a contemporary abstract, this Roman shade hangs on a standard exterior door and hides a window 24 by 40 inches.

Stitch: Basketweave.

Canvas: No. 10 mono canvas, 30 by 49 inches.

Yarn: About 36 ounces of Persian wool.

Other Materials Needed:

- Lightproof fabric for lining, 1 inch larger all around than the finished needlepoint.
- Cotton twill tape: three strips, each 50 inches long and at least ½ inch wide; this is used in place of commercial Roman shade tape, which is not strong enough to support a needlepoint shade.
- Fifteen plastic rings, each 1 inch in diameter.
- Traverse cord: three lengths, each 3 yards long.
- Brass curtain rod ⅜ inch in diameter, covered in fabric.
- Heavy-duty gripper tape, 27 inches wide.
- Wooden mounting board, 1 inch by 2 inches by 25 inches wide.
- Four screw eyes.

FROM DESIGN TO CANVAS

Bind the cut edges of the canvas with masking tape.

Following the instructions for enlarging the design in Part I, enlarge the design so that the width measures 26 inches; the length will be about 45 inches.

Center the enlarged design face up under the canvas and trace it onto the canvas with an indelible marker.

If your window is smaller, use as much of the design as you need. If your window is larger, extend the area by repeating a strip of the design at the top or the sides wide enough to fill your requirements.

STITCHING

Follow the color key for the design as you work the canvas and consult the color photograph. You can see that the main background shades from bronze to deep gold to yellow. This is done by stitching with strands of the closest shades at the same time, a process explained on page 14. This tweeding of strands creates a continuously shaded effect without sharp changes of color.

The black lines you have traced onto the canvas only delineate separate areas of color and should not be stitched.

Around all four sides extend the design for two extra rows.

FINISHING

Block the needlepoint.

Sew a row of machine stitching on the excess canvas just outside the needlepoint.

Attach the tape to the lining as follows:

Sew the cotton twill tapes to the

right side of the lining from the top edge to 1 inch short of the bottom; let the extra tape hang free. Sew one strip down the center and the others 4 inches in from each side (see Figure 1).

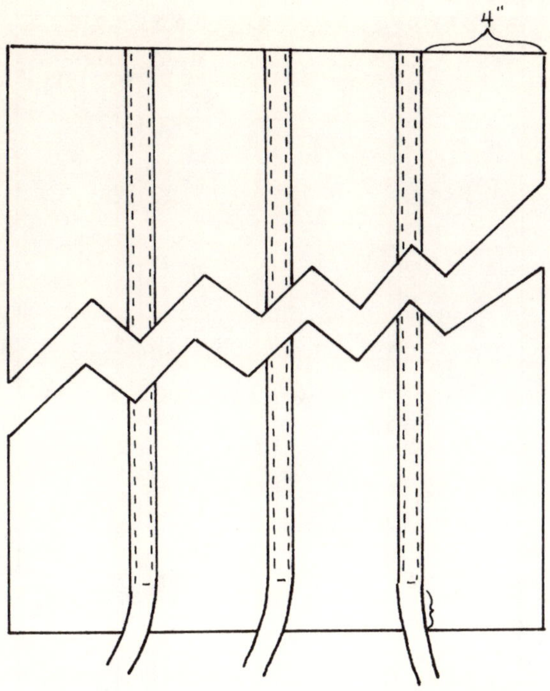

Figure 1

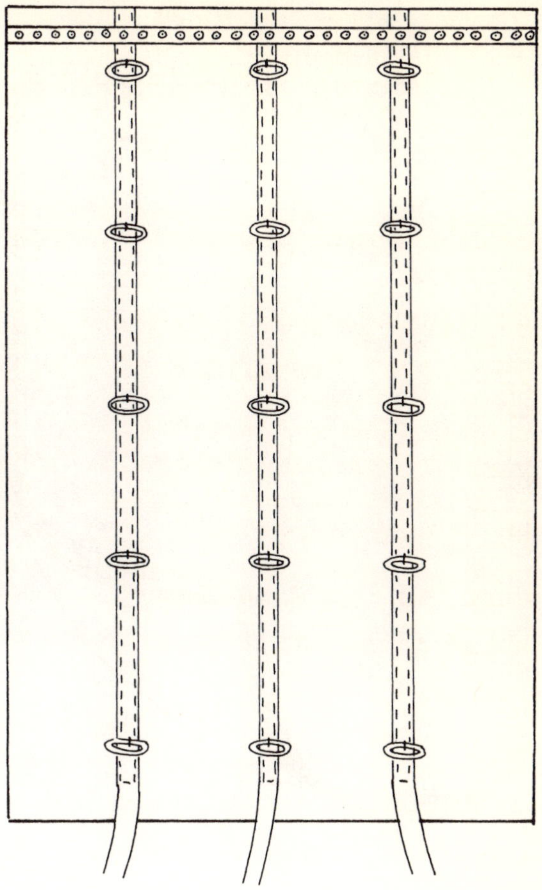

Figure 2

Sew one part of the gripper tape across the top of the lining, 1 inch down from the top edge. Stitch over the twill-tape strips as you come to them (see Figure 2). The other half of the gripper tape will be tacked to the door strip.

Sew the plastic rings securely to the twill tape, five to each strip, as follows: Sew one ring at the top 1 inch under the gripper tape. Sew another ring 3 inches from the bottom hem. Space the other three rings evenly along the strip; they will be about 10 inches apart. Sew rings to the other two strips in exactly the same places, making sure that each ring is even with its counterparts on the other strips (see Figure 2).

Lay the lining face up and place the needlepoint over it face down. Sew them together at the top and the two sides just inside the two-row seam allowance. Trim the unstitched canvas and extra lining to within an inch of the needlepoint, and cut the corners diagonally (see Figure 3). Turn the lined needlepoint right side out.

Pin the lining to the needlepoint in a few places so it doesn't slip, then blindstitch the twill strips to the back of the needlepoint. As you come to the rings, catch them securely to the needlepoint, taking care that your stitches don't show on the front. Remove the pins.

To hem the bottom, turn the extra two rows of needlepoint under, turn the lining under to match, and

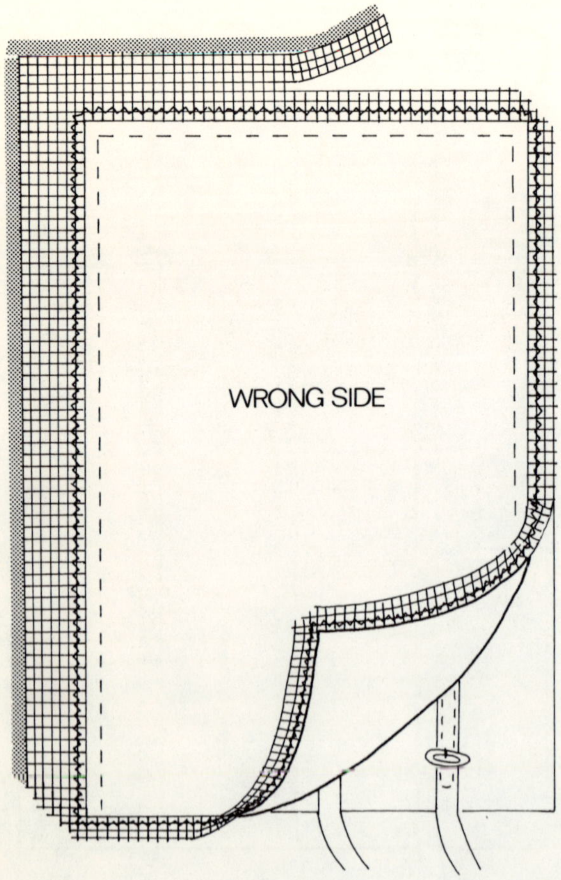

Figure 3

blindstitch the lining to the needlepoint.

Tack the hanging ends of the twill tape to the twill strips to form loops that clear the bottom of the shade by about 1 inch. Insert the fabric-covered curtain rod through the loops and secure it with extra tacking stitches (see Figure 4).

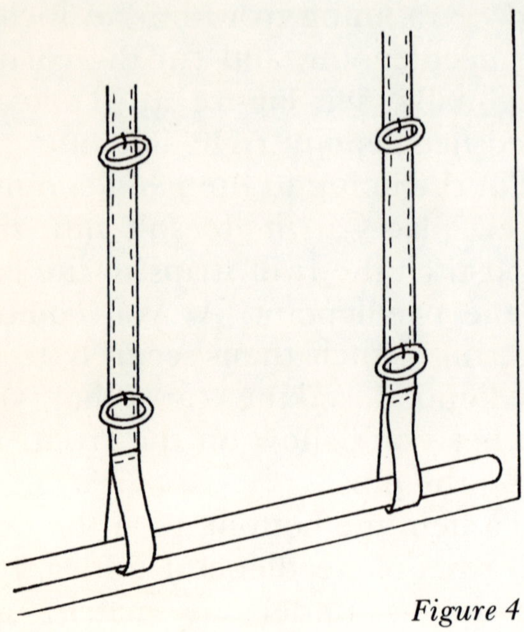

Figure 4

Tie one end of traverse cord to each of the three bottom rings, and thread each cord through the other rings on its twill tape. Let the long ends hang at the top (see Figure 5).

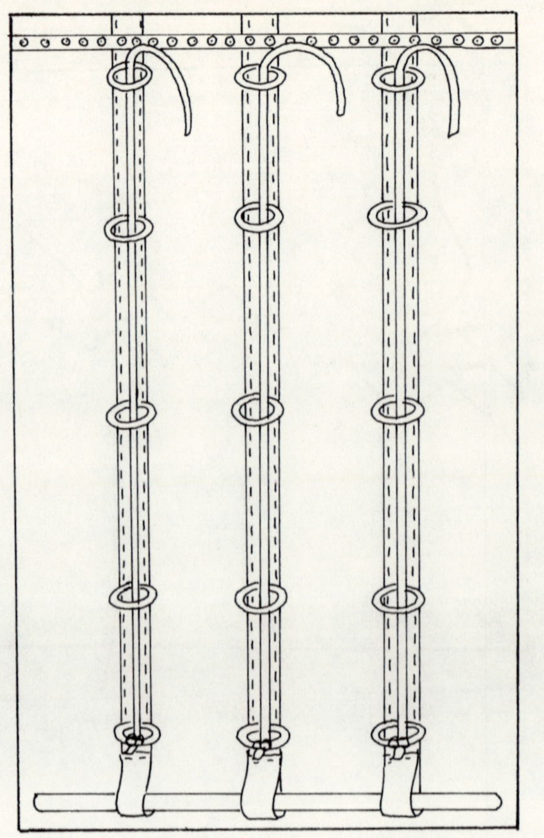

Figure 5

At the top of your door, nail or glue the mounting board with the wide side against the door. Tack the remaining half of the gripper tape at the top of the board to match its counterpart on the top of the shade (see Figure 6). Attach three screw eyes to the bottom of the board to correspond to the twill tape strips, and a fourth at the right end of the board (see Figure 6).

Snap the shade to the mounting board on the door. Pull each traverse cord through its corresponding screw eye on the board, then bring it through the screw eye at the right end

3
7
8
3
7
8
9
5
2
2
4
2
4
2
4
4
4
5
11
12
13
14
3
7
10
1
7
8
3
8
3
8
7
3
8
7
9
9
6
5
6
5
6
6

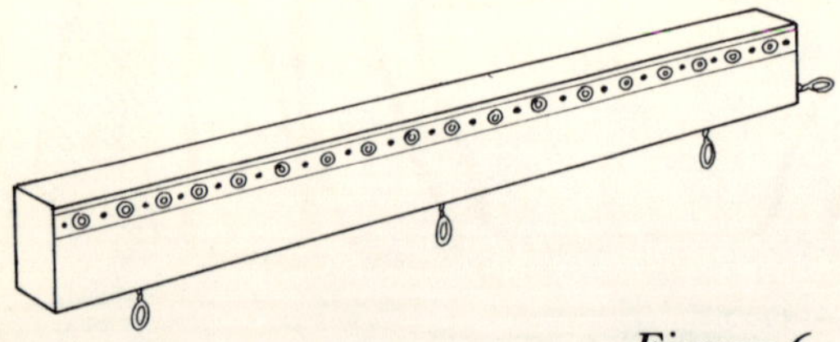

Figure 6

of the board and through any intervening screw eyes (see Figure 7). Adjust the cords until the shade rises and lowers evenly, then cut the ends off evenly and tie together (see Figure 7).

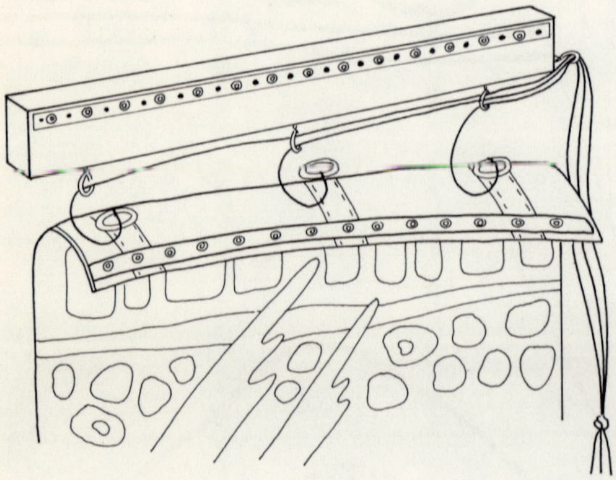

Figure 7

COLOR KEY

++++ dark brown

▨ medium pink

1 lavender

2 aqua shapes

3 medium yellow

4 cream

5 turquoise

6 taupe

7 hot pink

8 burnt orange

9 light gray

10 light pink

11 bronze

12 bronze and deep yellow; tweeded

13 deep yellow and gold, tweeded

14 deep yellow

Side Chairs–Upholstered and Slip Seat

A pair of side chairs offers the irresistible opportunity to stitch related but different designs, making both room and project more interesting. These particular chairs, which could easily double as dining chairs, sport a set of jungle animal heads, each mounted like a trophy on its appropriate skin marking. They are all project-size, that is, they can be traced right from the book pages onto the needlepoint canvas.

Both the animal heads and their skin markings are scaled to fit any chair seat about 16 inches square. If your seat—the sitting area, not including the side drops on upholstered chairs—is appreciably larger than 16 inches square, you should enlarge the head and its skin marking proportionately, following the instructions for enlarging designs in Part I. (A good rule of thumb is to enlarge the design so that the length of each animal face is about two thirds the depth of the seat, not including the side drop.) Your sitting area is not likely to be smaller than 16 inches square, but if you want to reduce this design for another project, see page 10.

Making a custom pattern for an upholstered chair seat. Whether you trace the design off the book page or enlarge it for a bigger chair seat, you will still have to make a custom pattern for your needlepoint because every chair is slightly different in its contours, its proportions, the depth of its side drops, and the thickness of its seat padding—all of which affect the area to be stitched.

To make the pattern, lay a piece of muslin over the seat and on it mark all the pertinent outlines (see Figure 1).

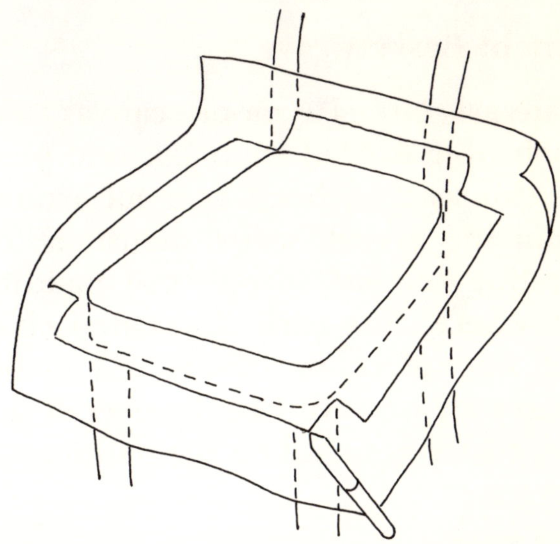

Figure 1

If you are planning to replace the chair padding, be generous in your outline of the sitting area because the new padding may be fuller than the worn stuffing. Mark only the finished dimensions of the needlepoint; seam allowances are given with the instructions.

Making a custom pattern for a slip-seated chair. Unfasten the seat panel of your chair and, if possible, use the existing seat fabric you have just removed as a custom pattern for your needlepoint. If you have to make a new pattern, lay a piece of muslin over the seat and on it mark the outlines of the area to be stitched (see Figure 2). Allow for new padding if needed.

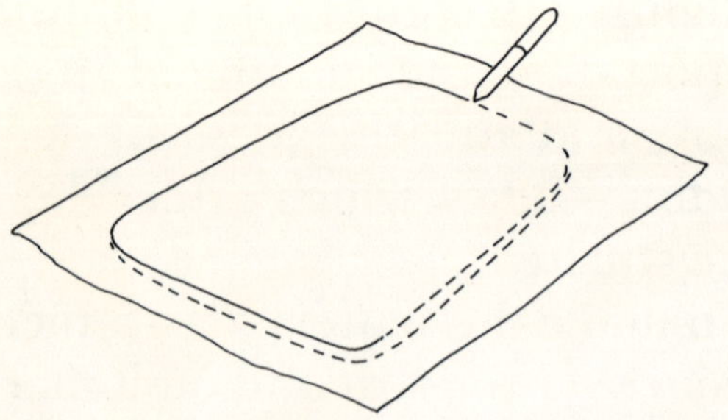

Figure 2

Stitch: Basketweave.

Canvas: No. 10 mono canvas. For each upholstered chair cut one piece of canvas 2 inches larger all around than the overall seat dimensions, including the side drops and padding allowance. For each slip-seated chair cut one piece of canvas 3½ inches larger all around than the overall seat dimensions, including the padding allowance.

Yarn: One ounce of Persian wool for every 36 square inches of needlepoint.

Other Materials Needed:
• Cambric for lining, 1 inch larger than the bottom of the chair seat.

FROM DESIGN TO CANVAS

Bind the cut edges of the canvas with masking tape.

Center the canvas over the muslin pattern and outline the dimensions of the seat on the canvas with an indelible marker (see Figure 3). You may want to darken the lines on the muslin for greater visibility.

Position the canvas over the design on the book page so that the animal face is centered horizontally but is

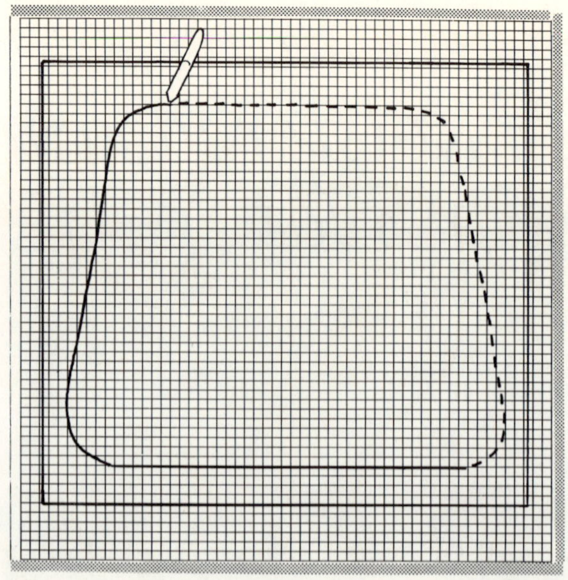

Figure 3

slightly forward of the true center vertically (see Figure 4). If you prefer, you can transfer the design to tracing paper first and then to the canvas. (Note: For the upholstered chair, don't be surprised if the head looks disproportionately small on the seat outline; the side drops require a sizeable area of stitching.)

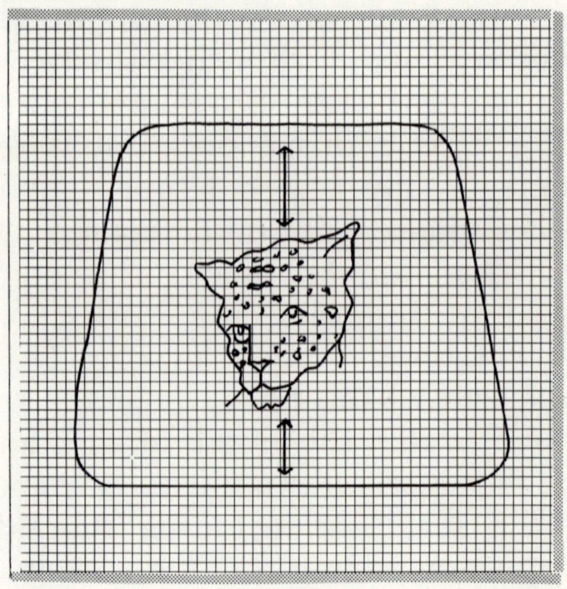

Figure 4

To transfer the skin markings to the canvas, you must first trace the markings from the book page onto tracing paper because the markings, although

- rust nose
- gold shadows
- green eyes
- black markings, nostrils, whiskers, mouth, eyeballs, eye lines, ear shadows
- 1 deep yellow shadows
- 2 pale yellow-beige background
- 3 white

project-size in scale, have to be repeated to fill the seat outline.

Place the tracing of the skin marking under the canvas at one front corner of the seat outline and trace it onto the canvas with an indelible marker (see Figure 5). Following the

Figure 5

instructions for extending designs in Part I, flop the tracing and trace the markings onto a contiguous part of the canvas (see Figure 6). Flop the

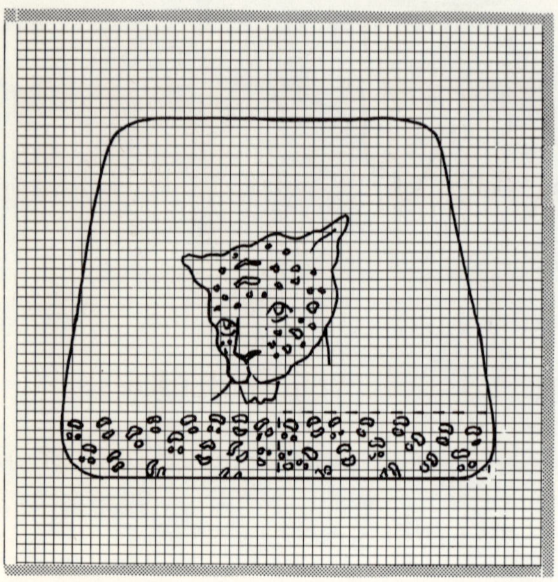

Figure 6

tracing as many times as you need to in order to cover the design area horizontally, then flop the tracing the short way as needed to fill the chair outline (see Figure 7). If any part of the skin marking falls under the animal head, ignore it and trace the markings up to but not inside the head outline (see Figure 7).

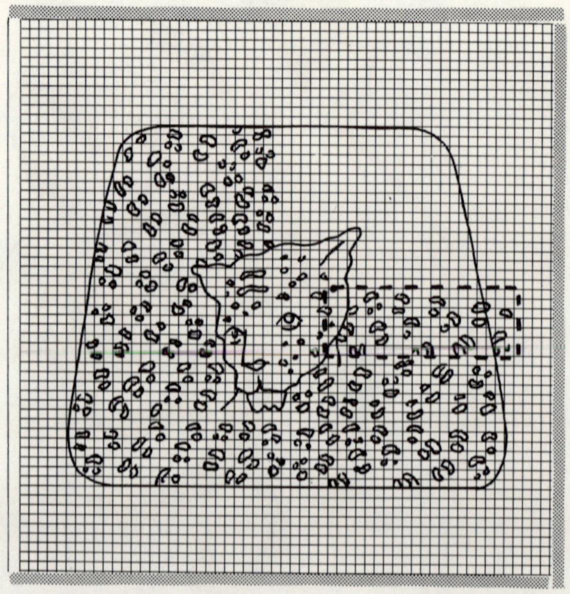

Figure 7

STITCHING

Follow the color key for the animal heads and the skin markings and refer to the color photograph as you work. The black lines you have traced onto the canvas only delineate separate areas of color and should not be stitched.

For the upholstered chair extend the design around all four sides 1 extra inch for turning under. For the slip-seated chair seat extend the design around all four sides an extra 1½ inches for turning under.

FINISHING THE UPHOLSTERED CHAIR

Block the needlepoint.

- gray
- rust
- yellow-green
- red-orange
- gold
- 1 pale yellow
- 2 medium yellow
- 3 white
- black spots, outline in eyes, eyeballs, whiskers, mouth

Sew a row of machine stitching on the excess canvas just outside the needlepoint.

Cut the excess canvas away on all four sides to within 1½ inches of the needlepoint, and cut the corners diagonally to within 1 inch of the stitching.

Remove existing cambric and upholstery from the chair; replace padding if needed.

Center the needlepoint over the padding and tack it loosely to the front and back in a few places (see Figure 8).

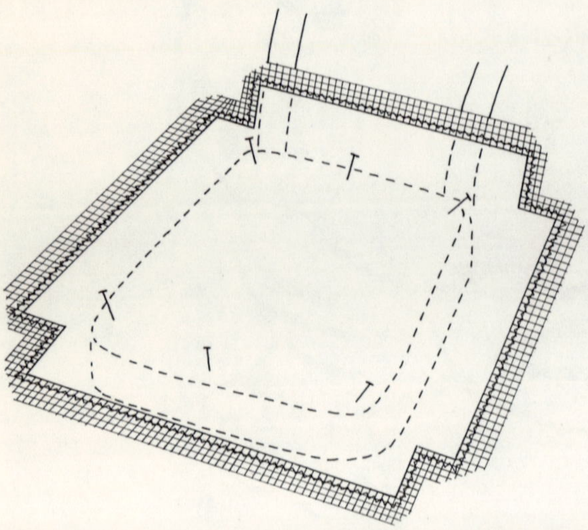

Figure 8

To upholster around each back corner post, turn a back corner of needlepoint forward on the chair seat. Starting at the corner of the needlepoint, cut a slit toward the back post, stopping just short of the post. Turn the two cut edges of the slit under (see Figure 9). Nail each edge to the bottom of the chair with upholstery tacks, pulling the needlepoint taut around the post (see Figure 10). Repeat for the other post, then tack the rear edge to the bottom of the seat (see Figure 10).

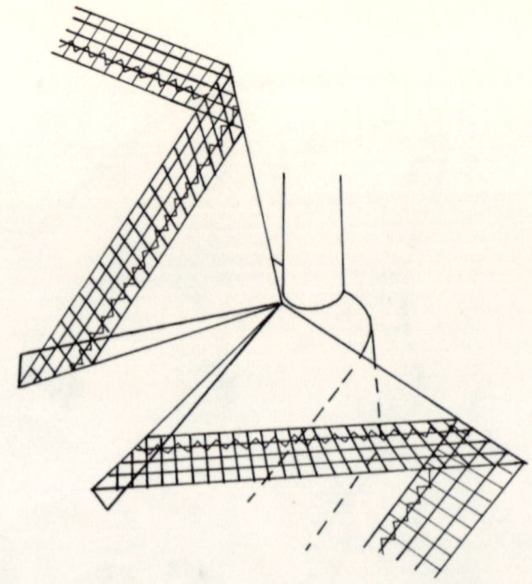

Figure 9

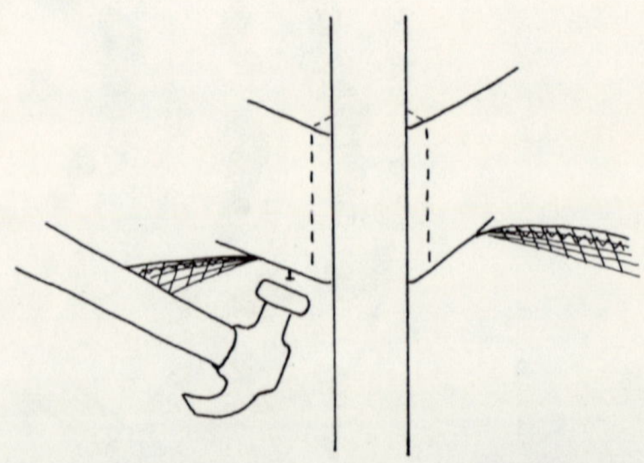

Figure 10

Remove the temporary tacks from the front corners, pull the needlepoint forward until it is smooth; then tack the front edge to the bottom of the seat, leaving the front corners open (see Figure 11).

Upholster the front corners as follows:

Where the needlepoint meets the leg at the side (see Figure 12), slit the needlepoint from *A* to *B* and cut the side edge from *C* to *D*.

Make a small hem at the cut edge *AB;* turn the overhang under and tack to the bottom of the seat (see Figure 13). Turn a small hem under at *CD* so that its hem meets the bottom of the seat frame, *BE*. Tack the needlepoint to the chair leg at its innermost edge, *EF*. Fold the front corner over to hide the tacks and anchor the needlepoint over the chair leg, if necessary, with small-headed, almost invisible gimp tacks (see Figure 14).

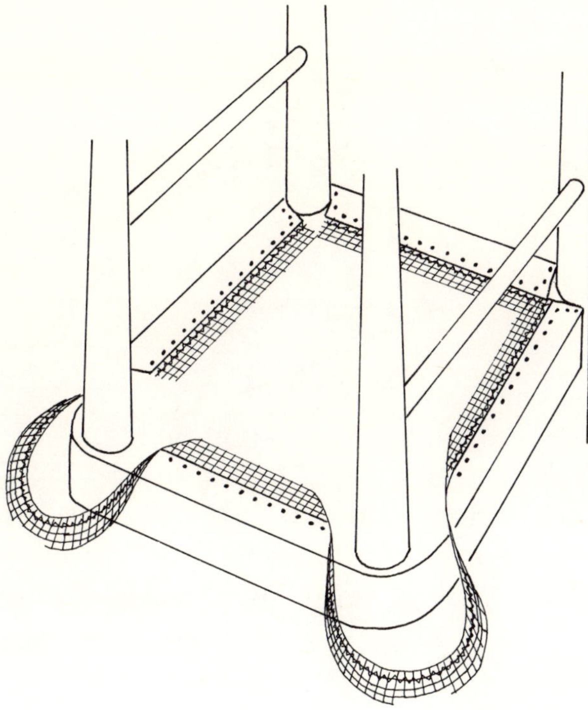

Figure 11

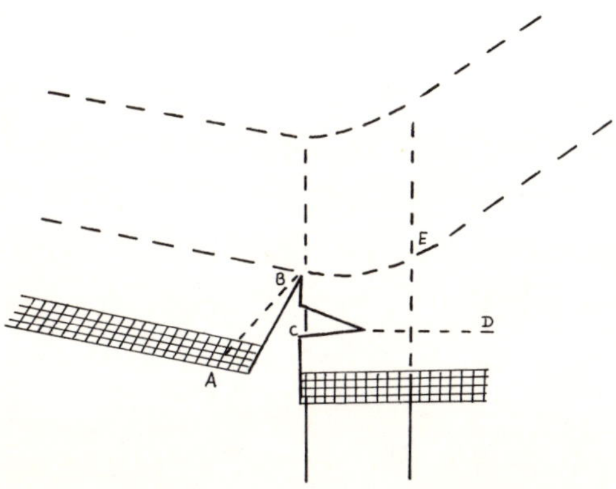

Figure 12

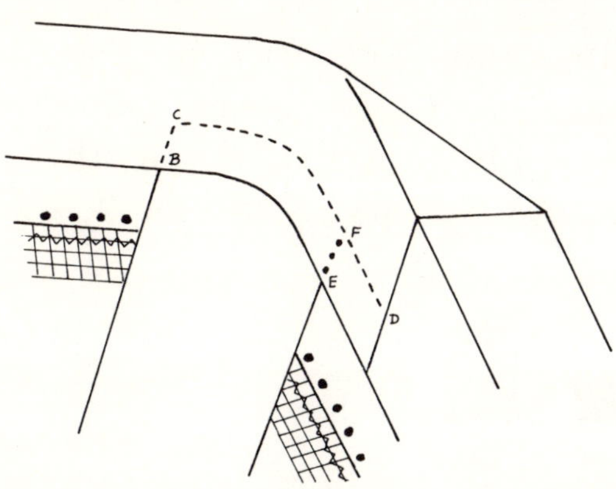

Figure 13

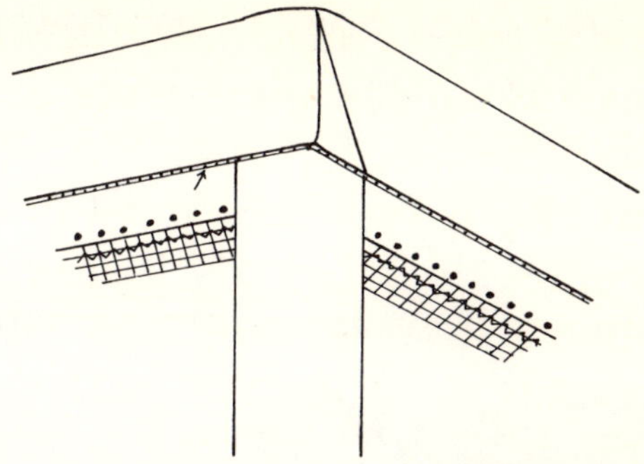

Figure 14

Turn the chair over and tack any loose edges to the chair frame. Lay the cambric over the tacked needlepoint and turn the four sides under to fit the seat bottom. Tack to the chair frame, pulling the lining taut and encircling the legs as you come to them (see Figure 15).

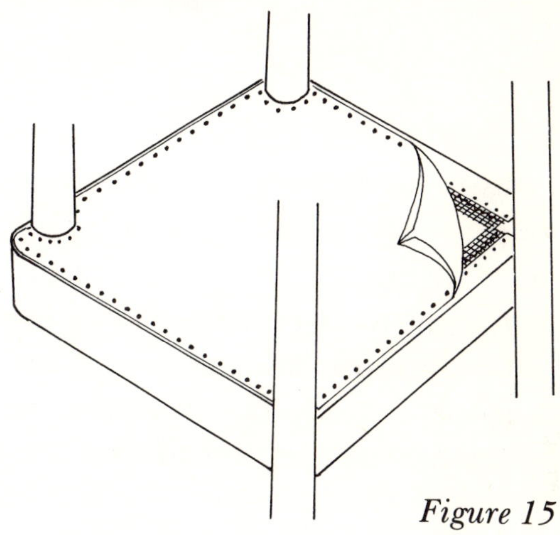

Figure 15

FINISHING THE SLIP-SEATED CHAIR

Block the needlepoint.

Sew a row of machine stitching on the excess canvas just outside the needlepoint.

Cut the excess canvas away on all sides to within 1½ inches of the needlepoint, and cut the corners diagonally to within 1 inch of the stitching.

If you haven't done so already, unscrew the seat panel and remove the existing fabric and cambric. Replace the padding if needed.

Lay the needlepoint face down on a clean table. Over it center the seat panel with its padded side down. Temporarily secure the needlepoint to the back of the panel by taping or tacking each side (see Figure 16).

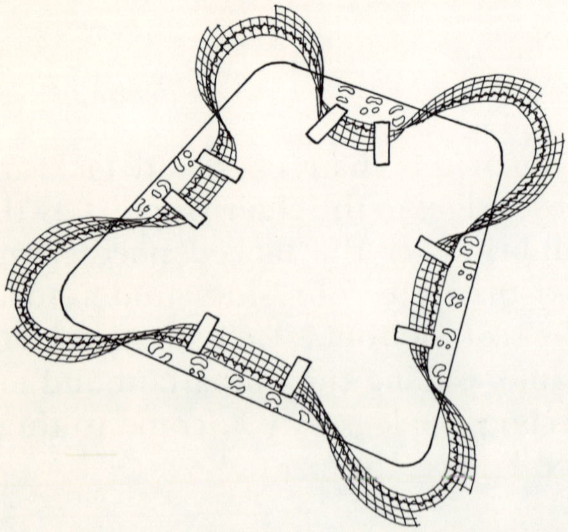

Figure 16

Starting at the center of one side, nail short upholstery tacks through the edge of the needlepoint every inch or so, working toward each corner. Do the same on the opposite side, pulling the needlepoint taut as you tack it. Tack the front edge in the same manner, again working from the center out toward the corners. At the back edge pull the needlepoint taut and smooth, then tack in the same way.

When you come to each corner, fit the needlepoint into neat folds if the corners are angular, or into narrow pleats if the corners are rounded (see Figure 17).

If the corners are excessively bulky, cut the excess canvas away and run a thin line of white all-purpose glue along the cut edges to prevent raveling.

Lay the cambric lining over the tacked seat panel and turn the edges under so that the lining almost covers the panel. Tack the lining to the seat

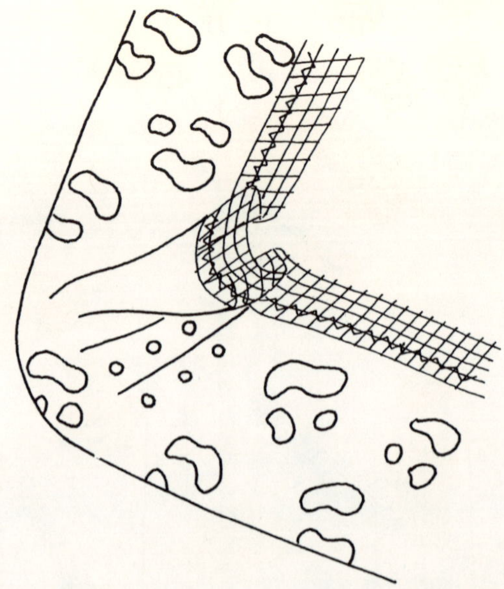

Figure 17

panel every inch or so through the needlepoint, mitering the corners neatly as you come to them (see Figure 18). Replace the covered seat panel in the chair frame.

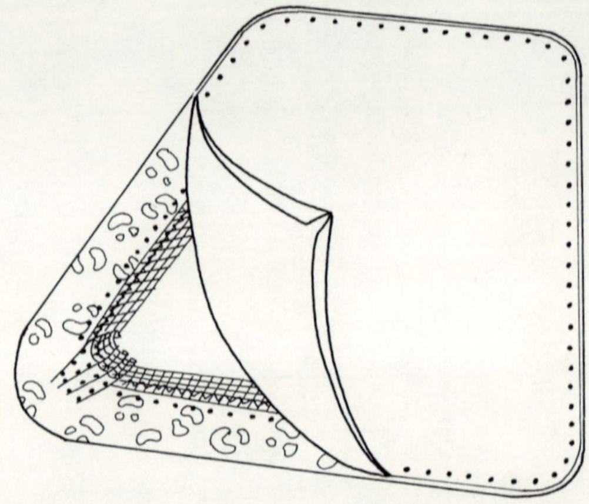

Figure 18

COLOR KEY

The color key for the tiger and leopard heads appears on their design pages. The color key for the skin markings follows:

- gold
- black
- 1 pale yellow
- 2 charcoal-brown

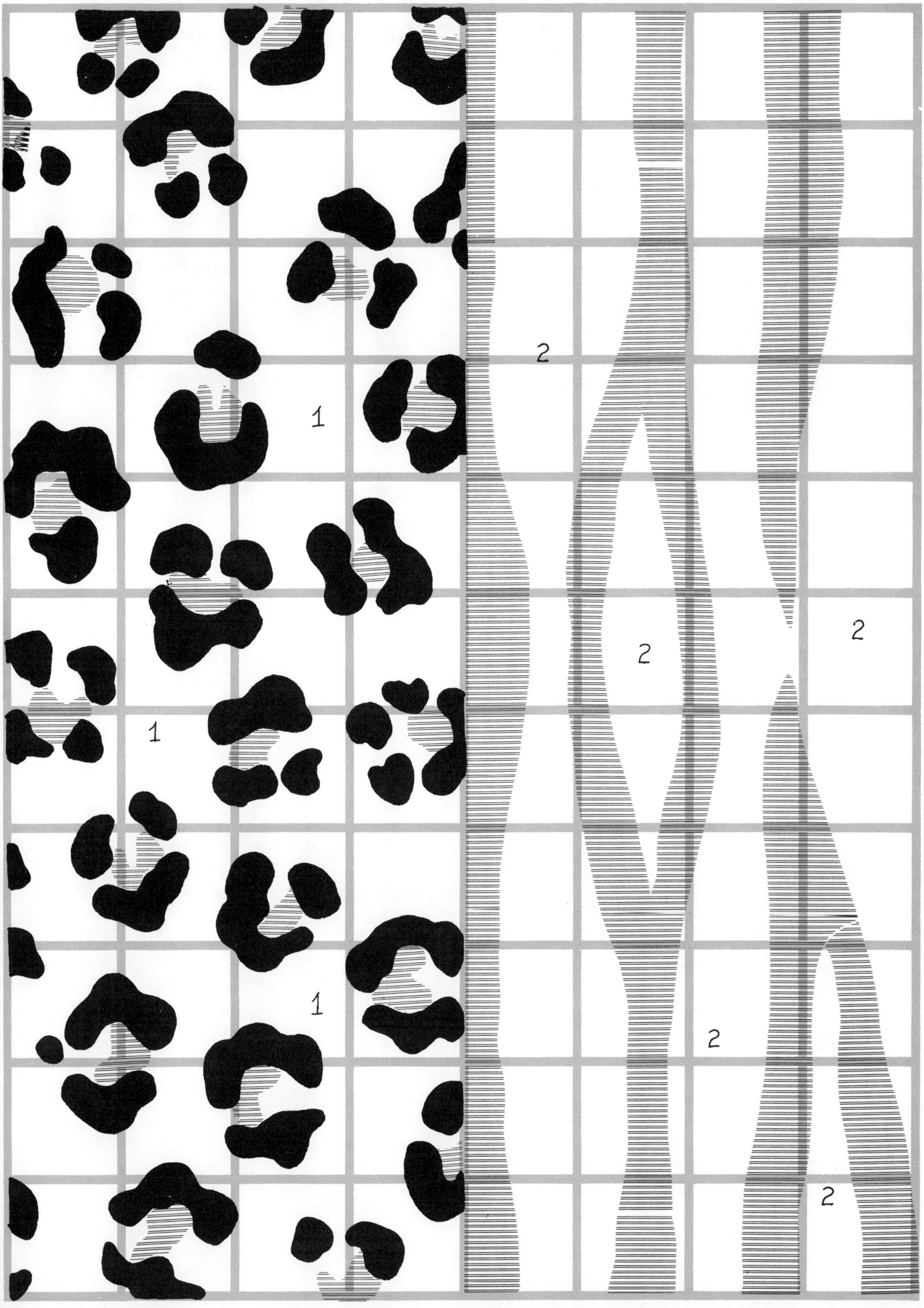
1
1
1
2
2
2
2
2

Kitchen Stool

With quick meals growing in popularity, why not make counter dining attractive as well as comfortable? With a set of zodiac signs you can customize a kitchen stool for each member of the family and bring welcome design and color to the kitchen at the same time. Or, indeed, you can treat yourself to your own astral monogram on a vanity stool, a footstool, or, with fuller stuffing, on a boxed pillow.

The zodiac design on page 93, like the eleven others in the Design Workbook, is project-size and can be traced from the book page onto canvas. It makes a splendid central motif for a circular pad of virtually any diameter; a 12-inch pad, for example, will fit the standard seat of an ice cream parlor stool. Finish it with a ruffled edge for a charming look in kitchen or powder room, or with welting for more tailored surroundings.

Making a custom pattern. Lay a piece of brown paper over the stool and on it outline the circumference of the seat with a dark marker. If your seat is not circular, simply outline the shape to be stitched.

Stitch: Basketweave.

Canvas: No. 10 mono canvas, a square cut 4 inches larger than the diameter or largest dimensions of the area to be stitched.

Yarn: 1 ounce of Persian wool for every 32 square inches of needlepoint.

Other Materials Needed:

- Fabric backing ½ inch larger all around than the finished needlepoint.
- Ribbon 2 or more inches wide and twice the circumference of the finished needlepoint, gathered to 1 inch longer than the circumference; or welting 1 inch longer than the circumference.
- Foam rubber, ½ inch thick, the size of the finished needlepoint.

FROM DESIGN TO CANVAS

Bind the cut edges of the canvas with masking tape.

Center the custom pattern face up under the canvas and trace the shape onto the canvas with an indelible marker.

Center the canvas over the zodiac sign on the book page. Following the instructions for tracing designs in Part I, trace the design from the book onto the canvas with an indelible marker. If you prefer, you can transfer the design to tracing paper first and then to the canvas.

STITCHING

Follow the color key for the design as you work. The black lines you have traced onto the canvas only delineate separate areas of color and should not be stitched.

Around all edges extend the design for two extra rows for a seam allowance.

FINISHING

Block the needlepoint.

Sew a row of machine stitching on the excess canvas just outside the needlepoint.

Lay the needlepoint face up and, starting at the back, lay the gathered ribbon over it with the gathering seam directly over the needlepoint seam allowance and the ruffles pointing in (see Figure 1). If you are welting the pad, place the welting the same way over the needlepoint, that is, with the welted edge pointing in. Baste, then sew the ruffle (or welting) to the needlepoint on top of the gathering (or welting) seam. When the edging is attached all around, join its ends together (see Figure 2).

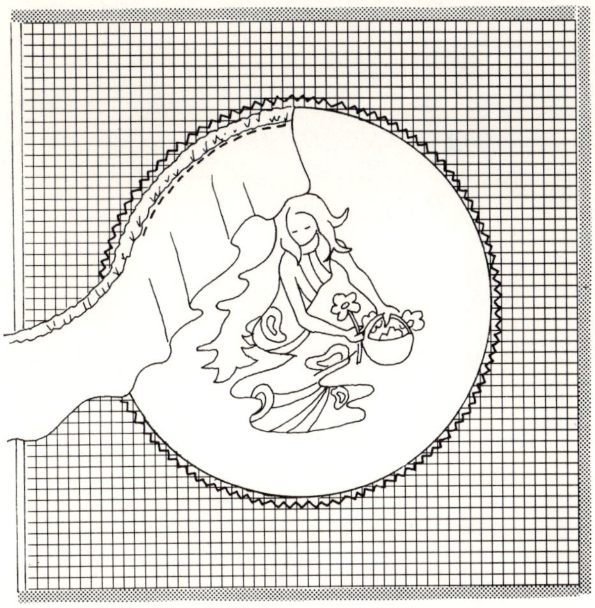

Figure 1

Place the ruffled (or welted) needlepoint and the backing fabric right sides together. Baste, then sew over the ruffle (or welting) seam, leaving an 8-inch opening in the back (see Figure 3).

Figure 2

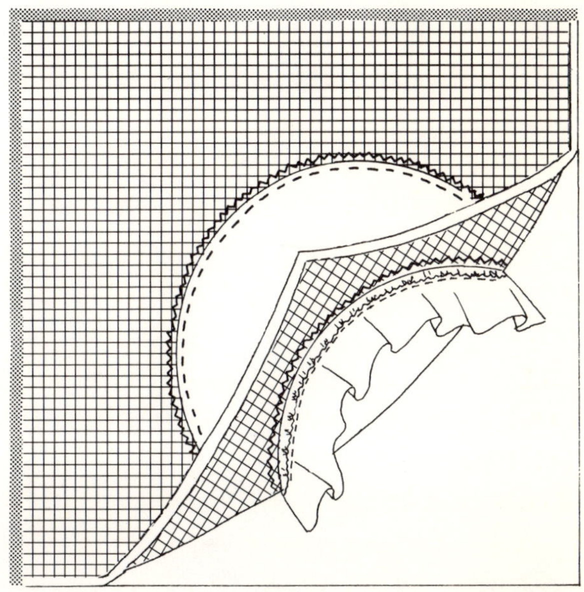

Figure 3

Trim the unstitched canvas and fabric backing to within ½ inch of the needlepoint, notching it at intervals around the curve (see Figure 4).

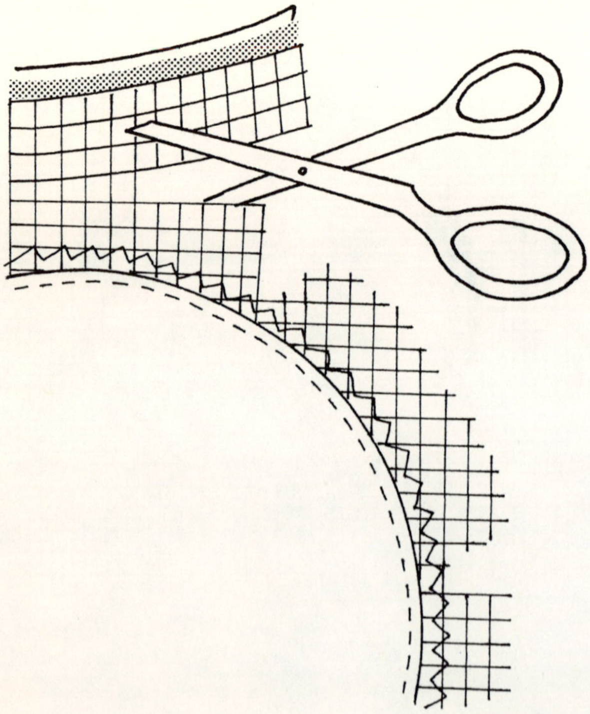

Figure 4

Turn right side out, insert the foam rubber pad, and blindstitch the opening.

COLOR KEY

The color key for the zodiac signs appears below as well as in the Design Workbook, where the rest of the zodiac designs are given.

Symbol	Color
	red-orange
	royal blue
1	pale yellow
2	deep yellow
3	light green
4	kelly green
5	flesh
6	beige lines in hair
7	dark brown
	white
	black lines for eyes, around face, and on basket

Virgo
7
7
5
5
1
3
4
7
5
1
1
5
2
2
7
2
7
2
2
2
1
4
1
2
2
4
1

Oriental Rug

The designs in Oriental rugs can be curvilinear or geometric, realistic or stylized, muted or bold in color. The rugs themselves can be grand in scale and concept, worthy of shahs and emperors, or they can be modest in size, the prayer rug of one person who kneels on it five times a day facing Mecca to pray.

This particular design, a stylized pomegranate tree, or tree of life, is derived from a Samarkand multiple prayer rug called a *saph,* which provides a prayer niche, or *mihrab,* for each member of the family. In a *saph* the same *mihrab* design is usually repeated in different colors in each of the separate compartments, with slight variations in the spandrel area over each prayer niche; the overall design of this project follows that tradition. The rug would make a handsome wall hanging, as would any one or two of its component units.

Stitch: Basketweave; edging.

Canvas: No. 5 interlocking canvas, 26 by 52 inches.

Yarn: About 55 ounces of Pat-Rug wool.

Other Materials Needed:
- Lining, 1 inch larger on all sides than the finished rug.
- Thin, nonskid rubber backing: four small pieces each about 4 inches square or triangular.

FROM DESIGN TO CANVAS

Bind the cut edges of the canvas with masking tape.

Following the instructions for enlarging designs in Part I, enlarge the design so that the width is 16 inches; the height will be about 22 inches. The design in the book is exactly half the width and height of *one* of the three identical compartments in the rug.

Center the enlarged design face up under the canvas and trace it onto the canvas with an indelible marker.

Now move the enlarged design under the canvas to the left, abutting the side edges of the design, and trace the enlargement onto the canvas with an indelible marker, with this exception: Omit the striped spandrel that appears over the prayer niche (see Figure 1). Trace the design onto the right third of the canvas in the same manner, again omitting the striped spandrel at the top.

Enlarge the two other spandrel designs on the design page to measure twice their width and height. Position one of the spandrel designs under the left panel and trace it onto the canvas with an indelible marker. Repeat for the right panel, using the other spandrel design (see Figure 2).

STITCHING

Follow the color key for the design and refer to the color photograph as you work. As you can see, the same colors are used in all three compartments, but they appear in different places in each variation. Follow the color scheme for the center compartment and work your own variations for the two side panels.

Figure 1

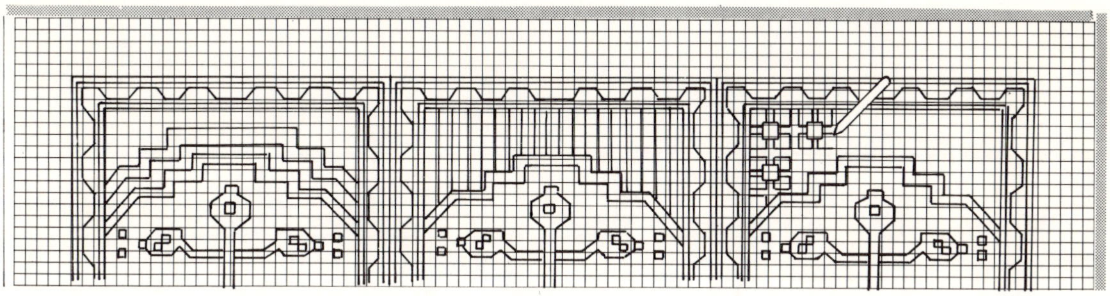

Figure 2

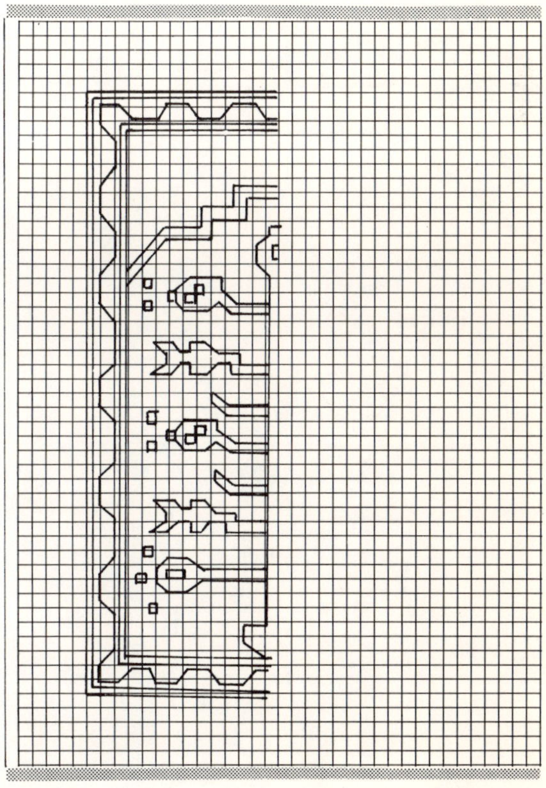

Figure 3

The black lines you have traced onto the canvas only delineate separate areas of color and should not be stitched.

If you want each compartment of the rug to be absolutely geometrical, you should stitch one vertical half of each panel entirely (it doesn't matter which half) and then work the other half in its mirror image by duplicating the number of stitches you have already worked on the first half (see Figure 3). If you don't demand precision in your work—and the original Samarkand weavings did have handwoven variations—simply work the

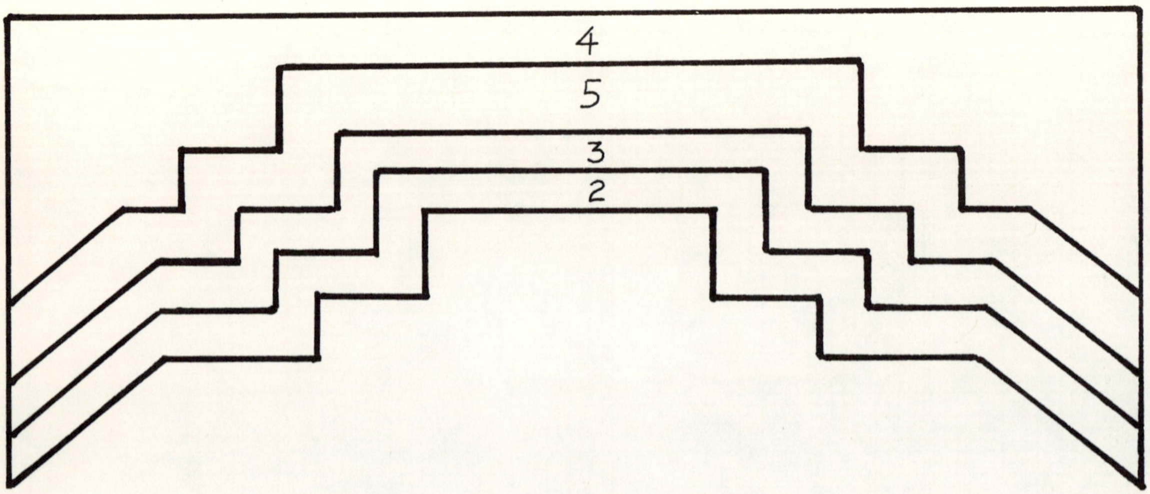

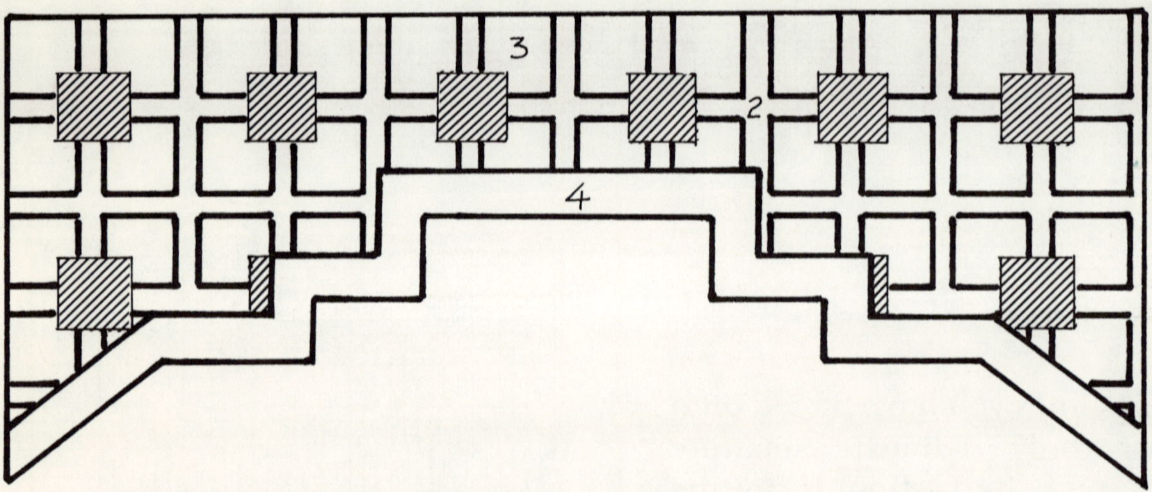

brass

1 yellow

2 red

3 turquoise

4 light blue

5 navy

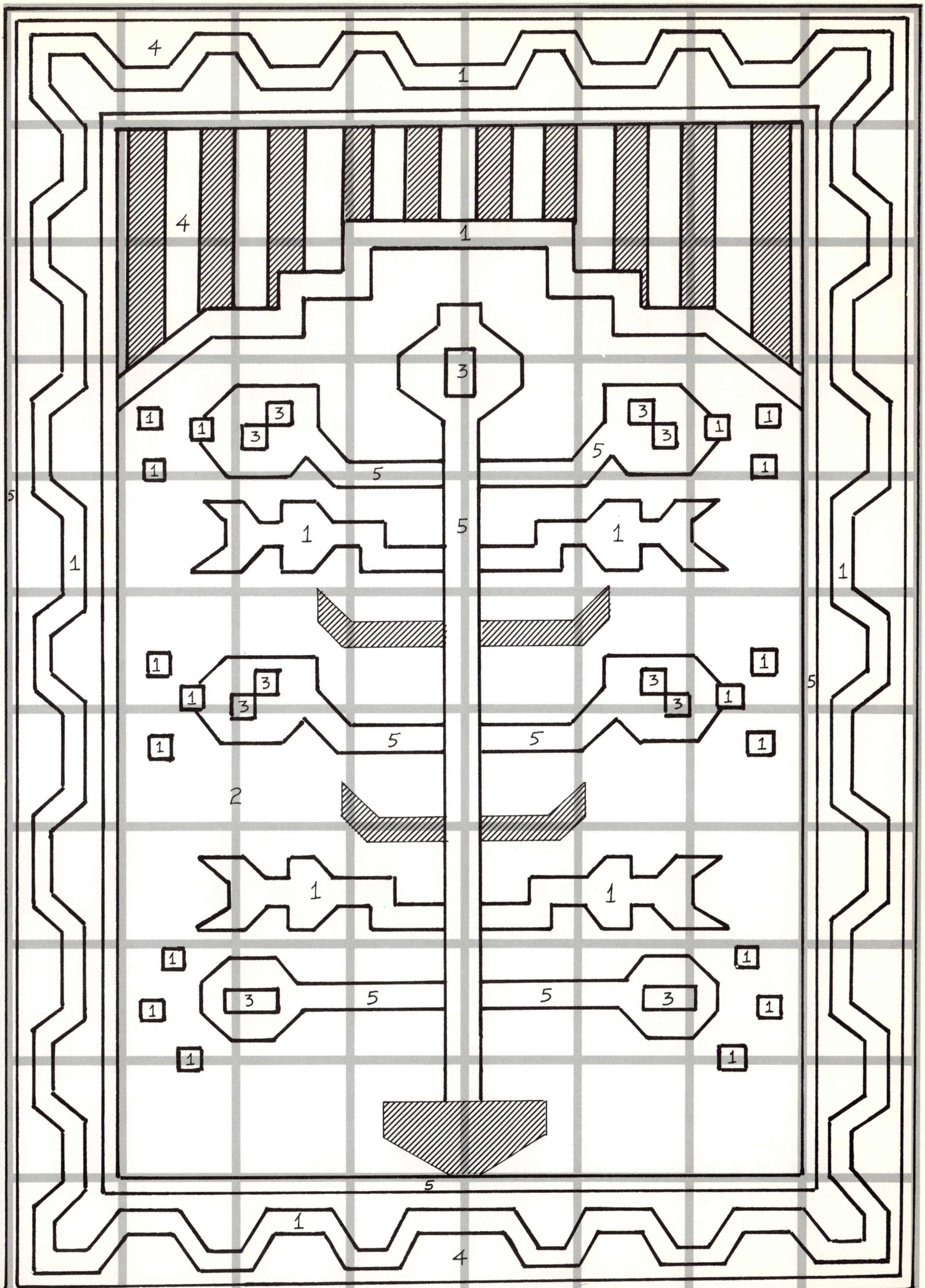

4
1
4
1
3
1
1
3
3
3
3
1
1
5
5
1
1
5
1
1
1
1
1
3
3
3
3
1
1
5
5
1
1
2
1
1
1
1
1
3
5
5
3
1
1
1
1
5
5
1
4
1
5

design as a whole without concern for a mirror image.

Around all four edges stitch up to but not including the last row of the border.

FINISHING

Block the needlepoint.

Along all edges carefully cut the canvas one row outside the existing needlepoint, leaving one thread all around. Finish the sides with the edging stitch, including in it both the outer, unstitched thread and the last actual stitch. For adequate coverage be sure to insert a few stitches in the corner mesh (see Figure 4).

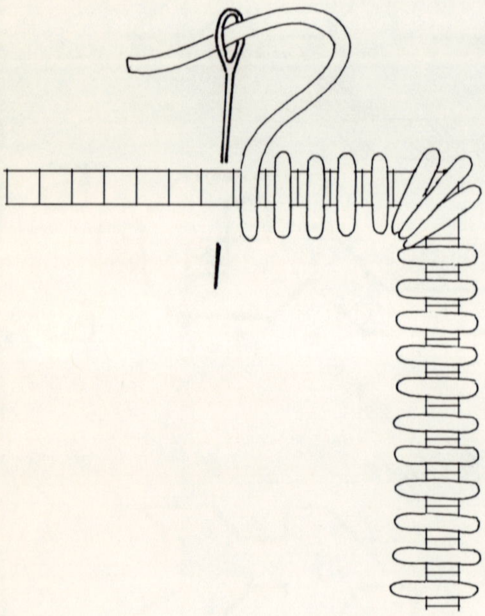

Figure 4

Lay the finished rug facedown and over it place the lining, right side up; anchor the lining in place with a few pins. On the top and two sides turn the lining under about 1 inch so that it just clears the edge of the rug; blindstitch the lining to the back of the needlepoint. Miter the corners as you come to them (see Figure 5). On the

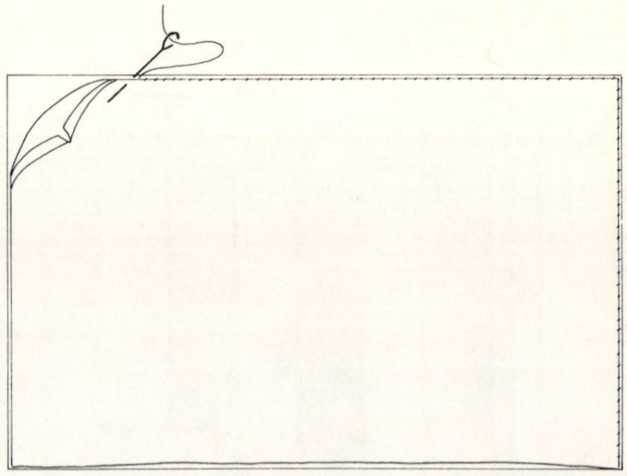

Figure 5

bottom, hem the lining without tacking it to the needlepoint so that it hangs free, which will allow you to shake out any accumulations of dust. Remove the pins.

At the four corners of the lining sew patches of nonskid backing material (see Figure 6).

Figure 6

COLOR KEY

The color key for the entire center panel and the two side spandrels appears on one of the design pages. For the main body of each side panel, use the same colors, but for variety, place them in different positions within the design (see the color photograph of the finished rug).

Pillows

Once you have learned the basic techniques of pillow making, you have at hand the tools for almost-instant decorating, for pillows—and their close relatives, bolsters, cushions, and pads, all of which require similar finishing techniques—are an easy and inexpensive way to inject new color, texture, and design into a room.

The following three pillows illustrate the most common pillow-making techniques: The butterfly design has a knife edge and welting; the tulip pillow is made with a boxing strip and welting; and the allover floral design has boxed corners in a style also known as a "kneeler" because it is widely used in churches. You can see from the color photographs that the butterfly and tulip pillows are coordinates, using related colors on the same bamboo background. All the design components for those two pillows are derived from the Design Workbook.

Floral Pillow with Boxed Corners

Stitch: Basketweave.

Canvas: No. 10 interlocking canvas, 20 inches square.

Yarn: 8 ounces of Persian wool, including about 4 ounces for background.

Other Materials Needed:
• Backing fabric of velvet, corduroy, or upholstery material of your choice, 15 inches square.
• Soft inner pillow to fit inside the finished needlepoint pillow or a slab of foam rubber 13 inches square and 1½ inches thick.

FROM DESIGN TO CANVAS

Bind the cut edges of the canvas with masking tape.

Following the instructions for enlarging designs in Part I, enlarge the design to a 16-inch square.

Center the enlarged design face up under the canvas and trace it onto the canvas with an indelible marker.

STITCHING

Follow the color key for the design and refer to the color photograph as you work. The black lines you have traced onto the canvas only delineate separate areas of color and should not be stitched.

Around all edges, including the cut-out corners, extend the design for two additional rows for a seam allowance.

FINISHING

Block the needlepoint.

Sew a row of machine stitching around all the edges (see Figure 1).

Figure 1

Trim the excess canvas along all edges to within 1 inch of the finished needlepoint (see Figure 2).

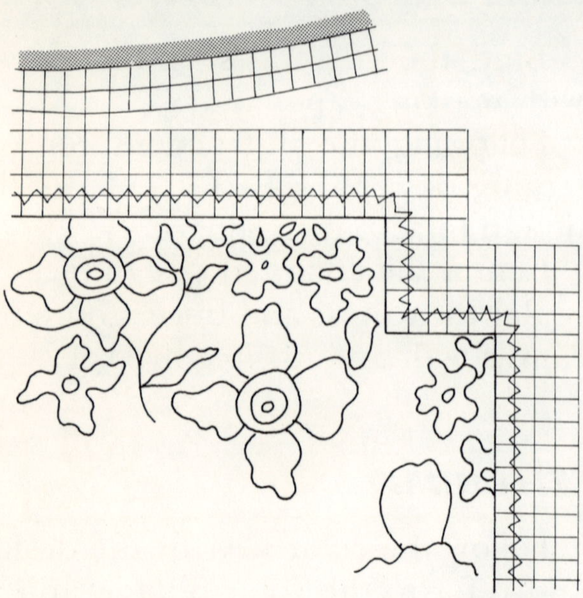

Figure 2

To make one box corner, follow these instructions:

Place right sides of the needlepoint together and sew a seam by hand or machine just inside the two-row seam allowance, from the corner, *A,* to the point of the bottom seam, *B* (see Figure 3).

Finish the other three corners in the same manner.

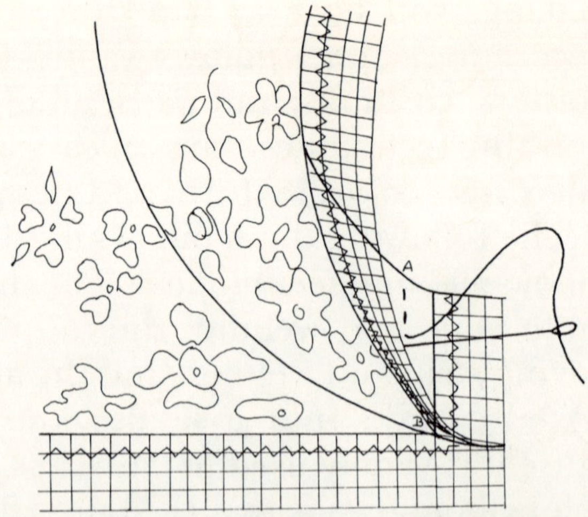

Figure 3

Lay the backing fabric face up. With the boxed needlepoint still inside out, baste and then sew the needlepoint to the backing on the seam line (*BD,* Figure 4); start at one corner and stop just after you have turned the fourth corner, leaving most of one seam open for stuffing the pillow.

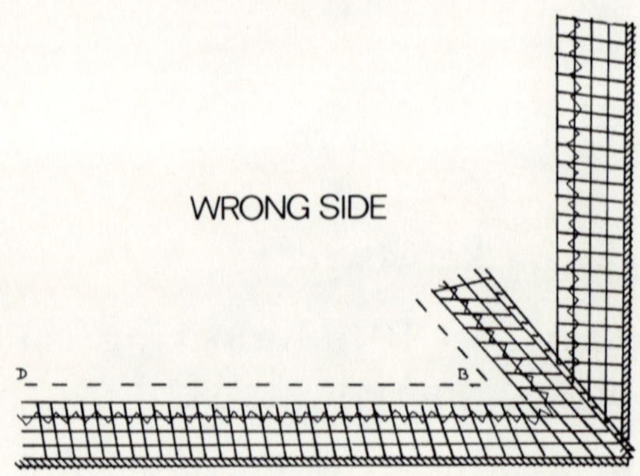

Figure 4

Turn right side out and stuff with the soft inner pillow for a puffy look or with the foam rubber for a trim box pillow. Blindstitch the open seam.

COLOR KEY

The color key for the floral pillow appears on its design page.

orange	3 purple
light green	4 red-orange
lavender	5 pale yellow background
brown	6 white
1 bright yellow	dark green
2 gold	

Butterfly Pillow with Knife Edge

Figure 1

Stitch: Basketweave.

Canvas: No. 5 interlocking canvas, 17 inches square.

Yarn: 8½ ounces of Pat-Rug wool.

Other Materials Needed:
- Backing fabric of velvet, corduroy, or other material of your choice, ½ inch larger all around than the finished needlepoint.
- Welting 1 inch longer than the perimeter of the finished needlepoint (about 53 inches).
- Inner pillow to fit inside the finished needlepoint pillow.

Figure 2

FROM DESIGN TO CANVAS

Bind the cut edges of the canvas with masking tape.

Lay the canvas on the book page so that there are about 2 inches of excess canvas on the bottom and each side; there will be about 4 inches of canvas outside the top outline (see Figure 1).

Following the instructions for tracing designs in Part I, trace the design from the book onto the canvas with an indelible marker. At the top edge continue the bamboo pattern for an additional 2 inches so that the pillow design, using the same bamboo pattern (it is also given in the Design Workbook in the same scale), is 13 inches square (see Figure 2). If you prefer, you can transfer the design to tracing paper first and then to the canvas.

STITCHING

Follow the color key for the design and refer to the color photograph as you work. The black lines you have traced onto the canvas only delineate separate areas of color and should not be stitched.

Around all edges extend the design for two additional rows for a seam allowance.

FINISHING

Block the needlepoint.

Sew a row of machine stitching on the excess canvas just outside the needlepoint.

Lay the needlepoint face up and, starting at the back, lay the welting over it with the welted edge pointing in and the seam of the welting directly over the seam allowance of the needlepoint (see Figure 3). Baste, then sew the welting to the needlepoint on top of the welting seam. When the welting is attached all around, join its ends together and seam it to the needlepoint (see page 19).

Place the welted needlepoint and the backing fabric right sides together. Baste, then sew over the welted seam, leaving a 9-inch opening in the back (see Figure 4). Trim the unstitched canvas and fabric backing to within ½ inch of the needlepoint, notching the welting strip at the corners where necessary (see Figure 5).

Turn right side out, insert the inner pillow, and blindstitch the opening.

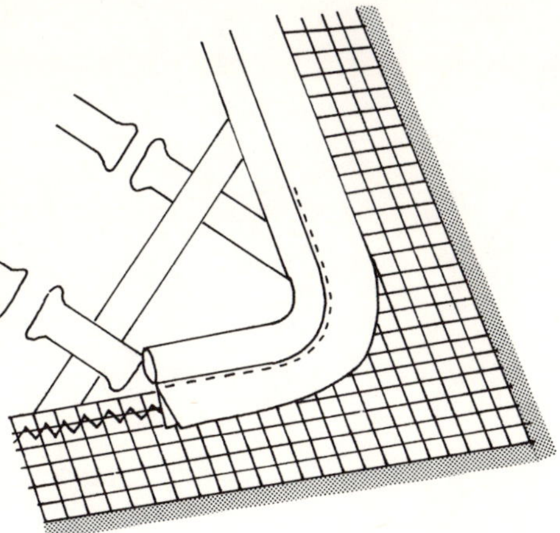

Figure 3

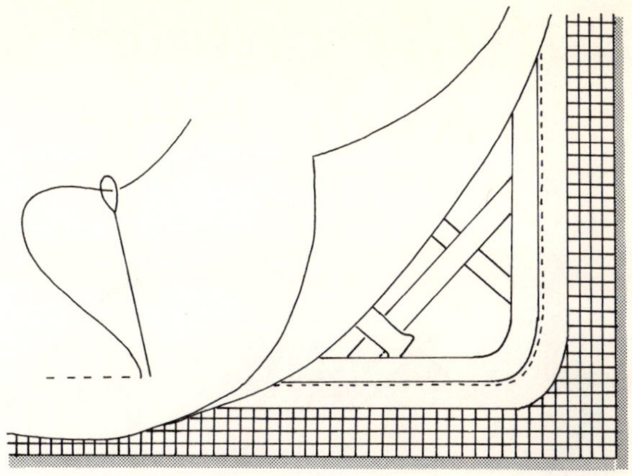

Figure 4

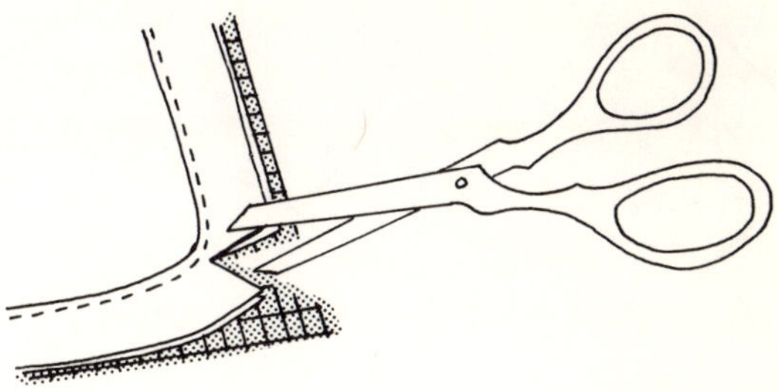

Figure 5

COLOR KEY

The color key for the butterfly pillow appears on its design pages.

2
1
3
5
2
4
3
4
1
5

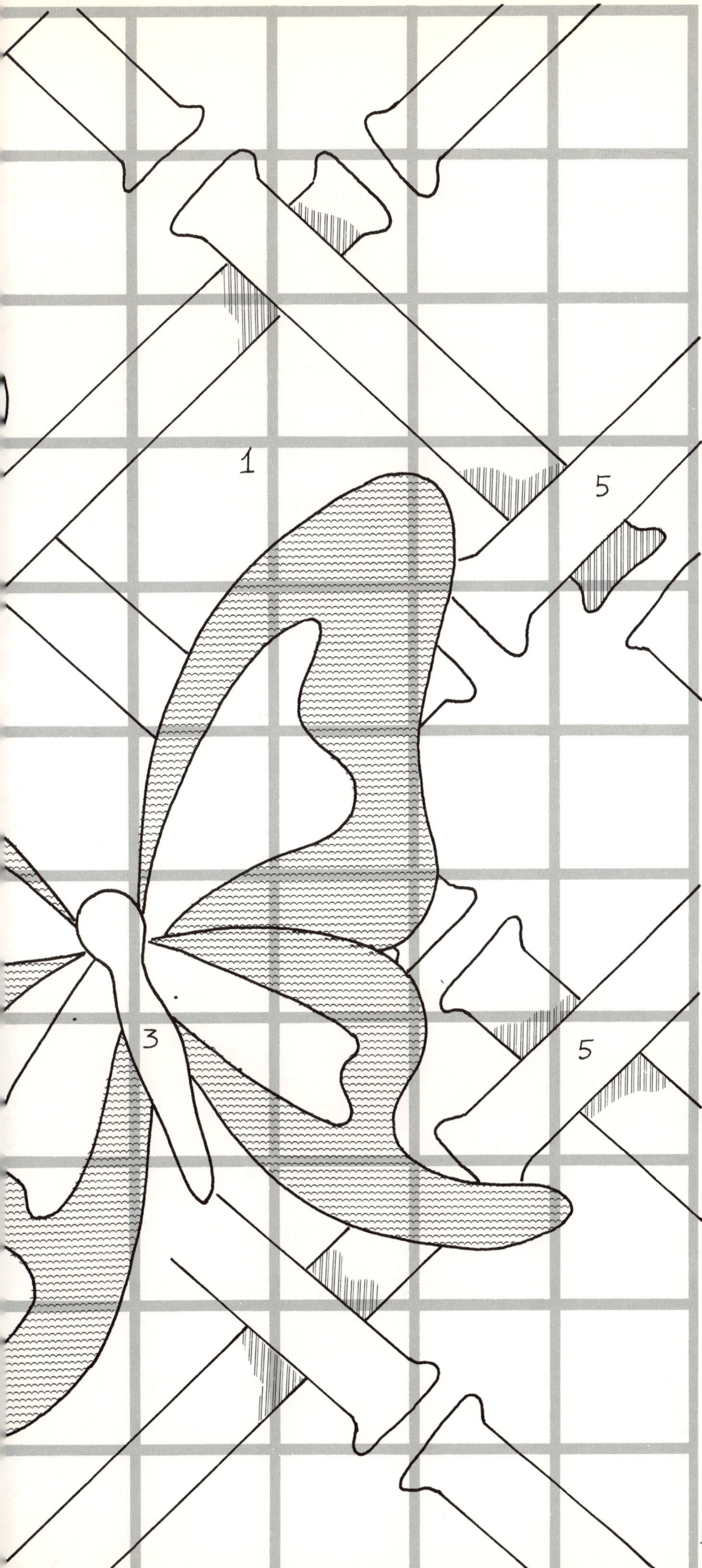

- red-orange
- gold
- white
- 1 brown background
- 2 green
- 3 beige
- 4 light orange
- 5 pale yellow

Tulip Pillow with Boxing Strip

Figure 1

Stitch: Basketweave.

Canvas: No. 5 interlocking canvas, 17 inches square.

Yarn: 8½ ounces of Pat-Rug wool.

Other Materials Needed:
- Backing fabric of velvet, corduroy, or other material of your choice, ½ inch larger all around than the finished needlepoint.
- Boxing strip of the same fabric, 3 inches wide and 1 inch longer than the perimeter of the pillow (about 53 inches).
- Two strips of welting, each the length of the boxing strip.
- Inner pillow to fit inside the finished needlepoint pillow.

FROM DESIGN TO CANVAS

Bind the cut edges of the canvas with masking tape.

In the center of the canvas outline a 13-inch square with an indelible marker. Lay the lower left section of canvas over the triple tulip spray on the book page (see Figure 1). Following the instructions for tracing designs in Part I, trace the tulip spray from the book onto the canvas with an indelible marker. Now move the canvas so that the upper right section falls over the single tulip spray (see Figure 1) and in the same manner trace the single tulip spray from the book onto the canvas with an indelible marker. If you prefer, you can transfer both tulip sprays to tracing paper first and then to the canvas.

Set the canvas aside while you trace the bamboo background from the Design Workbook onto tracing paper.

Place the tracing of the bamboo under one corner of the canvas and trace it onto the canvas with an indelible marker. Move the tracing to a contiguous part of the canvas so that its lines abut and match the already traced bamboo, and trace the bamboo a second time (see Figure 2). Continue

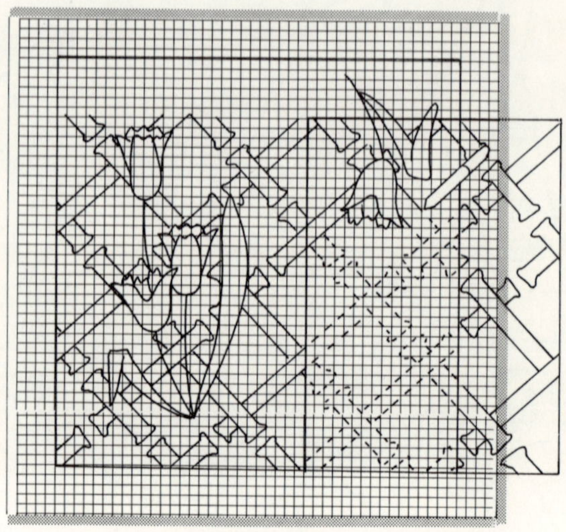

Figure 2

to move the tracing of the bamboo under the canvas, matching abutting lines, and to transfer the bamboo to the canvas until you have filled the entire background area. Wherever the bamboo falls on an already traced tulip spray, do not trace that portion of the bamboo onto canvas; you want to create the illusion that the bamboo pattern actually continues under the flowers. But do remember to resume the bamboo wherever it should be seen—through or around the petals or leaves of the flowers (see Figure 2).

STITCHING

Follow the color key for the design and refer to the color photograph as you work. The black lines you have traced onto the canvas only delineate separate areas of color and should not be stitched.

Around all edges extend the design for two additional rows for a seam allowance.

FINISHING

Block the needlepoint.

Sew a row of machine stitching on the excess canvas just outside the needlepoint.

Lay the needlepoint face up and, starting at the back, lay the welting over it with the welted edge pointing in and the seam of the welting directly over the seam allowance of the needlepoint (see Figure 3). Baste, then sew the welting to the needlepoint on top of the welting seam. When the welting is attached all around, join its ends together and seam it to the needlepoint (see page 19). Notch the welting at the corners so that it lies flat (see Figure 4).

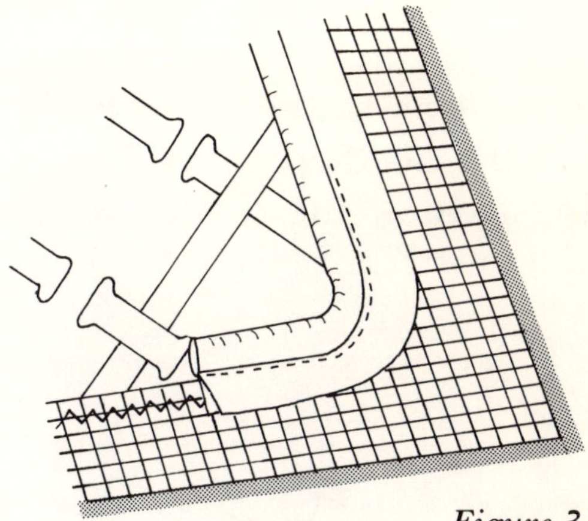

Figure 3

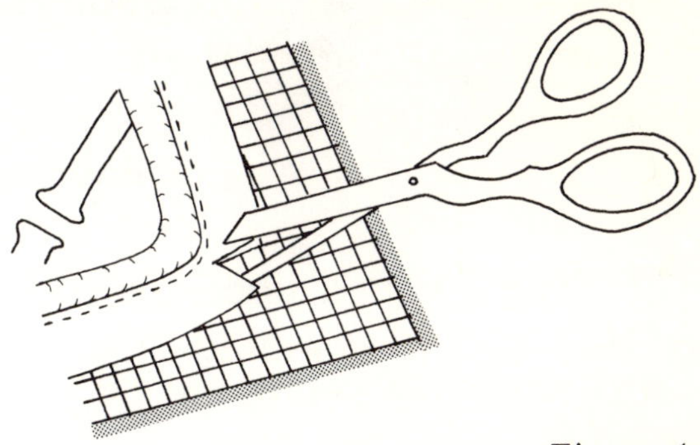

Figure 4

Lay the backing fabric face up and sew the second welting strip to it in the same manner as described above, leaving a ½-inch seam allowance on the backing fabric.

Lay the needlepoint face up. Starting in the center of the back of the pillow, lay the boxing strip face down over the needlepoint so that its seam allowance is directly over the seam of the welting (see Figure 5). Around all

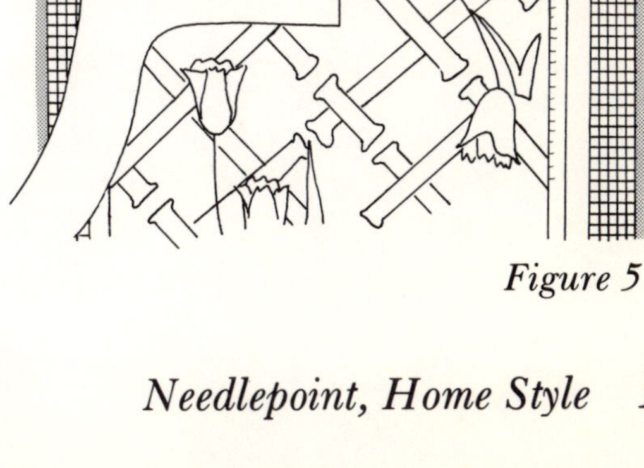

Figure 5

four sides baste and then sew the boxing strip to the welted needlepoint. When you reach your starting point at the center of the back edge, join the two ends of the boxing strip together. Trim the excess canvas to within a ½ inch of the needlepoint and notch the boxing strip at the corners so that it lies flat (see Figure 6).

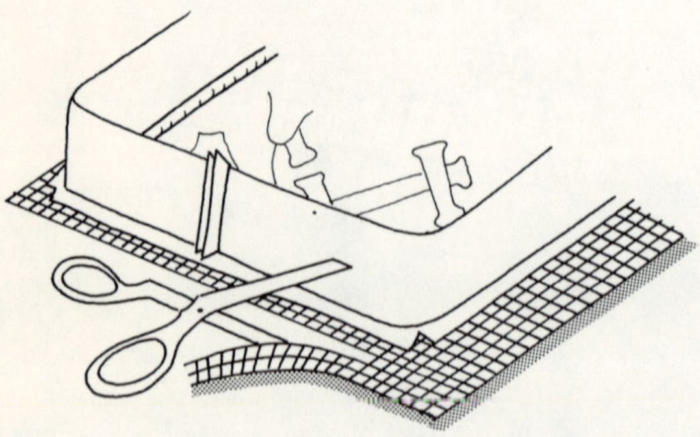

Figure 6

Lay the welted backing fabric face up. With the welted and boxed needlepoint still inside out, sew the boxing strip to the backing as described above; that is, with the seam allowance of the boxing strip directly over the seam of the welting on the backing fabric (see Figure 5), baste and then sew the boxing strip to the welted backing, leaving an 8-inch opening in the seam (see Figure 7).

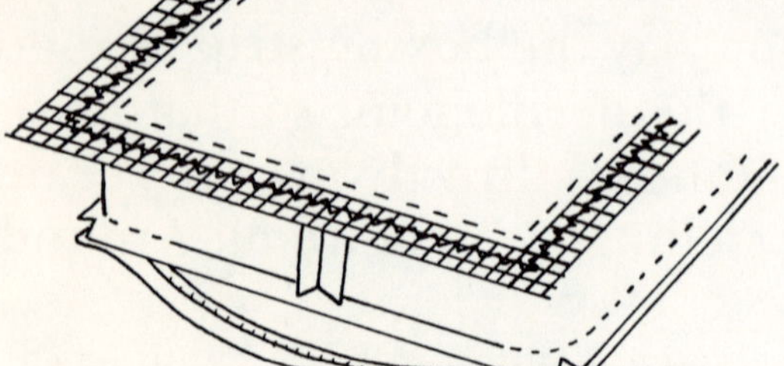

Figure 7

Trim the excess canvas to within a ½ inch of the needlepoint and notch the boxing strip at the corners.

Turn the project right side out and insert the inner pillow. Blindstitch the opening closed.

COLOR KEY

The color key for the tulips appears on its design page. The color key for the bamboo appears in the Design Workbook and also on the design pages for the coordinating butterfly pillow.

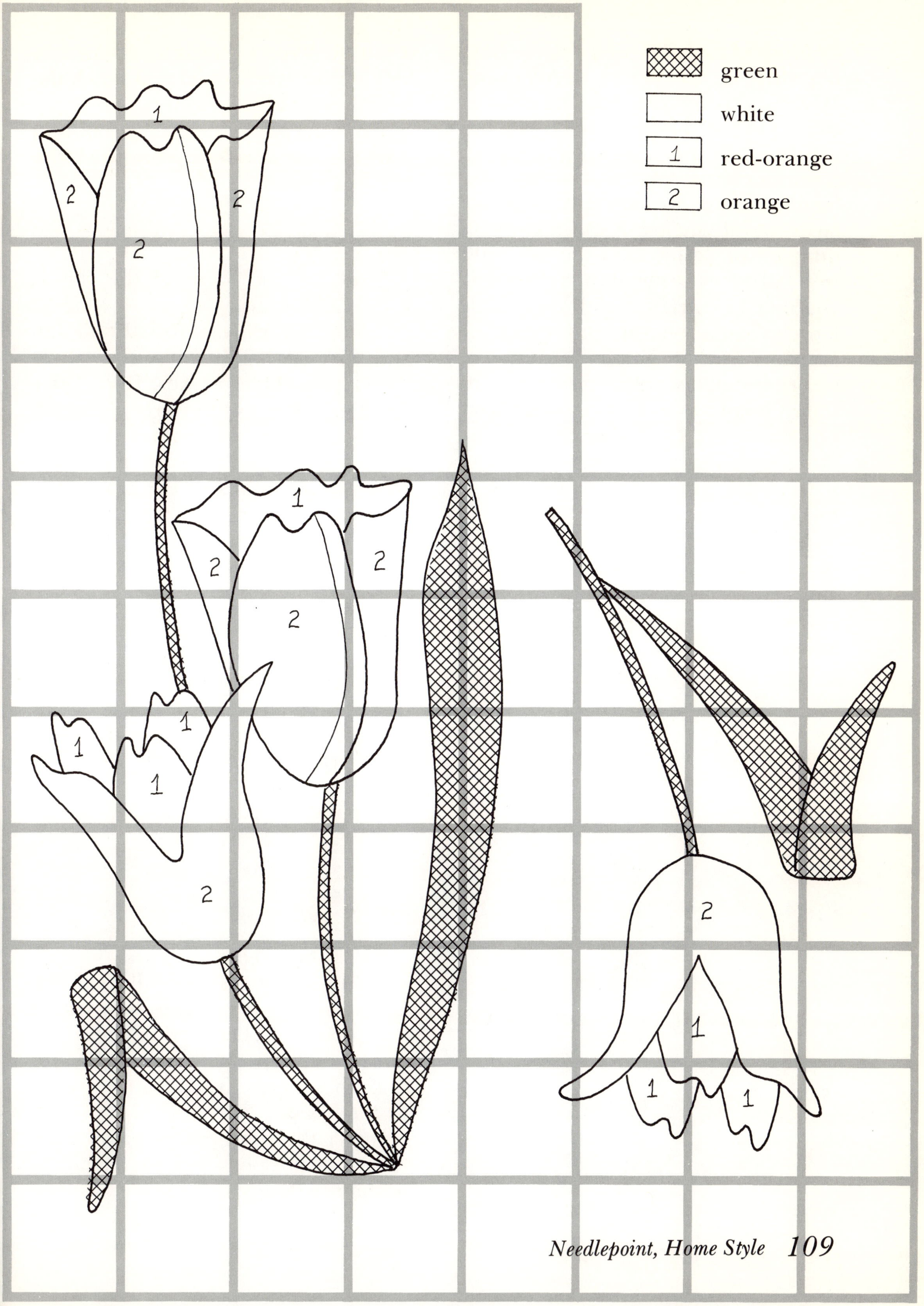
green
white
1 red-orange
2 orange

Shoulder Bag

Signature bags are having great popularity, but if you are one of a growing number of fashionable people who won't display the initials of a designer, you may be intrigued with this motif, loosely based on the *guls* (coats of arms) of Turkoman tribes, which are incorporated as tribal signatures in their Oriental rugs and weavings. You can substitute a set of initials for the interior design in the central octagon if you want to personalize the design or give it as a very special gift.

The needlepoint panel fits into an outer pocket in a handsome prefinished shoulder bag (see "Source," below) and is held in place by strips of Velcro, which grip the finished stitching securely (see Figure 1). This ingenious construction not only circumvents costly finishing of the pocketbook but allows the panel to be replaced at will, offering the possibility of a wardrobe of needlepoint styles and colors.

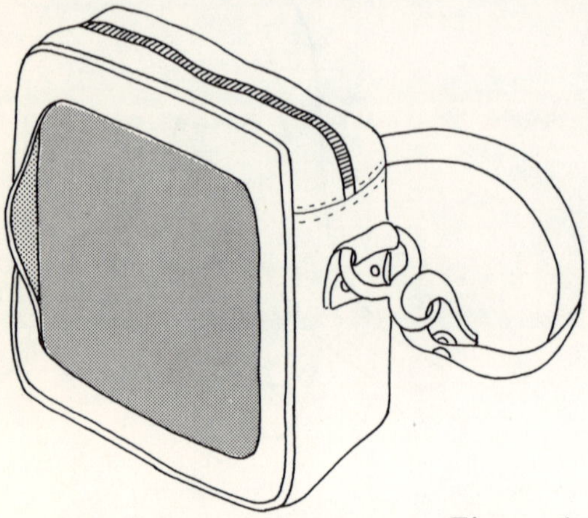

Figure 1

Stitch: Basketweave.

Canvas: No. 10 interlocking canvas, 13 by 11 inches.

Yarn: About 2½ ounces of Persian wool.

FROM DESIGN TO CANVAS

Bind the cut edges of the canvas with masking tape.

Center the canvas over the design and trace the outline onto the canvas with an indelible marker. Don't trace the design itself onto canvas; you will find it much easier to work from the graph, which will ensure geometric accuracy. Each box of the graph designates one stitch.

STITCHING

Fold the canvas in half and then in half again to establish the exact center point (which will occur in the central black rectangle). Follow the color key for the design and refer to the color photograph as you work from the graph.

Around all edges stitch up to the outline.

FINISHING

Block the needlepoint.

Along all edges carefully cut the canvas two rows outside the existing needlepoint. There is no need to finish the canvas edges any further since they will be framed and covered by the bag.

Insert the needlepoint panel carefully into the pocket of the bag, centering the design (see Figure 2). Press

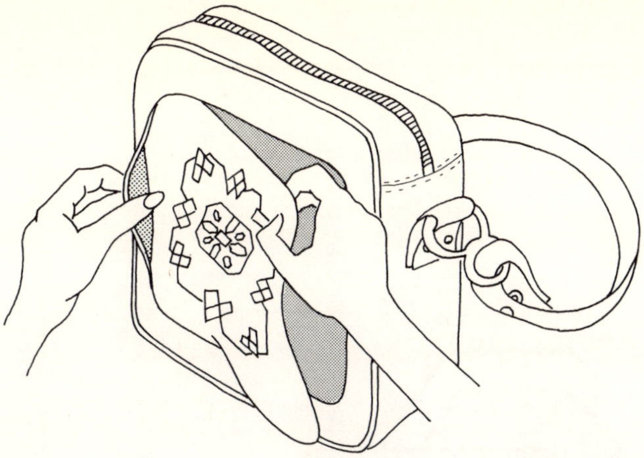

Figure 2

the sides of the bag to the needlepoint so that the underlying Velcro strips grip the needlepoint.

COLOR KEY

	×	brown
1	□	beige
2	•	black
3	○	white
4	\	rust

SOURCE

The leather shoulder bag (TP#102) is available from Toni Totes of Vermont, Inc., Rte. 100, South Londonderry, Vt. 05155; it comes in navy, honey brown, red, bone, and black and retails for $37.00 at the time of publication. A canvas version (TP#110) is available in navy, red, brown, black, yellow, denim, camel, and light green; it retails for $18.00 at the time of publication. Either bag can also be ordered through a retail needlework shop near you.

2
3 3
4
3
4
3
1
1
4
2
2
1
1
2
3
4
1
3 3
1

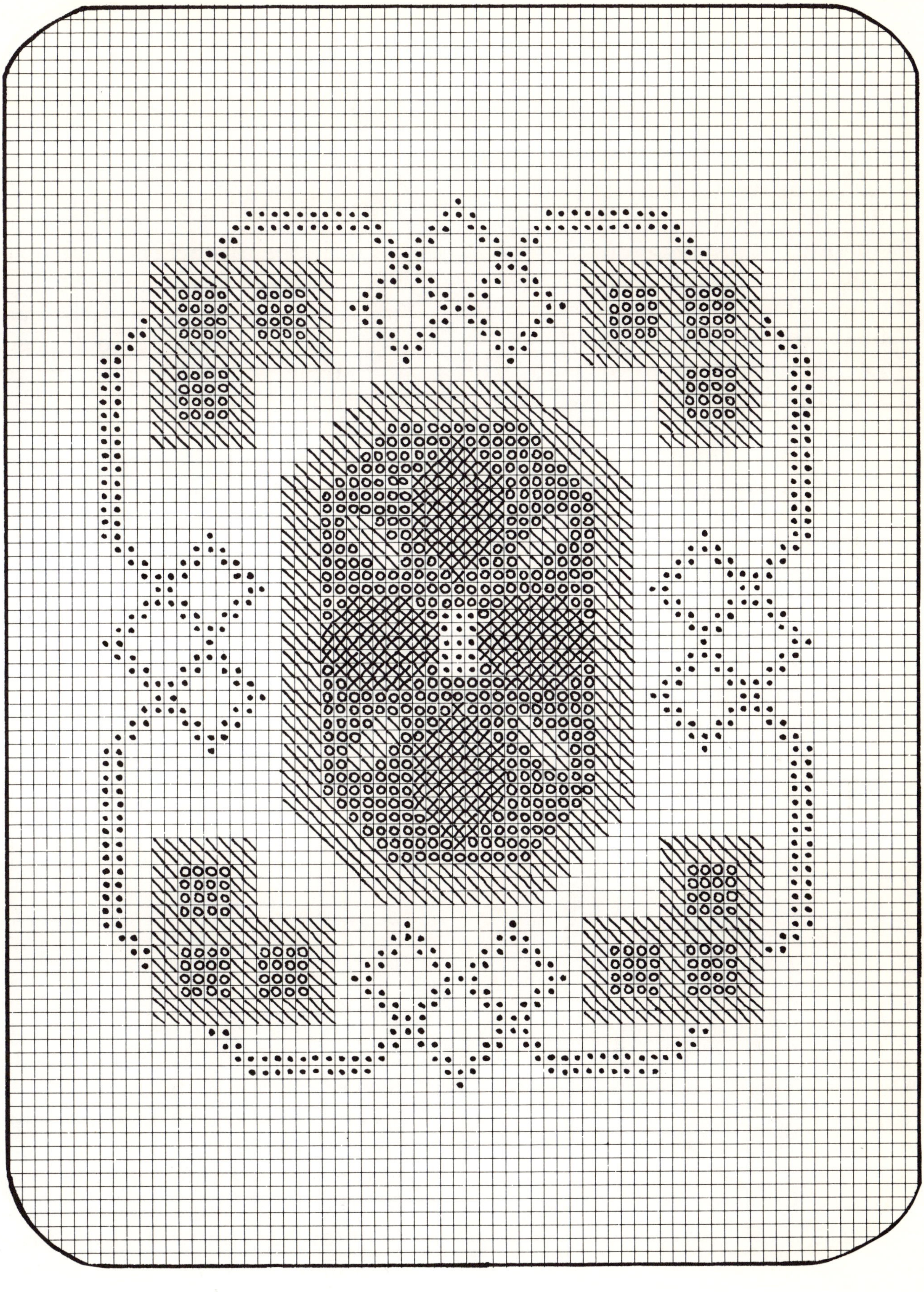

Tote Bag

Stitch: Basketweave.

Canvas: No. 5 interlocking canvas, premounted.

Yarn: About 8 ounces of Pat-Rug wool.

The pleasures of tote bags have always been apparent, but for the needlepoint enthusiast the difficulties of mounting needlepoint into a professional-looking bag seemed either almost insurmountable or unduly expensive. Both objections are now neatly bypassed by this trim prefinished tote (see "Source," below). It measures 14 by 12 by 4 inches, with a generous needlepoint panel of 13½ by 10¾ inches virtually filling one entire side of the tote. For the large-canvas devotee, its most felicitous feature is that the premounted canvas is No. 5 interlocking.

For the actual stitching of the canvas the tote bag unzips into two completely separate halves, and a vinyl flap, which will protect the finished stitching, lifts up for easy access to the canvas (see Figure 1).

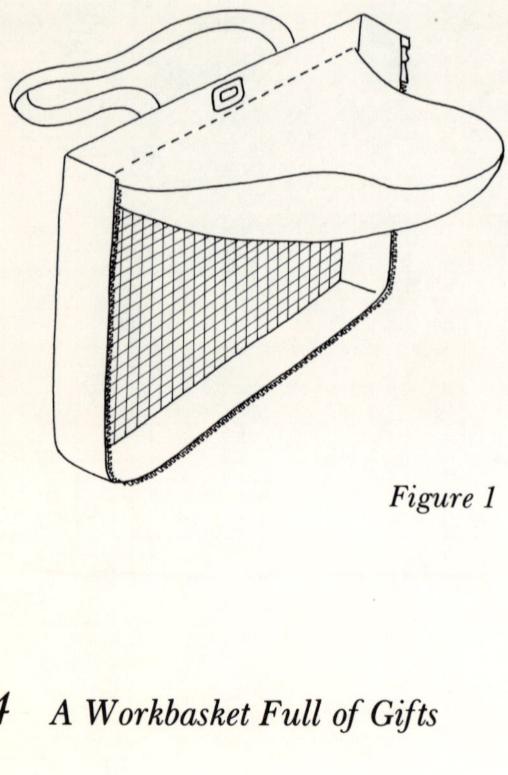

Figure 1

FROM DESIGN TO CANVAS

Unzip the unstitched canvas half of the tote and lift up the vinyl flap inside. Lay the left side of the canvas over the design on the book page. If the boxing strip of the tote makes it difficult for you to lay the canvas out flat over the design, perch the book on top of a deep box so that the boxing strip doesn't get in the way (see Figure 2). Trace the design from the book onto the canvas with an indelible marker. Because the design is narrower than the width of the canvas, you will also have to trace part of the design onto the right side of the canvas; the entire design won't fit a second time (see Figure 3). If you prefer, you can transfer the design to tracing paper first and then to the canvas.

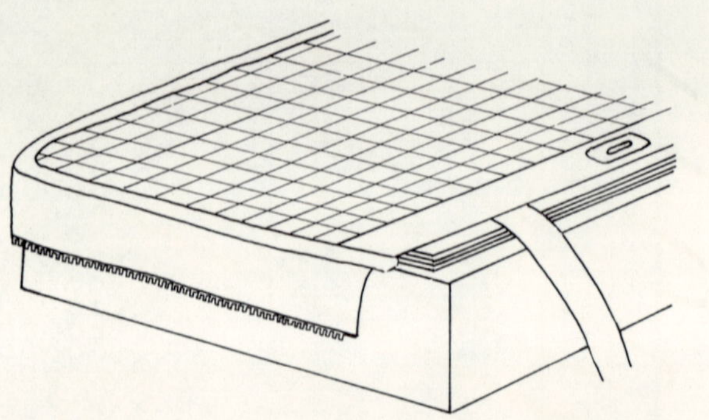

Figure 2

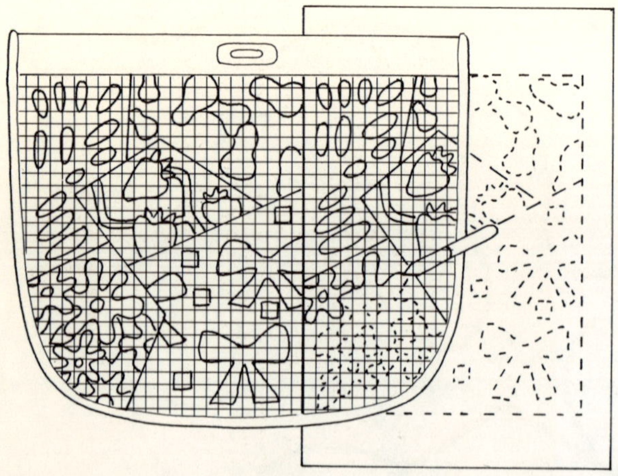

Figure 3

STITCHING

Follow the color key for the design and refer to the color photograph as you work. The black lines you have traced onto the canvas only delineate separate areas of color and should not be stitched.

To keep the distortion of the canvas as slight as possible, work the basketweave stitch by the "push/pull" method (see pages 11–12), that is, by forming each stitch with two separate strokes rather than in one continuous flowing motion. Tuck the outermost row of stitches under, or as close as you can to, the prefinished binding (see Figure 4).

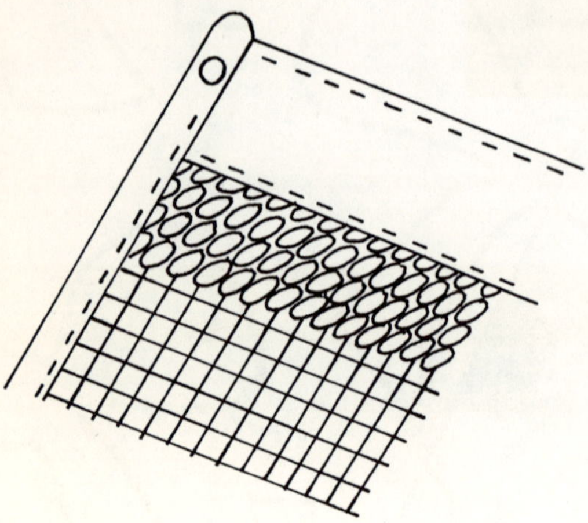

Figure 4

FINISHING

Block the needlepoint, if necessary, following the instructions given in Part I for blocking prefinished projects.

COLOR KEY

(crosshatch)	kelly green
(solid)	black
1	golden yellow
2	lemon yellow
3	gold
4	yellow-green
5	beige
6	medium brown
7	brown
8	red
9	orange

SOURCE

This prefinished tote bag is available in brown, black, navy, bone, and white; it retails for $25.00 at the time of publication. For a retail source near you, write the manufacturer, Markann Mfg. Corp., 69 Warren St., New Rochelle, N.Y. 10801.

Tote Bag, page 114

Tulip Pillow, page 106, and Butterfly Pillow, page 102

Photo Album, page 43

Tennis Racquet Cover, page 36

Peacock Bellpull, page 54

Bulletin Board, page 72

Picture Frame, page 41

Floral Pillow, page 99

Jewel Box, page 129

Mirror, page 68

Inlaid Box and Lighter, page 132

Cheese Board, page 127

Vest for a Man

If the value of a gift were measured in the time—that most precious commodity—required for its creation, then this needlepoint vest would surely be the worthiest of presents. It combines the skills of needlepoint with the patience of a tailor, and the result is indeed a splendid vestment.

The following instructions are given for a medium-size vest (chest measuring 38–40 inches; waist, 32–34 inches). The vest itself fits loosely, and there is room for play both in the overlap of the two front pieces and in the adjustable belt in back; if there are significant differences in any measurement in the vest that you want to make, buy a small- or large-size vest pattern and make the necessary adjustments according to that pattern.

Stitch: Basketweave.

Canvas: No. 10 mono canvas; two pieces, each 14 by 27 inches.

Yarn: About 11 ounces of Persian wool.

Other Materials Needed:
- Fabric for backing, such as a lightweight wool, 28 inches wide by 24 inches long.
- Lining for vest: ⅔ yard of lining material that has a minimum width of 44 inches.
- Welting to trim armholes, neck, and front of vest: about 14 feet of ready-made welting, or else custom-made in the same fabric used for backing.
- Two pairs of decorative buttons, each button about ¾ to 1 inch in diameter, with a 3-inch double chain attached to one button in each set (these sets are available at notions counters).
- Small buckle for back belt.

FROM DESIGN TO CANVAS

Bind the cut edges of the canvas with masking tape.

Following the instructions for enlarging designs in Part I, enlarge the outline of the right side of the vest so that it measures 11½ inches from *A* to *B* (see Figure 1). The needlepoint pattern includes a standard ⅝-inch seam allowance. Also note on the enlarged outline the center front of the vest (*CD* on Figure 1).

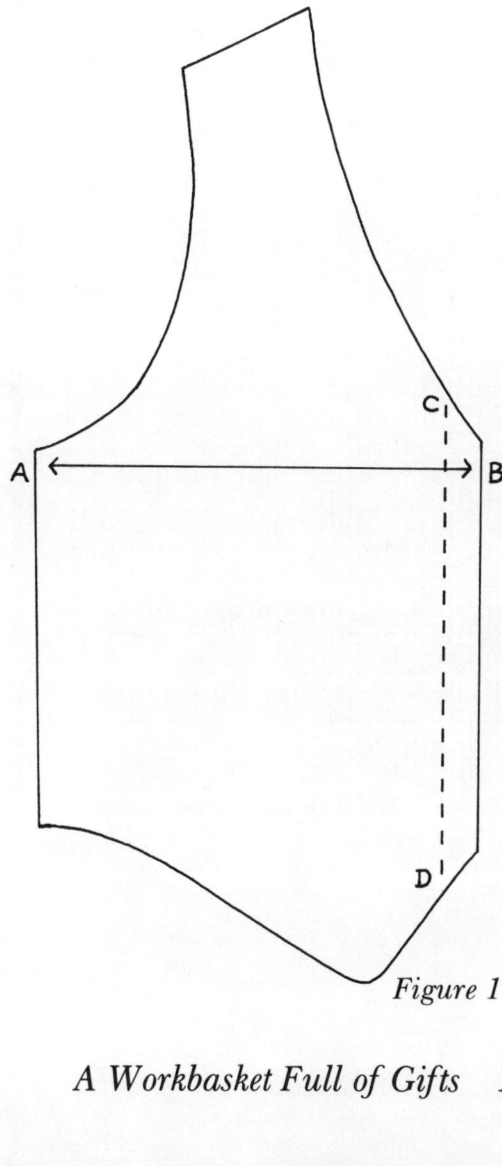

Figure 1

Center the enlarged design face up under one piece of canvas and trace it onto the canvas with an indelible marker. Also note the center line, *CD,* on the canvas.

To get a mirror image for the left side of the vest, turn the enlargement over and on the back of it trace all lines with a dark marker. You can see the original lines better if you hold the outline up to a light.

Center this reverse image of the enlarged design face up under the second piece of canvas and trace it onto the canvas with an indelible marker. Note the center line, *CD,* on this piece of canvas as well (see Figure 2).

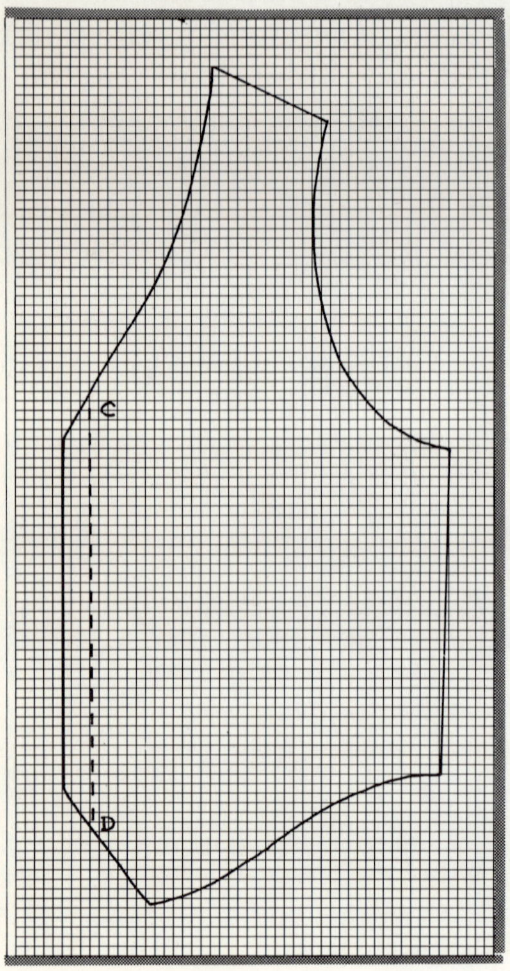

Figure 2

Transfer the design from the book page to a piece of tracing paper with a dark marker. Include the dotted line *EF.*

Place the tracing of the design under the canvas for the right side of the vest, lining up the dotted line, *EF,* on the tracing under the center line, *CD,* on the canvas (see Figure 3).

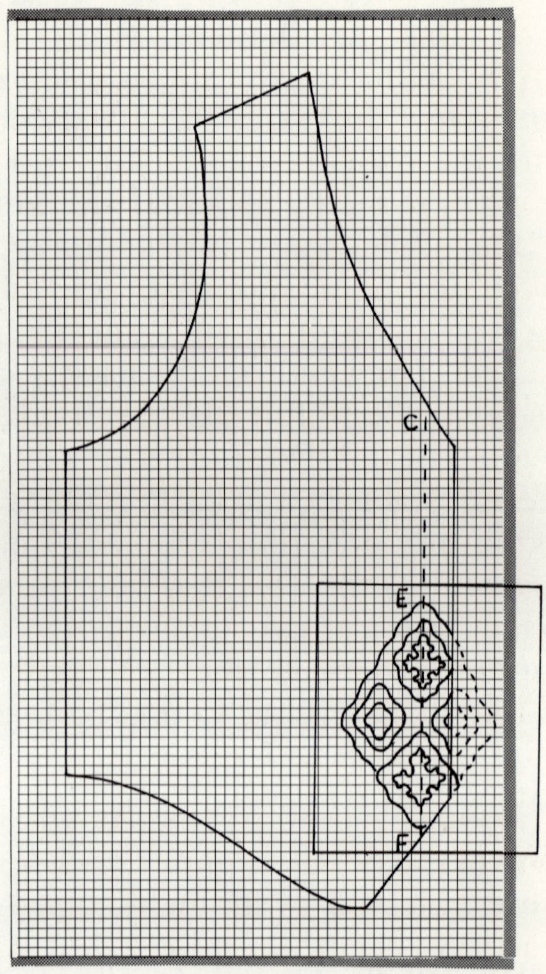

Figure 3

Trace the design onto the canvas with an indelible marker (don't trace the guideline, *EF.)* Move the tracing to a contiguous part of the canvas so that the design continues without interruption and trace the same design a second time (see Figure 4). Continue to move the tracing of the design under the canvas in the same manner until you have filled the entire outline of the vest panel. As you can see in

Figure 4, along the edges you will have partial diamond shapes.

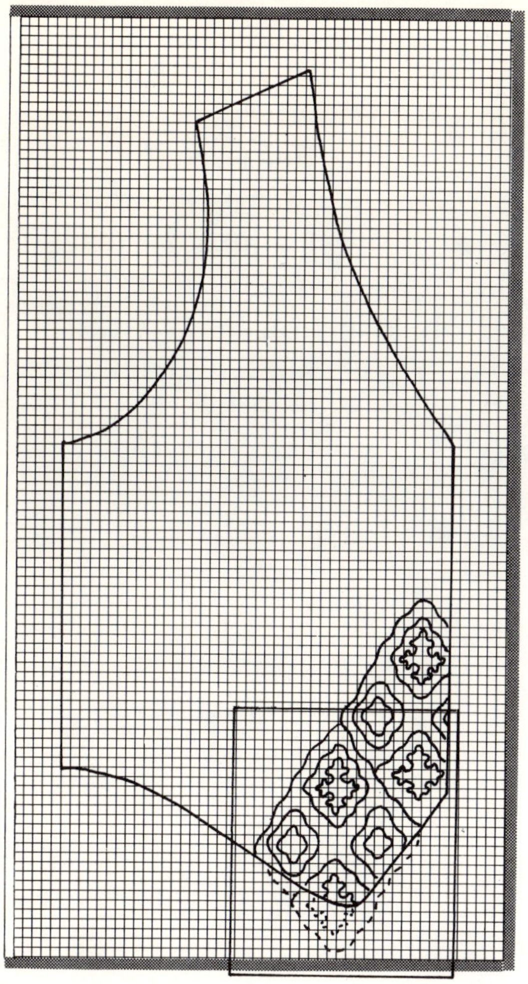

Figure 4

To match the two sides of the vest so that the design appears continuous when the vest is buttoned, place the tracing of the design under the canvas for the left vest panel, line up the dotted line, *EF,* on the tracing under the center line, *CD,* on the canvas (see Figure 5). Trace the design onto the canvas with an indelible marker as described above, moving the tracing around under this piece of canvas until the entire outline is filled.

STITCHING

Follow the color key for the design and refer to the color photograph as

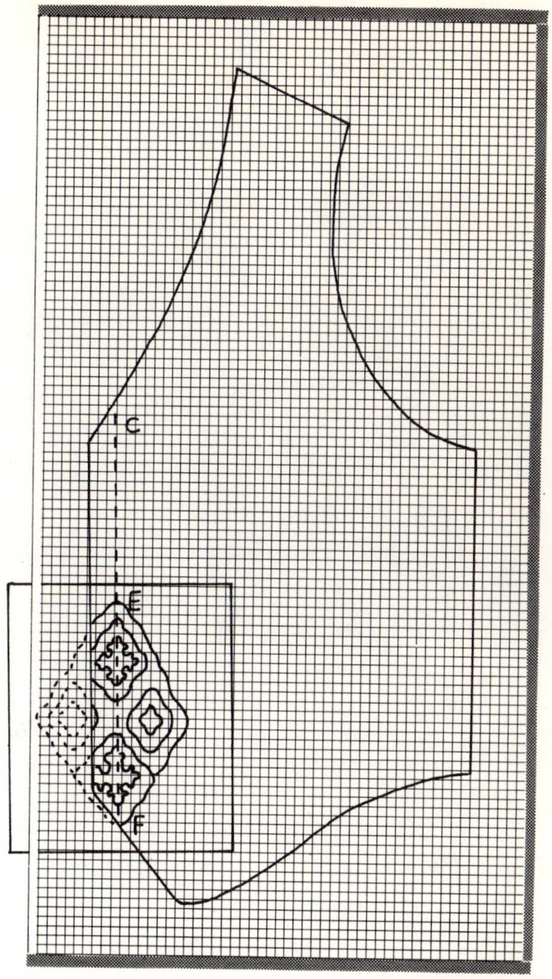

Figure 5

you work. The black lines you have traced onto the canvas only delineate separate areas of color and should not be stitched.

You can work this pattern from the traced design entirely for a loose, free-form look. If you want each diamond segment to be exactly the same as all the others, work from the graphed design, in which each square equals one stitch.

FINISHING

Block the needlepoint.

Sew a row of machine stitching on the excess canvas just outside the needlepoint. Cut the excess canvas away to within 1 inch of the needlepoint on all sides.

Cut the two back pieces and two belt sections from the backing fabric, according to the cutting layout in Figure 6. Each piece includes the standard ⅝-inch seam allowance.

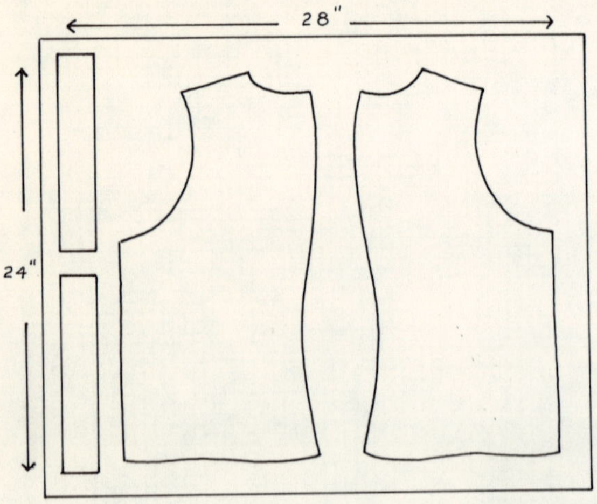

Figure 6

Stitch the center back seam (see Figure 7). Press seam allowances open.

Fold each belt section in half the long way with right sides together. Sew one short end as well as the long seam, leaving the other end open; cut the corners diagonally at the sewn end (see Figure 8). Turn each belt strip

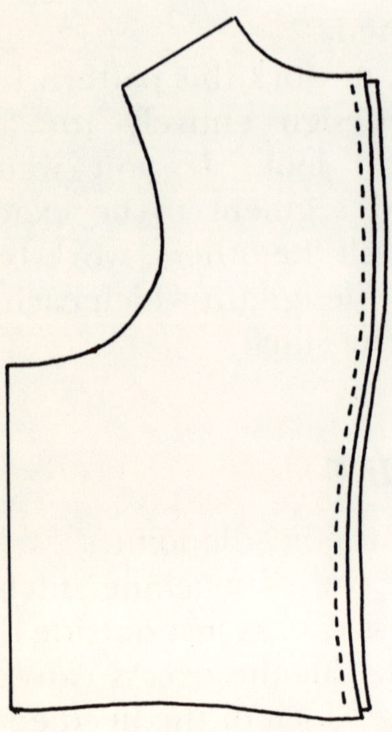

Figure 7

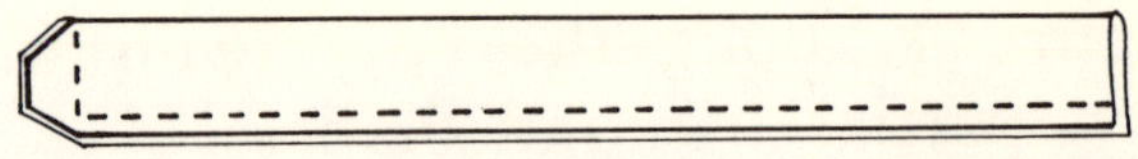

Figure 8

right side out through the open end and press the belt flat.

Baste each belt section, seamed edge pointed toward the hem, to the back of the vest about 3 inches from the bottom, with the short open edge of each belt section flush with the side seam allowances of the back (see Figure 9. Tack the belt securely in a few places.

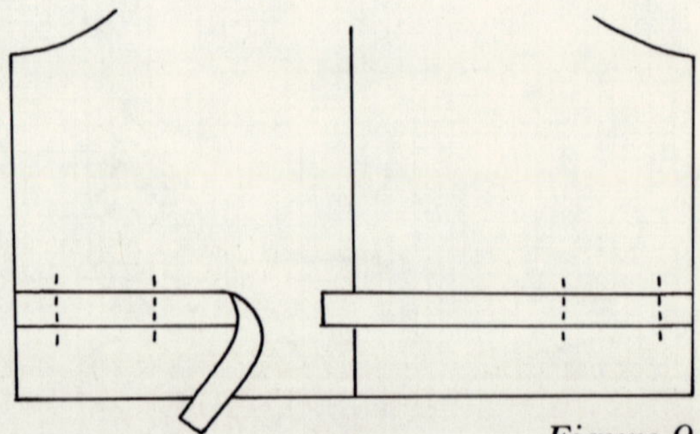

Figure 9

Fasten buckle to the left belt section and secure (see Figure 10).

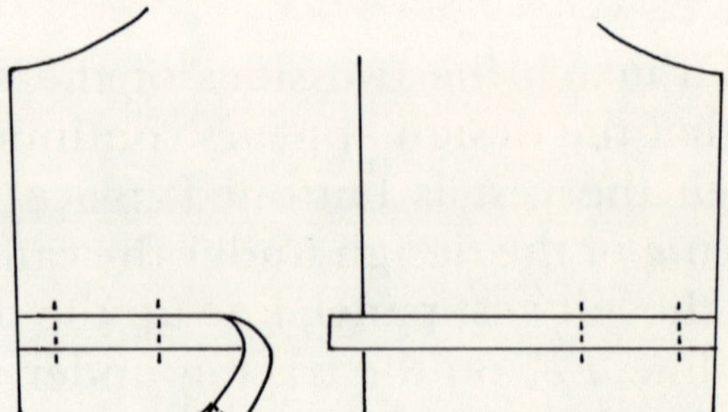

Figure 10

Lay the back of the vest right side up and over it position the two front needlepoint panels face down. Baste and then sew the front panels to the back at the shoulder and side seams along the ⅝-inch seam allowance of the backing fabric (see Figure 11). Turn the vest right side out.

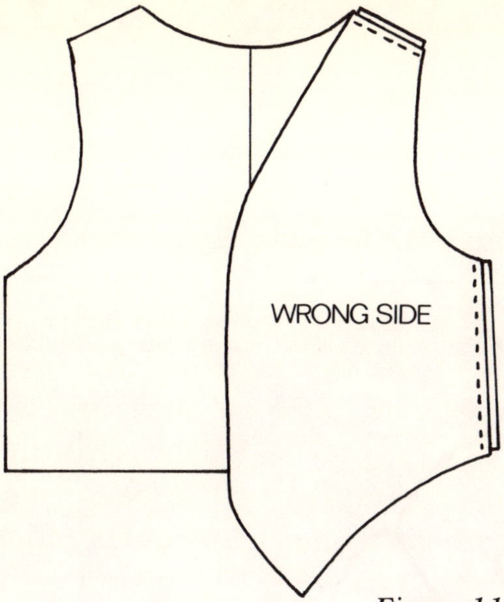

Figure 11

Welt each armhole as follows: With the vest right side out, pin the welting around the armhole with the welted head facing in toward the neck of the vest and the seam line of the welting directly over the seam allowance of the vest backing and of the needlepoint (see Figure 12). Baste, then sew the welting to the vest on the seam line. When the welting is attached all around, join its ends together (see Figure 13). Clip or notch the seam allowances at the curves. Turn the welting under and hem to the inside of the vest (see Figure 14).

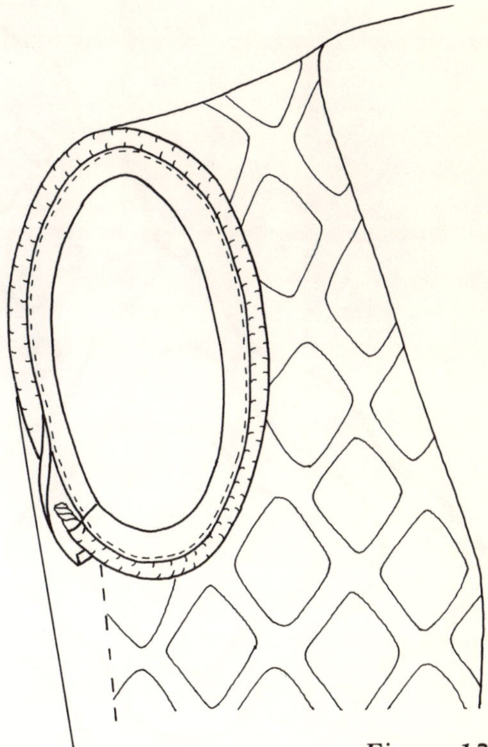

Figure 13

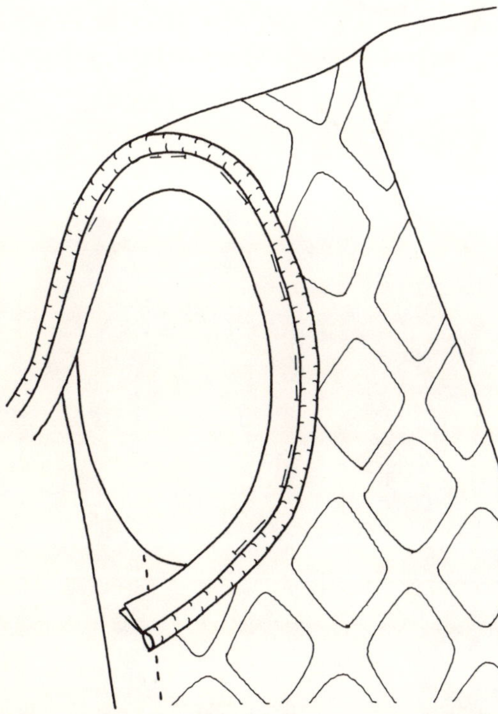

Figure 12

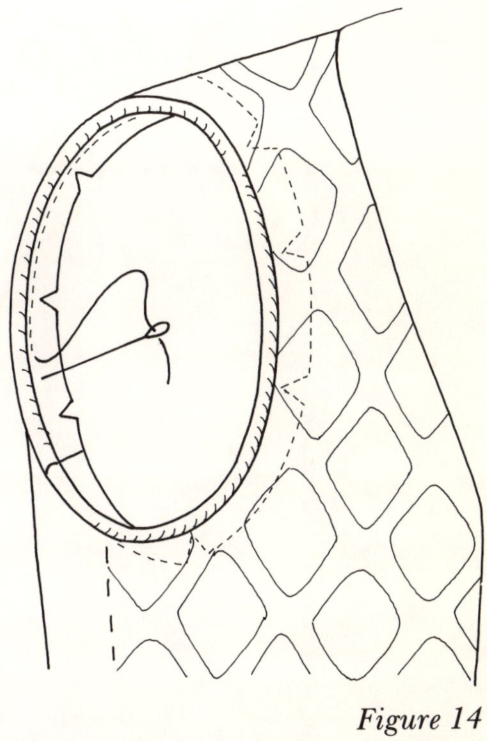

Figure 14

E
1
1
5
1
2
3
4
4
3
2
F

(stippled)	medium brown
(blank)	off white
1	gold
2	rust
3	medium blue
4	navy
5	gray

Welt the front needlepoint panels and the neck as follows: Start at one side seam and work up one needlepoint panel, around the neck, and down the other needlepoint panel to the opposite side seam; join the welting to the right side of the needlepoint with the welted head facing in and the seam line of the welting directly over the seam allowance of the needlepoint and of the backing fabric around the neck (in the same way as in Figure 12); leave an extra ½ inch of welting at each side seam to be hidden by the back hem (see arrow, Figure 15).

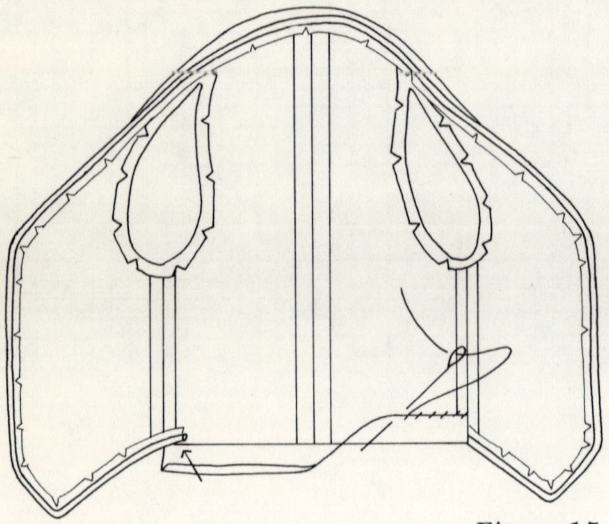

Figure 15

Baste, then sew the welting to the vest on the seam line and clip or notch the seam allowances at the curves and corners. Turn the welting under and hem to the inside of the vest (in the same manner as in Figure 14).

Turn under the hem of the vest back and with it the ends of the welting at each side seam; blindstitch to the backing fabric (see Figure 15).

Lay the left needlepoint panel over the right panel in its "closed" position; the invisible center guidelines, *CD*, will meet, and the design will appear continuous across the front of the vest (see Figure 16). On the left side sew the two buttons with chains, each 1½ inches in from the welting and about 5 inches from each other. On the right panel sew the two matching buttons so that the chains fit comfortably; each button will be about 3 inches from its mate (see Figure 16). You may want to anchor the vest with two hooks sewn under the welting of the left panel and with matching eyes sewn inconspicuously on the right panel.

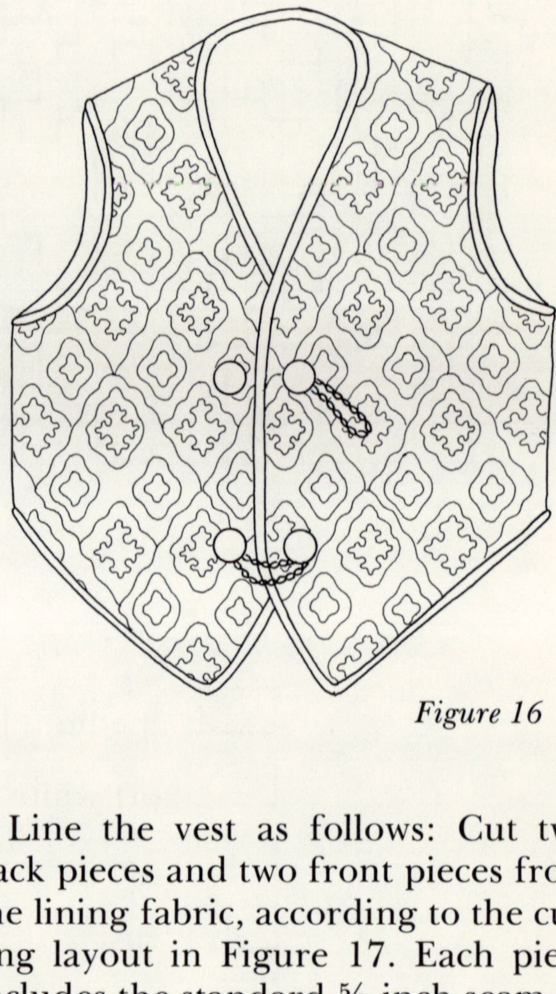

Figure 16

Line the vest as follows: Cut two back pieces and two front pieces from the lining fabric, according to the cutting layout in Figure 17. Each piece includes the standard ⅝-inch seam allowance.

Stitch the center back seam of the lining (see Figure 7). Press the seam allowances open.

Lay the back of the lining right side up and over it position the two front sections of lining, right sides down, so that the shoulder and side seams

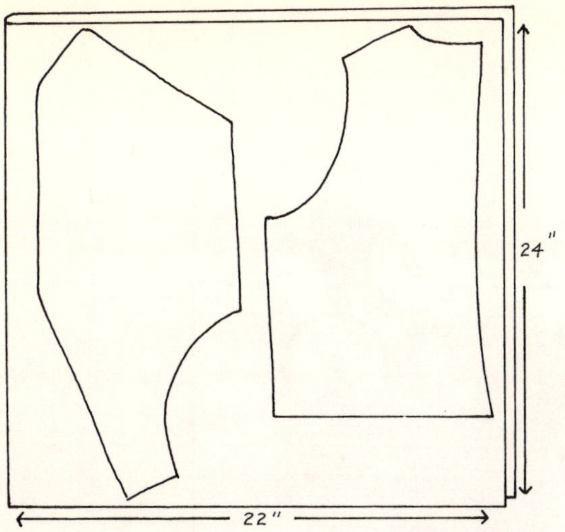

Figure 17

match. Baste and then sew the front panels to the back at the shoulder and side seams along the ⅝-inch seam allowance (as in Figure 11). Turn the lining right side out.

Pin the lining in place inside the finished vest, wrong sides together, fitting the lining around the neck and the armholes first. Turn under the seam allowance of the lining and blindstitch it to the seam allowance of the welting around the armholes, the neck, and the needlepoint panels. Across the back of the vest hem the lining to itself and let it hang free.

COLOR KEY

The color key for the vest appears on one of its design pages.

(wavy pattern)	yellow
(solid black)	brown
1	beige
2	red-orange
3	red
4	gray
5	light green
6	green
	off white background

Cheese Board

In very short order you can stitch a square of fruit and cheese, then serve the needlepoint delicacy under glass in a charming cheese board (see "Source," below). The needlepoint is 5 inches square, the board into which it fits is 6 by 12 inches, and together they make the nicest kind of hostess gift.

Stitch: Basketweave.

Canvas: No. 10 interlocking canvas, 8 inches square.

Yarn: ¾ ounce of Persian wool.

FROM DESIGN TO CANVAS

Bind the cut edges of the canvas with masking tape.

Center the canvas over the design on the book page. Following the instructions for tracing designs in Part I, trace the design from the book onto the canvas with an indelible marker; include the square outline. If you prefer, you can transfer the design to tracing paper first and then to the canvas.

STITCHING

Follow the color key for the design and refer to the color photograph as you work. The black lines you have traced onto the canvas only delineate separate areas of color and should not be stitched.

Work up to and including the outline row.

FINISHING

Block the needlepoint.

Unscrew the back panel and remove the square mounting board supplied by the manufacturer; it will be slightly smaller than the finished needlepoint.

Lay the finished needlepoint face down and over it center the mounting board, white side down. Place a thin line of white all-purpose glue (such as Elmer's Glue-All) along one back edge of the mounting board and fold the needlepoint over onto the glue; clip with clothespins (see Figure 1). Do the same with the opposite edge, pulling the needlepoint taut and making sure that the rows of stitching are aligned on the front.

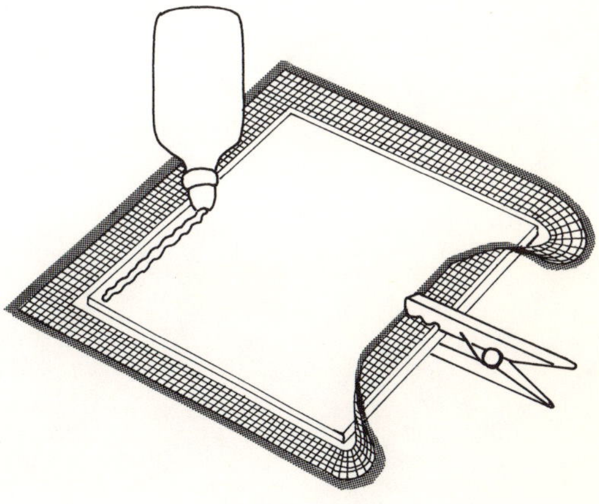

Figure 1

Repeat the gluing on the two remaining edges. Let all four sides dry well.

On all four sides trim the excess canvas away to within two rows of the finished stitching. Cut the four corners diagonally; tuck each corner into a miterlike fold and glue to the back of the mounting board (see Figure 2).

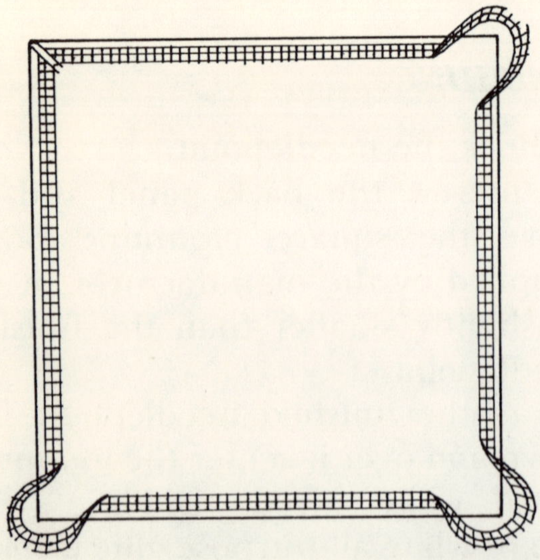

Figure 2

Clean the glass gently on the inside, being careful not to press out too hard from the inside. Place the mounted needlepoint face down on the glass. Replace the back panel and the mounting screws. For a more finished appearance, you can glue felt rounds over the screws.

COLOR KEY

The color key for the cheese board appears on its design page.

SOURCE

The cheese board is available from Sudberry House, Inc., Box 421, Old Lyme, Conn. 06371, who will either mail the item direct or suggest a local retail source near you; it retails for $9.95 at the time of publication. The same needlepoint panel will fit into a 6-inch-square trivet, which looks like the left hand side of the cheese board; the trivet, also distributed by Sudberry House, retails for $6.95.

Jewel Box

A flurry of leaves waft across the lid of this velvet-lined jewel box (see "Source," below), providing a 6-by-9-inch needlepoint panel in the 7-by-10-inch top. The stitched inset locks into place in an ingenious construction that doesn't require elaborate finishing or mounting techniques. Moreover, the multidirectional botanical design can be used just as effectively in a vertical format as, for example, in the photo album on page 43, which calls for the same size needlepoint panel and utilizes the same mounting technique.

Stitch: Basketweave.

Canvas: No. 10 interlocking canvas, 10 by 13 inches.

Yarn: 1¾ ounces of Persian wool.

FROM DESIGN TO CANVAS

Bind the cut edges of the canvas with masking tape.

Center the canvas over the design on the book page. Following the instructions for tracing designs in Part I, trace the design from the book onto the canvas with an indelible marker. If you prefer, you can transfer the design to tracing paper first and then to the canvas.

STITCHING

Follow the color key for the design and refer to the color photograph as you work. The black lines you have traced only delineate separate areas of color and should not be stitched.

Work up to but not beyond the outline of the design so that the finished needlepoint measures exactly 6 by 9 inches.

FINISHING

Block the needlepoint.

Sew a row of machine stitching on the outermost row of needlepoint on all four sides (see Figure 1).

Figure 1

Along all sides carefully cut the canvas one row outside the existing needlepoint, leaving one thread all around (see Figure 2).

Set aside the white plastic mounting board that you will find stored in the recessed frame of the jewel box lid. Slip two adjacent sides of needlepoint under the recessed frame and slide the white mounting board under the needlepoint (see Figure 3). Using any

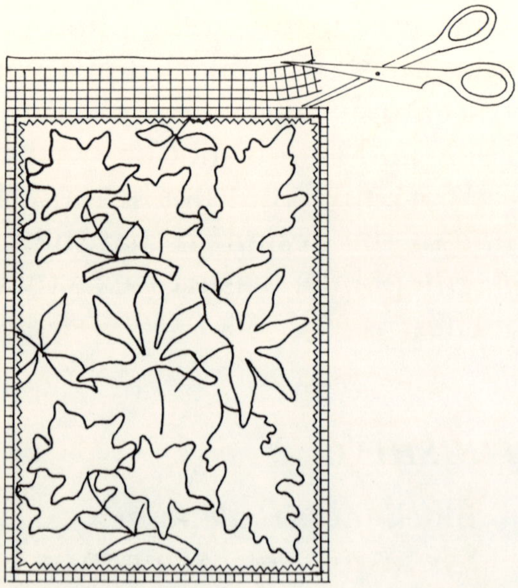

Figure 2

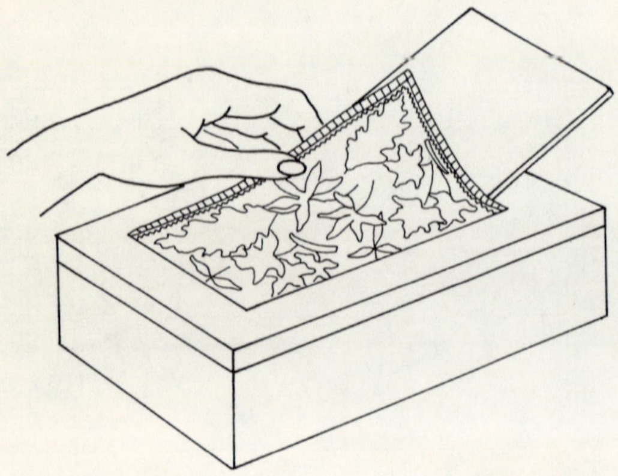

Figure 3

flat, dull tool, such as a spatula or a butter knife, wedge the other two sides of the needlepoint under the frame (see Figure 4).

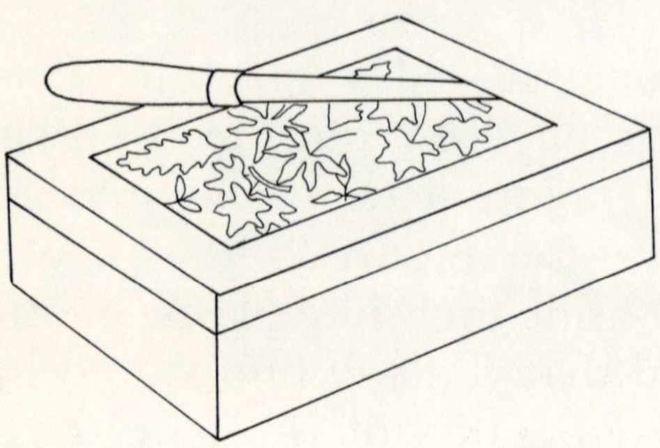

Figure 4

COLOR KEY

The color key for the jewel box appears on its design page.

SOURCE

The jewel box is made of simulated leather in ivory, white, black, brown, red, green, blue, lime, and lemon; it retails for $17.50 at the time of publication. You can order it by mail from Giftiques Unlimited, P.O. Box 412, Little Neck, N.Y. 11363, or your local needlework shop can probably order it from the manufacturer, Adolph Burkland, 28–18 Steinway St., Long Island City, New York, N.Y. 11103.

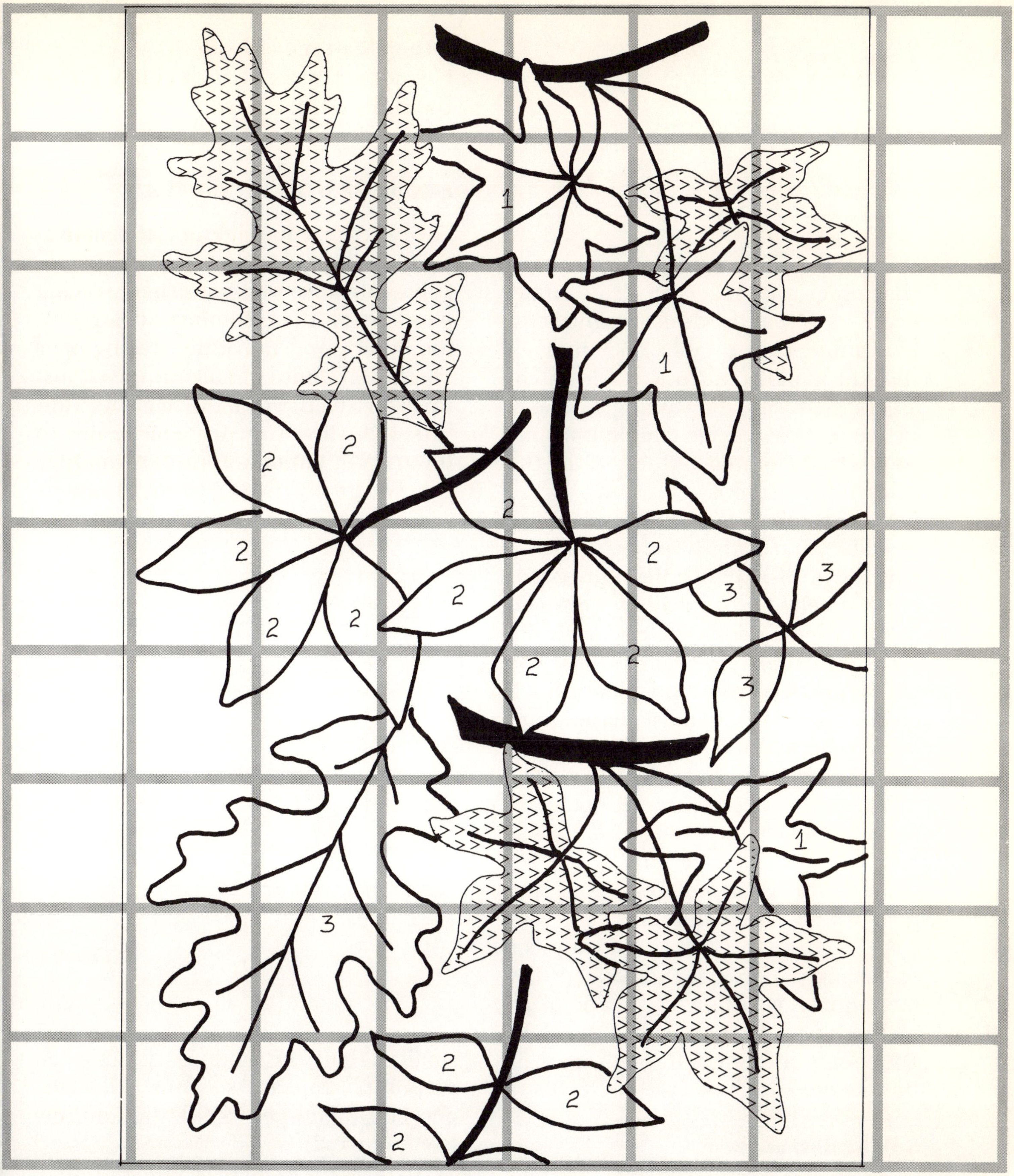

- yellow-green
- brown
- dark green lines
- 1 olive
- 2 kelly green
- 3 blue-green
- off-white background

Inlaid Boxes

A prettily decorated box makes a charming gift that can lead many lives—as a handy desk organizer, a handsome coffee table dispenser of cocktail napkins, a vanity-table catch-all for hair clips or earrings, or as a cigarette box (to be coupled with a similarly decorated lighter, as in the color photograph).

Fortunately, many such boxes are available, particularly in craft stores, which can display needlepoint panels handsomely. Look for a box whose lid has a raised wooden gallery around a recessed center panel into which the needlepoint is inset and glued. Such boxes come in various shapes and sizes to accommodate their many potential uses.

The geometric design on both box and lighter panels suggests inlaid ceramic tiles. The design can be repeated and extended to cover a surface of any size or shape.

Making a custom pattern. Lay a piece of tracing paper over the panel of the box and on it outline the shape of its recessed section with a dark marker. Draw only the finished dimensions of the needlepoint.

Stitch: Basketweave.

Canvas: No. 10 mono canvas, 2 inches larger on all sides than the outline of the needlepoint.

Yarn: 1 ounce of Persian wool covers 32 square inches.

Other Materials Needed:
- Cotton batting 1 inch smaller than the finished needlepoint.

FROM DESIGN TO CANVAS

Bind the cut edges of the canvas with masking tape.

Lay the custom patterned tracing paper over the geometric design on the book page; move the tracing over the design until it encompasses just that part of the design that you want to stitch, then transfer the design to the tracing paper with a dark marker (see Figure 1). If the custom pattern is

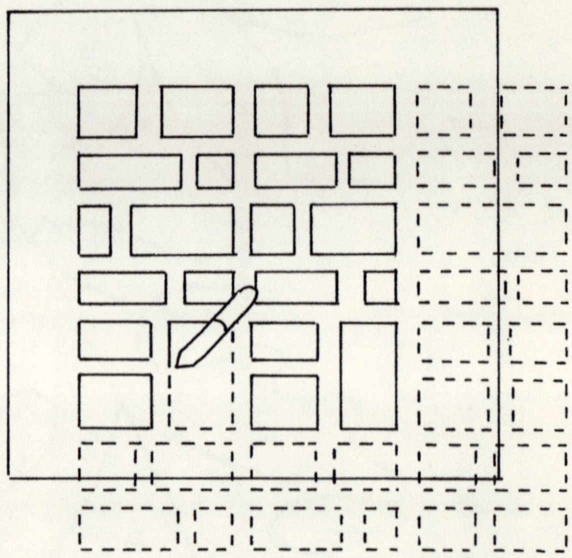

Figure 1

smaller than the outline of the needlepoint, repeat sections of the geometric design to fill the outline (see Figure 2).

If you want to incorporate an initial or monogram from the Design Workbook, trace it onto the tracing paper where you want to position it and space the geometric design around it (see Figure 3).

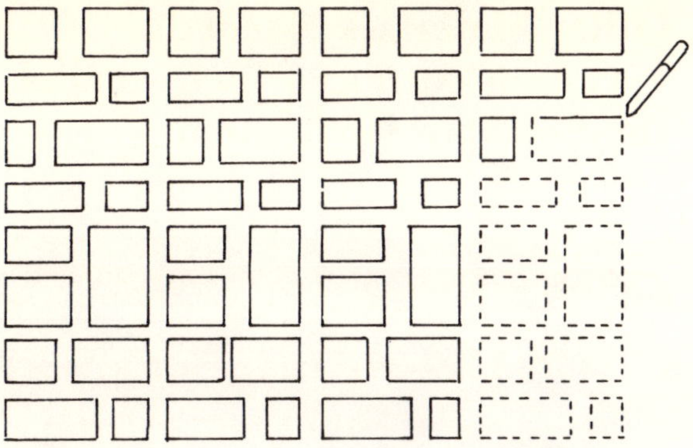

Figure 2

Figure 3

Once your entire design has been laid out on the tracing paper, center it face up under the canvas and trace both the outline of the panel and its design onto the canvas with an indelible marker (see Figure 4).

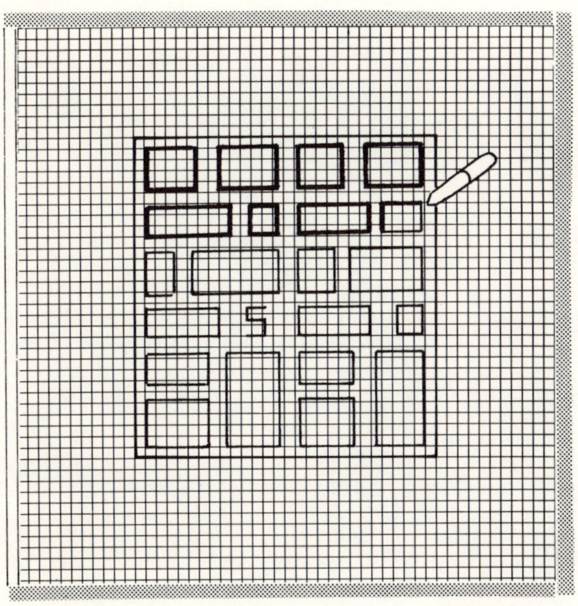

Figure 4

STITCHING

Follow the color key for the design and refer to the color photograph as you work. The black lines you have traced onto the canvas only delineate separate areas of color and should not be stitched.

On all edges stitch right up to but not beyond the outline of the needlepoint.

FINISHING EACH INLAID NEEDLEPOINT PANEL

Block the needlepoint.

Sew a row of machine stitching on the excess canvas just outside the needlepoint.

Cut the excess canvas away on all sides to within ¾ inch of the needlepoint. Cut the corners diagonally to within ½ inch of the stitching.

Miter the corners and hem the sides, tacking the turned-back canvas to the back of the needlepoint (see Figure 5).

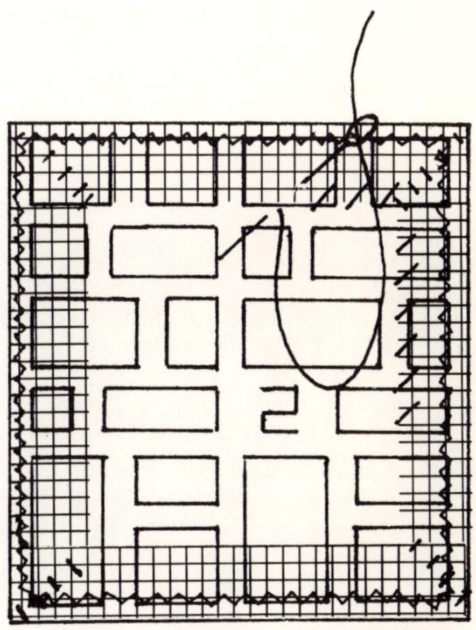

Figure 5

Spread a thin coating of white all-purpose glue in the recessed section of the box and press the cotton batting into the center of it. Spread a little more glue over the cotton batting, then press the mitered needlepoint into place (see Figure 6). Weight the inset with a heavy book for a day until the glue dries.

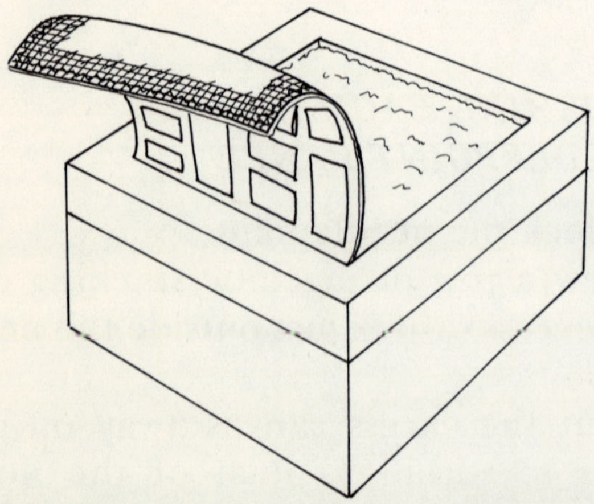

Figure 6

COLOR KEY

The color key for the geometric design appears on the design page.

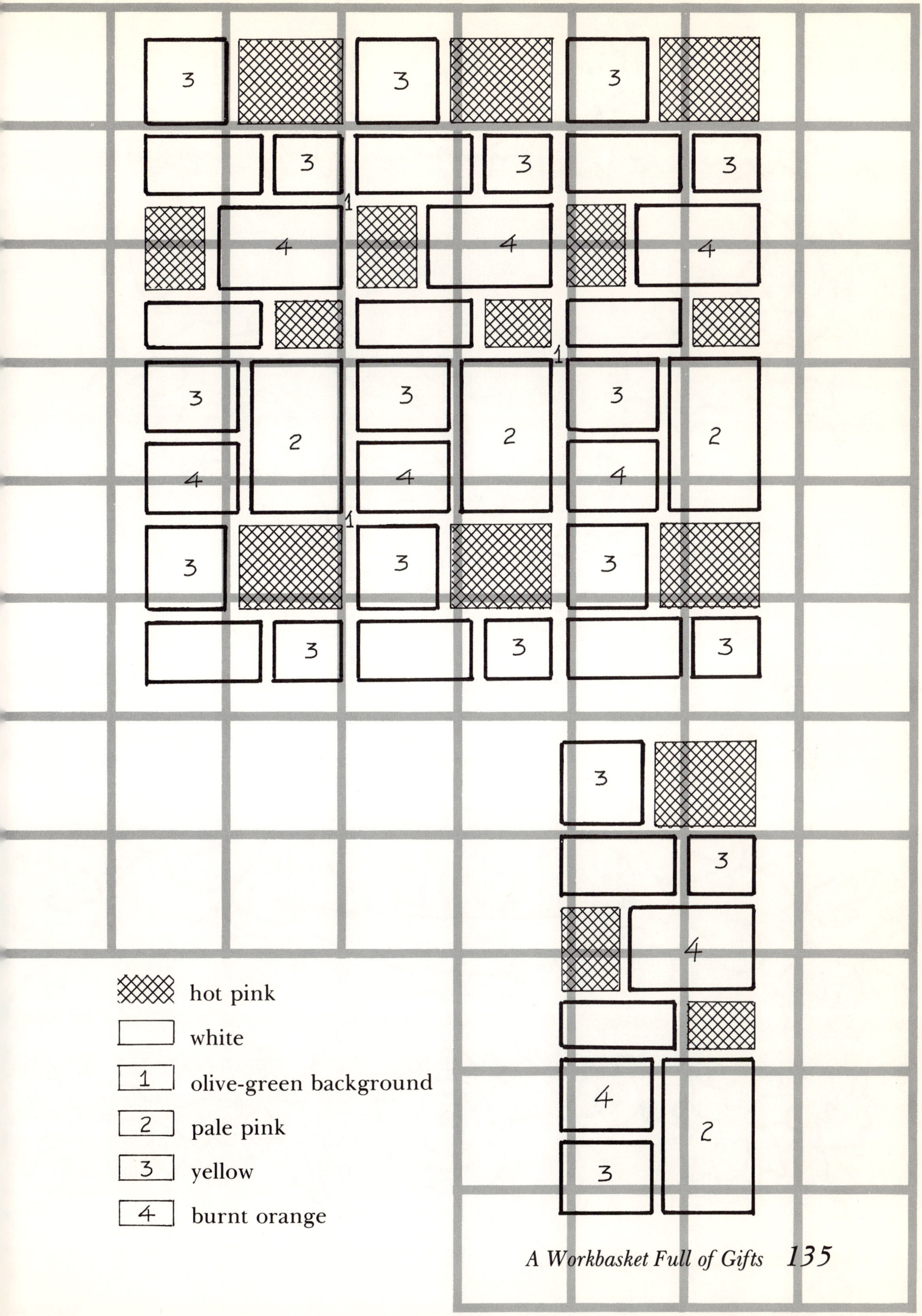
hot pink
white
1 olive-green background
2 pale pink
3 yellow
4 burnt orange

Baby Carriage Cover

The expressions of joy and benediction for future well-being that accompany the birth of a child can be offered in many ways, and none more delightful than a tapestry stitched with love and care, perhaps by grandmother. This design, recalling the charm of Early American folk art, has fitting intimations of immortality—a tree of life and doves of peace bearing floral messages of purity and innocence, all entwined in leafy garlands and all in the muted pastel tones of the nursery. The stitchery snaps onto any ready-made carriage cover and snaps off when the cover needs cleaning. Once the toddler has outgrown the pram, it can become a wall hanging for a child's room.

Stitch: Basketweave; edging.

Canvas: No. 10 interlocking canvas, 18 by 22 inches.

Yarn: 8½ ounces of Persian wool, which includes about 4 ounces for background and 2 ounces for a 1-inch border all around.

Other Materials Needed:
- A carriage cover (sometimes called a shawl), usually about 40 inches square.
- Two lengths of gripper tape, each pair 16 inches long.
- For a wall hanging a wooden mounting board 14 inches long, 1 to 2 inches deep, and ½ inch thick.

FROM DESIGN TO CANVAS

Bind the cut edges of the canvas with masking tape.

Following the instructions for enlarging designs in Part I, enlarge the design so that the width is 13 inches; the height will be about 17 inches.

Center the design face up under the canvas and trace it onto the canvas with an indelible marker.

STITCHING

Follow the color key for the design and refer to the color photograph as you work. The black lines you have traced onto the canvas only delineate separate areas of color and should not be stitched.

Around all four sides stitch a 1-inch border (ten rows), picking up any of the colors in the design to coordinate with the nursery decor or the color of the carriage blanket. The needlepoint is planned to fit comfortably in a common lightweight carriage. If your baby's carriage differs significantly in dimensions, extend or reduce the borders as needed.

FINISHING

Block the needlepoint.

Along all four sides cut the canvas to within one thread of the stitched needlepoint. Using yarn the color of the border, work the edging stitch over both this canvas thread and the outermost row of needlepoint (see Figure 1). For adequate yarn coverage, remember to insert extra edging stitches in the corner meshes.

Lay the finished needlepoint wrong side up and blindstitch one part of

Figure 1

gripper tape across the top edge, turning under ½ inch at each end (see Figure 2). Attach one half of the other strip of gripper tape to the bottom edge of the needlepoint in the same manner.

Figure 2

Position the needlepoint on the carriage cover carefully, allowing room at the sides and bottom to tuck under the carriage mattress. Then blindstitch each gripper tape "mate" strip to the carriage cover (see Figure 3) to match the corresponding strip of tape on the needlepoint.

If you want to mount the needlepoint as a wall hanging, remove (or replace) the upper, receiving strip of gripper tape from the blanket, then

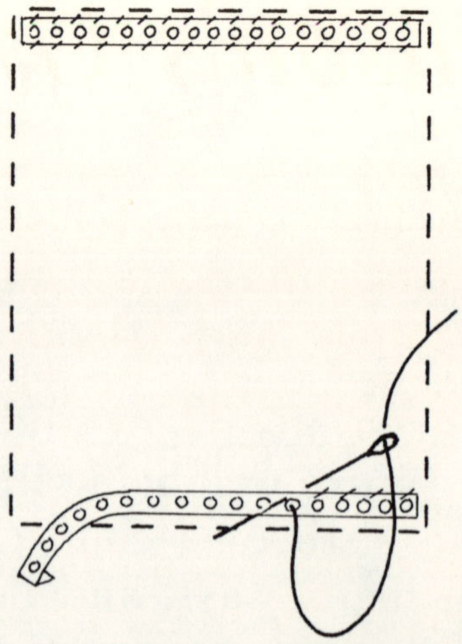

Figure 3

tack it to the mounting board, tucking each end under 1 inch (see Figure 4). Press the top edge of the needlepoint to the mounting board so that both halves of the gripper tape engagc. Lct the bottom edge hang free. Suspend the mounting board from the wall by means of two extended nails or hooks.

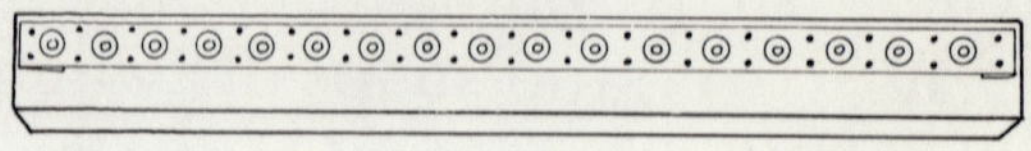

Figure 4

COLOR KEY

- deep yellow
- hot pink
- 1 cream
- 2 fuchsia
- 3 medium pink
- 4 light blue
- 5 medium blue
- 6 deep blue
- 7 light green leaves
- 8 brass
- dark green stems

Season's Greetings

The holiday season is celebrated joyously with song, special cakes and cookies, seasonal punches, and most of all, with family and friends. Why not with needlepoint? Herewith a group of stitchable ideas to make a part of your holiday traditions year after year: Stockings for the mantle, ornaments for the tree, and a welcoming wreath for the door that can double as a centerpiece at Christmas dinner or be transformed into a display holder for Christmas cards.

Christmas Wreath

Stitch: Basketweave.

Canvas: No. 10 mono canvas, 18 inches square.

Yarn: 5 ounces of Persian wool, which includes 1½ ounces of white for the center.

Other Materials Needed:
- Stiff cardboard, 14 inches in diameter, on which to mount the wreath.
- Red felt for lining, the size of the finished needlepoint.
- Red velvet ribbon, ¼ inch wide, one length 26 inches long for the inner band, another length 8 inches long for a tab hanger.
- Piece of red felt 8 inches wide and 48 inches long for the card holder.
- Upholsterer's needle.

FROM DESIGN TO CANVAS

Bind the cut edges of the canvas with masking tape.

Fold the canvas in half and then in half again. Crease the fold lines, then lay the canvas out flat.

The design for the wreath on page 143 is project-size, but shows only one quarter of the total area to be stitched, so it must be copied onto the canvas four times. To do this, lay a piece of tracing paper over the book page and onto it trace the design with a dark marker.

Lay the tracing face up under one quadrant of the canvas so that each short side meets a horizontal or a vertical fold (see Figure 1); it doesn't matter which quadrant you fill first since you will trace this quarter-wreath once in each quadrant. With an indelible marker transfer the design from the tracing to the canvas.

Following the instructions for extending designs in Part I, turn the tracing over and move it under the canvas to a contiguous quadrant, making sure that all matching lines abut (see Figure 2). Trace the quarter-wreath onto this quadrant of canvas with an indelible marker. Repeat the process, flopping the tracing each time, until the quarter-wreath has been traced four times to form a complete circle (see small figure on the design page).

With a dark marker write your family name on a piece of paper in your own hand; scale it boldly so that it fits nicely into the center circle. Align and center your signature under the canvas and trace it in the center with an indelible marker (see Figure 3).

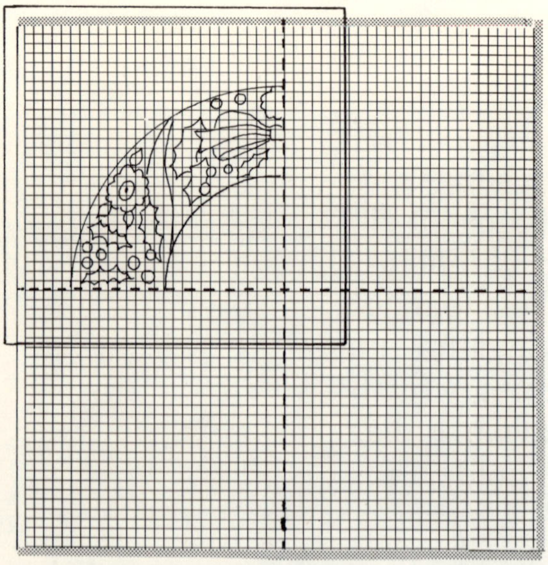

Figure 1

STITCHING

Follow the color key for the design as you work. The black lines you have traced onto the canvas only delineate separate areas of color and should not be stitched, except for the outlines and veins of the leaves, which the color key indicates should be dark green. Stitch the center of the wreath in white and your signature in green, red, or any favorite color.

Around the outside edge extend the design for three extra rows.

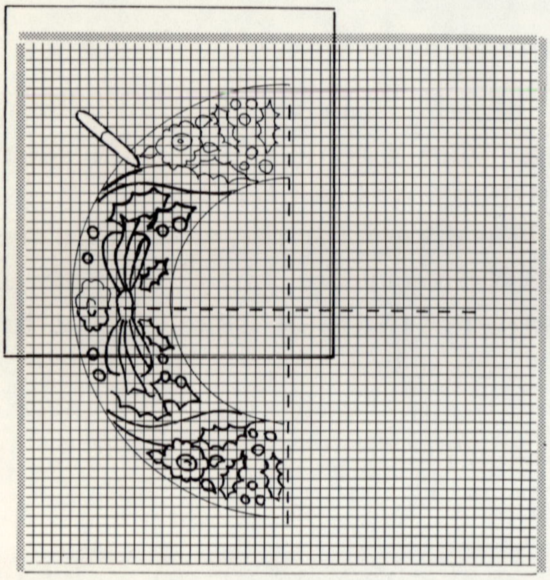

Figure 2

FINISHING

Block the needlepoint.

Sew a row of machine stitching on the excess canvas just outside the needlepoint.

Frame the white center circle with red velvet ribbon; lay it over the needlepoint and blindstitch in place (see Figure 4).

Cut the excess canvas away all around to within 1½ inches of the needlepoint. Glue the cut edges and let dry (see Figure 5).

Lay the needlepoint face down and center the board over it. Temporarily

Figure 3

Figure 4

Figure 5

anchor the needlepoint to the edge of the board with tape. Lace opposite sides of the circle together with an upholsterer's needle, working from top to bottom, then side to side, and then lacing across the intervening spaces (see Figure 6).

Lay the felt lining over the board and blindstitch it in place. As you come to the top of the wreath, double an 8-inch piece of ribbon and sew its ends to the inside of the felt lining so that it forms a loop for hanging (see Figure 7).

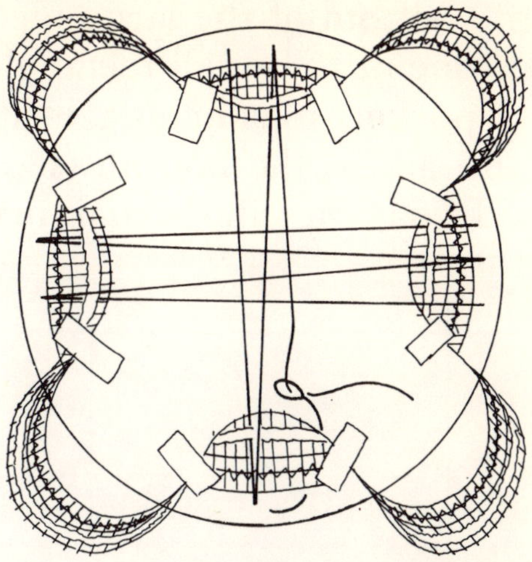

Figure 6

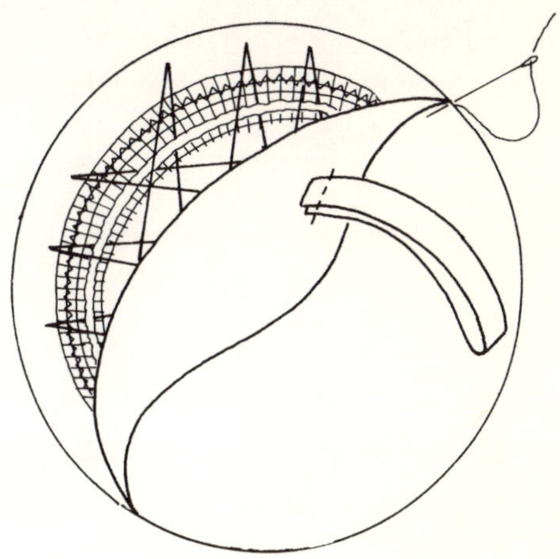

Figure 7

A FLORAL CENTERPIECE

To use the wreath as a centerpiece for your holiday table, tuck the loop under the needlepoint and set a bowl of pine cones or shiny golden balls over the center.

A CHRISTMAS CARD HOLDER

To transform the wreath into a Christmas card holder, follow these instructions:

From the long rectangle of red felt cut three small rectangles, each 6 inches long and 8 inches wide; this will leave a large piece of felt 30 inches long and 8 inches wide.

At the bottom of the large piece of felt sew one of the small rectangles to form a pocket, topstitching it at the sides and across the bottom (see Figure 8). Two inches above that, make a

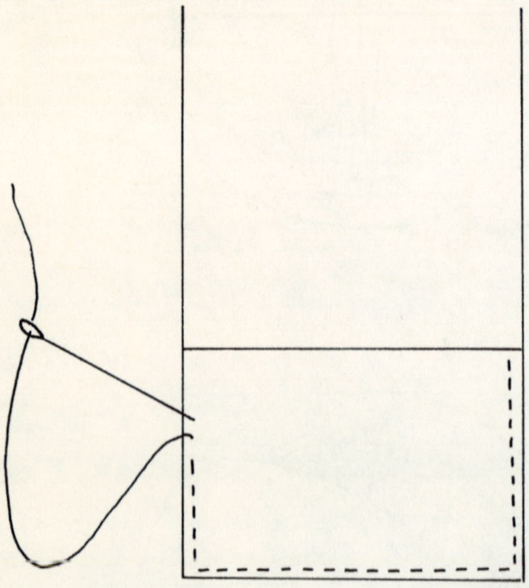

Figure 8

second pocket with another small rectangle. Repeat for the third pocket. Cover the top seams with decorative trim or ribbon (see Figure 9).

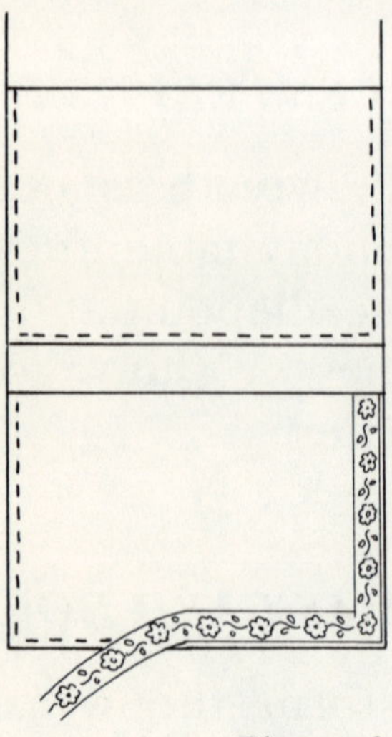

Figure 9

To attach the card holder to the wreath, sew snaps across the top of the felt and matching snaps to the felt lining on the back of the wreath (see Figure 10).

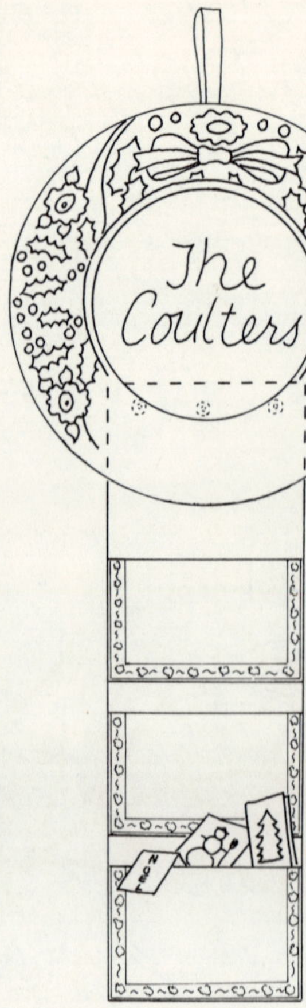

Figure 10

COLOR KEY

The color key for the wreath appears on the design page.

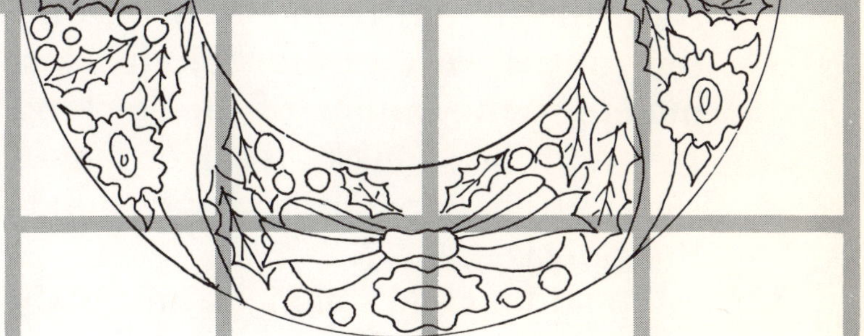

red ribbon, berries

pale yellow flowers

1 medium pink bow

2 dark pink shadow on bow

3 light yellow-green leaves

4 medium yellow-green holly leaves

5 brown flower center

6 kelly green background

7 white

dark green veins on leaves

Christmas Stockings

Stitch: Basketweave; edging.

Canvas: No. 10 interlocking canvas, 11 by 15 inches for each stocking.

Yarn: 2½ ounces of Persian wool for each stocking.

Other Materials Needed:
- Red or green felt for backing, ½ inch larger all around than each stocking.
- Strip of felt or ribbon 12 inches long for hanging each stocking.

FROM DESIGN TO CANVAS

Bind the cut edges of the canvas with masking tape.

Center the canvas over the design on the book page. Following the instructions for tracing designs in Part I, trace the design from the book onto the canvas with an indelible marker, including the outline of the stocking. If you prefer, you can transfer the design to tracing paper first and then to the canvas.

To add a child's name, transfer the letters you need from an alphabet on pages 184, 185, 186 to the tracing paper. Plan the name to fit into the top band on the stocking, centered and nicely spaced. You may want to lay the name out on graph paper first. Trace the letters onto the canvas with an indelible marker (see Figure 1).

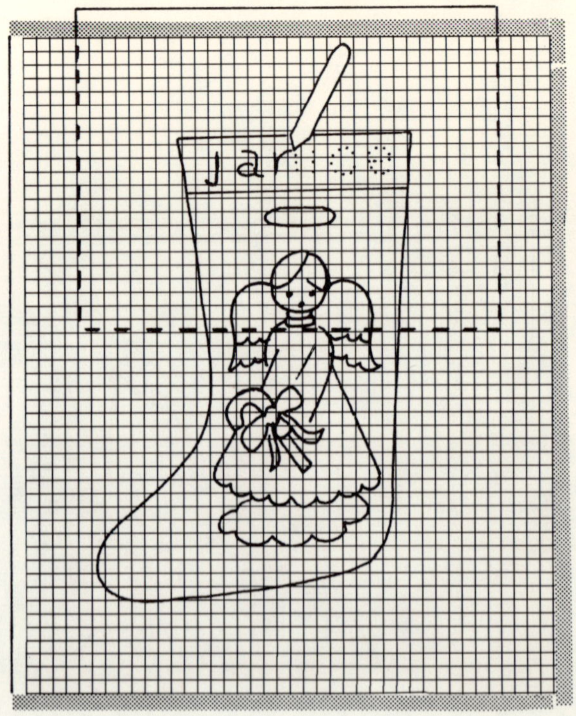

Figure 1

STITCHING

Follow the color key for the design and refer to the color photograph as you work. Stitch the letters in whatever Christmas colors strike your fancy, and be sure to keep them aligned. The black lines you have traced onto the canvas only delineate separate areas of color and should not be stitched unless clearly marked on the color key as "black."

Across the top edge, work up to but not including the last row of the design. Around the rest of the stocking extend the design for two extra rows (see Figure 2).

FINISHING

Block the needlepoint.

Sew a row of machine stitching on the excess canvas just outside the needlepoint all around the stocking except across the top.

Figure 2

Lay the needlepoint face down over the felt. Baste, then sew them together just inside the two-row seam allowance; leave the top opening unstitched (see Figure 3).

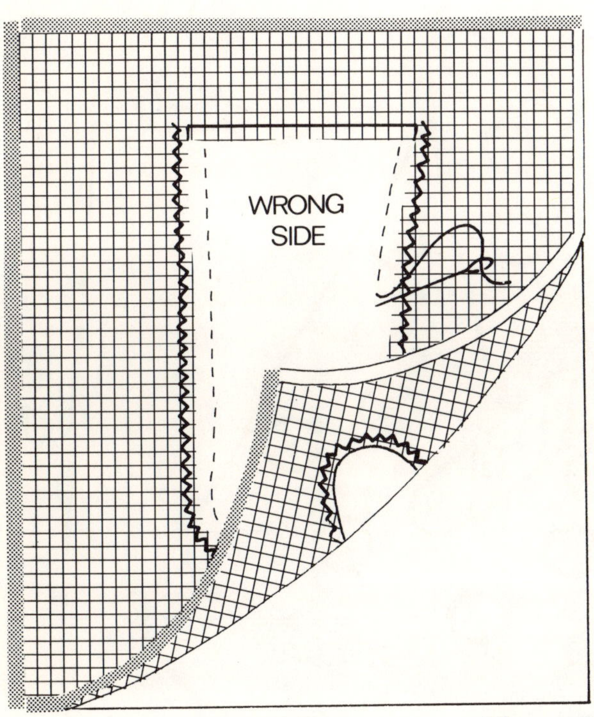

Figure 3

Across the top edge carefully cut the canvas one row outside the existing needlepoint, leaving one thread.

Finish the edge with the edging stitch (see Figure 4).

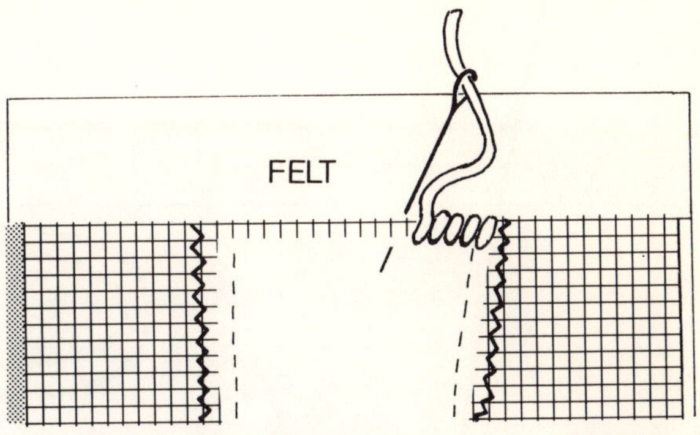

Figure 4

Cut the felt at the top edge to match the needlepoint. Around the rest of the stocking cut the excess canvas and felt to within 1 inch of the needlepoint, notching the corners and curves (see Figure 5). Turn right side out.

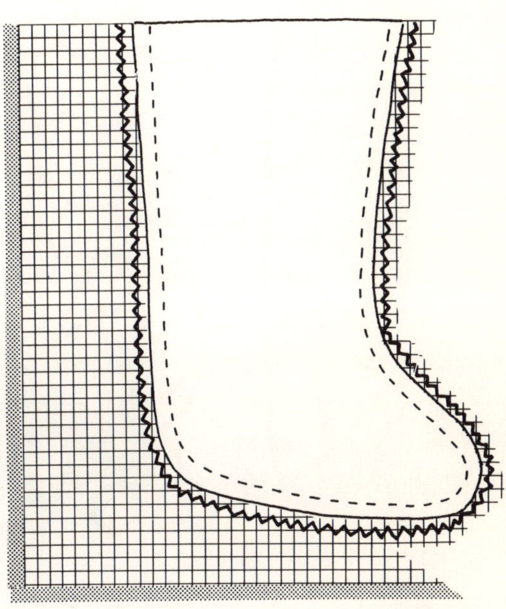

Figure 5

Fold the ribbon or felt strip in half and sew to the top of the felt backing (see Figure 6).

4
2
3
1
5
2
2
3
2
4
3
3
2
3
1
1
3
3
2
3
3
3
3
3

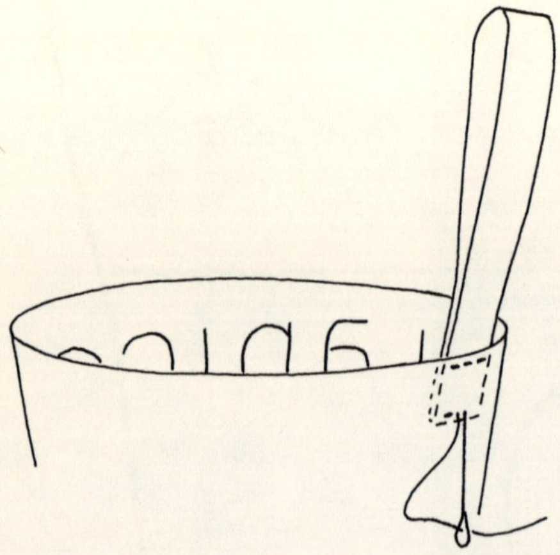

Figure 6

COLOR KEY

- light green
- deep blue
- black
- 1 flesh
- 2 red
- 3 bright yellow
- 4 white
- 5 kelly green
- 6 pale yellow

Christmas Tree Ornaments

Stitch: Basketweave.

Canvas: No. 10 mono canvas. For each ornament cut a rectangular piece of canvas 4 inches larger than the widest and longest dimensions.

Yarn: About ¾ ounce of Persian wool for each of the four large ornaments; a little less for the two smaller ones.

Other Materials Needed:
- Fabric for backing each ornament, 1 inch larger all around than each design.
- Cotton for stuffing.
- Cording 12 inches long for each ornament.

FROM DESIGN TO CANVAS

Center the canvas over the design on the book page. Following the instructions for tracing designs in Part I, trace the design from the book onto the canvas with an indelible marker. If you prefer, you can transfer the design to tracing paper first and then to the canvas.

STITCHING

Follow the color key for the design and refer to the color photograph as you work. The black lines you have traced onto the canvas only delineate separate areas of color and should not be stitched unless clearly marked as "black."

Around all edges extend the design for two extra rows.

FINISHING

Block the needlepoint.

Sew a row of machine stitching on the excess canvas just outside the needlepoint.

Lay the needlepoint face down over the lining. Baste, then seam them together, sewing just inside the two-row seam allowance; leave a 2-inch opening at the bottom (see Figure 1).

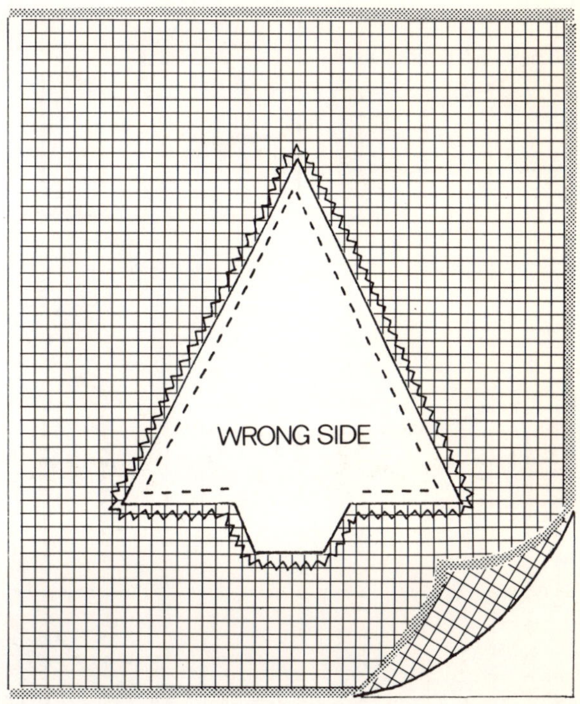

Figure 1

Trim away the tape, excess canvas, and backing all around to within 1 inch of the needlepoint, cutting all corners diagonally or notching them (see Figure 2).

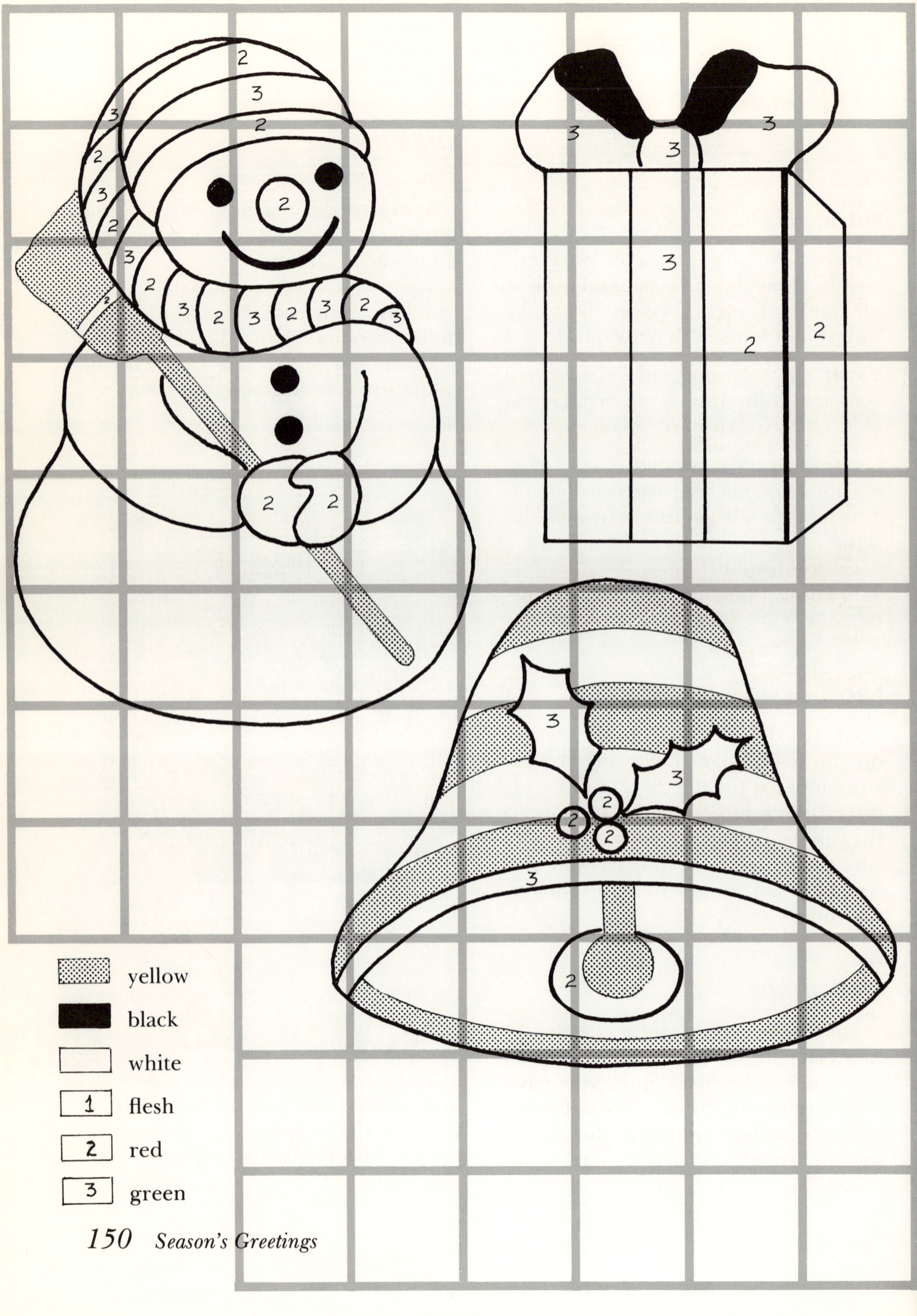
yellow
black
white
1 flesh
2 red
3 green

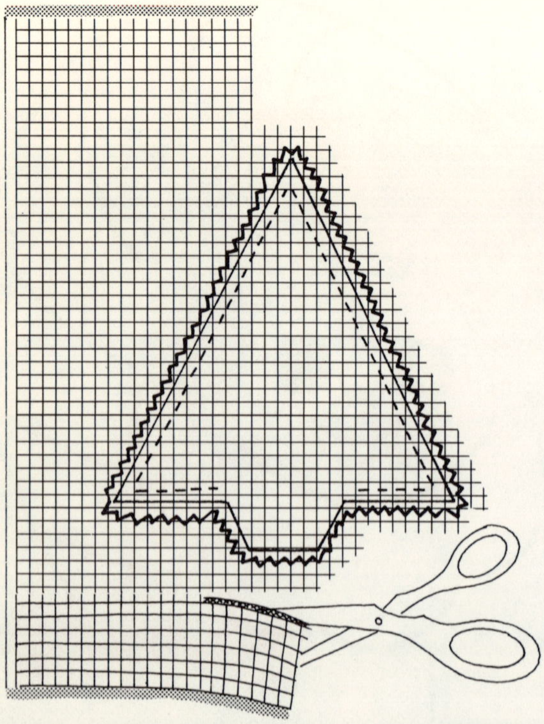

Figure 2

Turn right side out and stuff with cotton, working it into the corners. When the ornament is nicely plump, turn the lining and canvas edges under at the bottom opening and blindstitch together (see Figure 3).

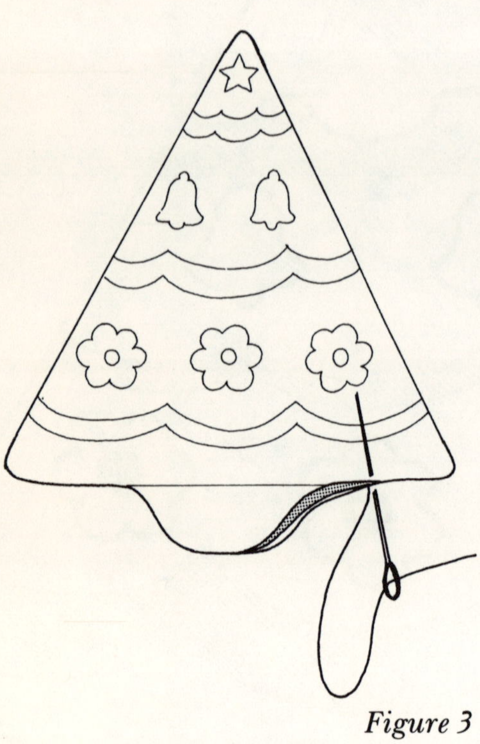

Figure 3

Fold a 12-inch length of cording in half and tack it in the middle to the top of each ornament for tying onto the tree (see Figure 4).

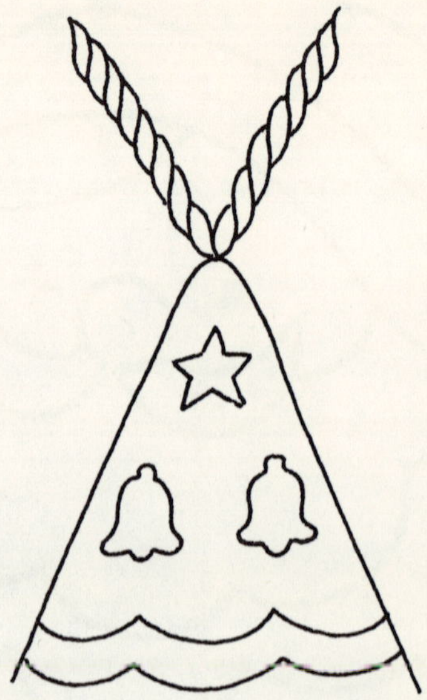

Figure 4

COLOR KEY

The color key for all six ornaments appears on one of the design pages.

PART III
The Design Workbook

USING THE DESIGN WORKBOOK

The pages of this workbook constitute a potpourri of patterns, a grab bag of mix-and-match motifs as well as already assembled compositions, all intended to expand your needlepoint horizons. These workbook designs can be used in several ways:

The simplest to use are the complete compositions—the bouquet on the first design page or any of the zodiac signs, for instance—which can be traced right off the page onto the canvas.

The most challenging and fun to use are the single motifs—flowers, leaves, butterflies, shells, fish, underwater foliage, animal heads—which can be combined in any fashion you like. For example, you can see some of the fish and seashells in an underwater scene on the wastebasket design (page 57), some of the same shells grouped differently in another pattern on the cover of the photo album (page 43), and a selection of leaves atop the jewel box (page 129).

There are many ways to expand the design possibilities of every single motif, once your imagination frees itself. Take the simple double tulip. You can use it just as it is as the centerpiece on a small object, say, the photo album (see Figure 1). You can

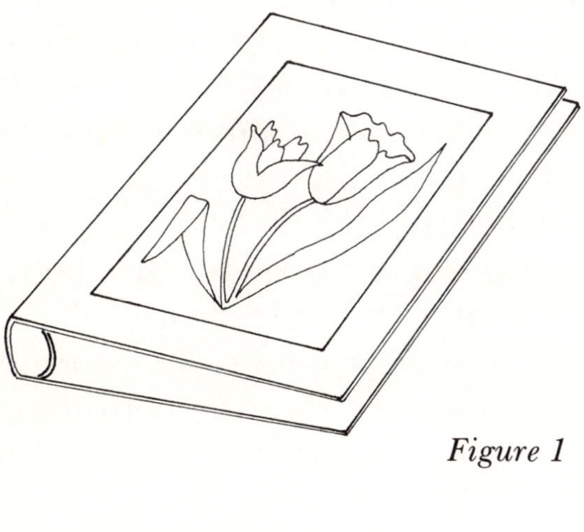

Figure 1

repeat one of the flower heads to make a triple bloom that fills a taller space (see Figure 2). You can extract

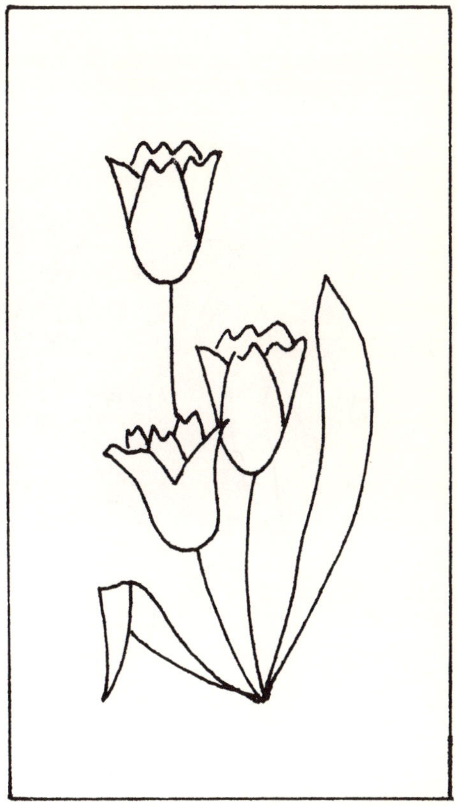

Figure 2

one of the two tulips and add that to the newly compound flower to fill an even larger space (see Figure 3)—and you now have the design for the tulip pillow minus the bamboo background (see color photo, facing page 116).

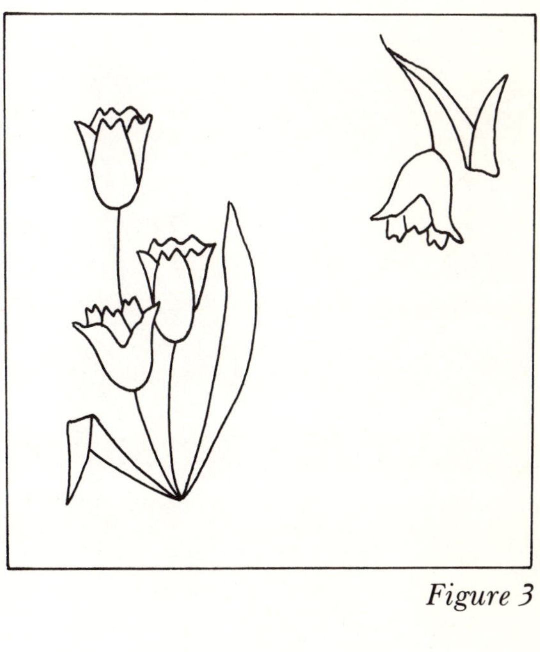

Figure 3

That same double-tulip motif from the Design Workbook could proliferate into still other patterns by reversing one or both of the flowers, or by tilting any of them (see Figure 4).

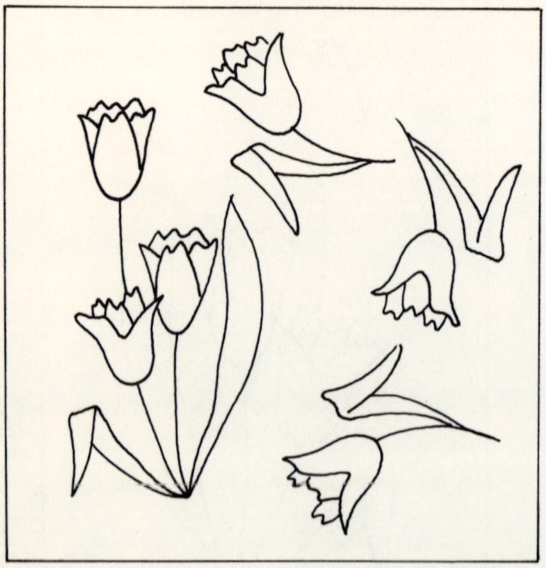

Figure 4

To plan a design using any one or more of the motifs from the Design Workbook, first outline the shape of the project on a piece of tracing paper, and with a black marker trace each motif you want to use onto separate pieces of tracing paper (see Figure 5).

Figure 5

Within the confines of the project outline, move the design elements around to try out various configurations and patterns. Once you are pleased with an arrangement, lay the tracing of the outline over the traced motifs and trace the entire composition onto the project-size, or master, tracing paper (see Figure 6). If you

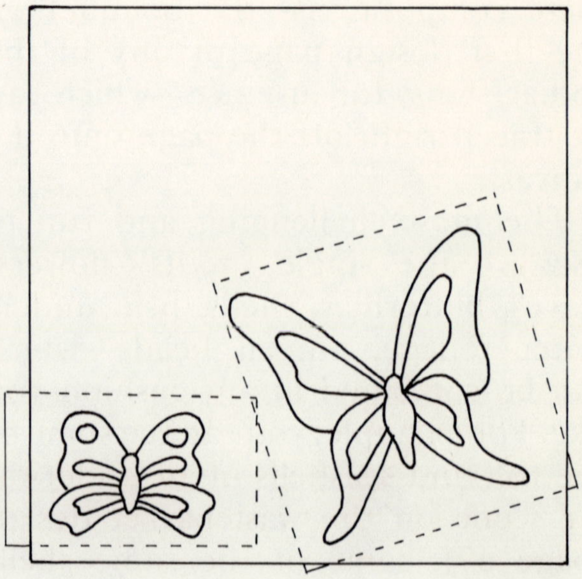

Figure 6

want to repeat the same component, trace it onto the master tracing once, then move the traced motif to another position and trace it off again, repeating that process as many times as needed (see Figure 7). If you want to reverse any motif and use its mirror image, simply flop the traced motif—you can see its black marking lines from either side of the tracing paper—and trace it onto the master tracing (see Figure 8).

If you want to superimpose one motif on part of another, position the one over the other and trace both, omitting those lines in the bottom motif that fall "underneath" the top motif; if you happen to be repeating the same motif, trace the bottom one, then reposition the tracing of the

Figure 7

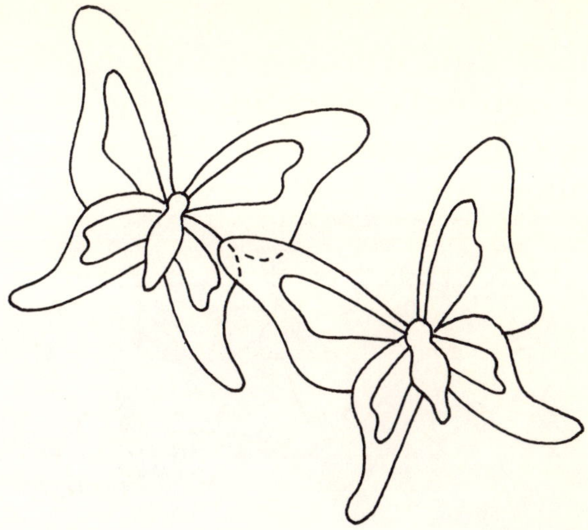

Figure 9

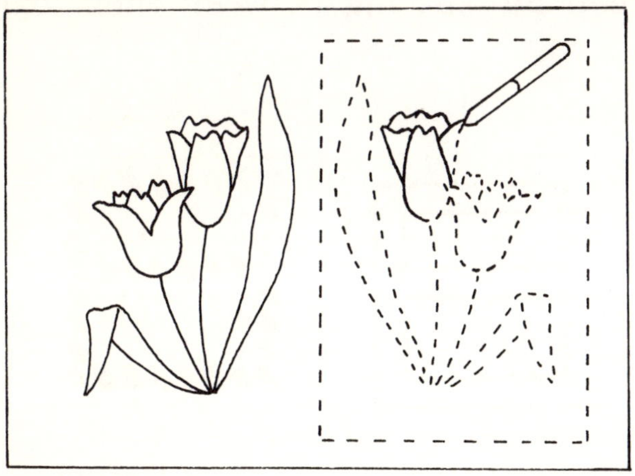

Figure 8

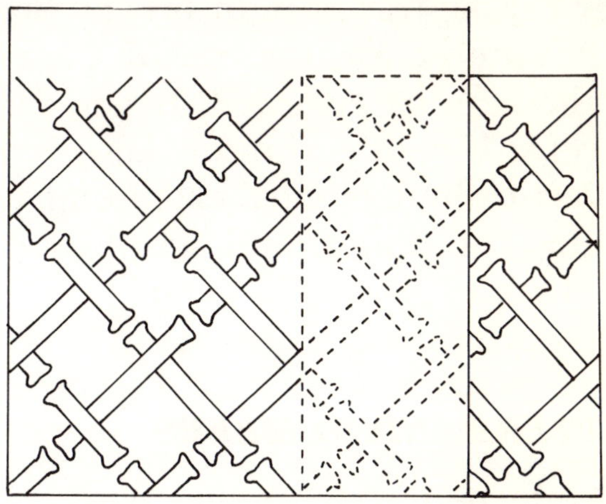

Figure 10

motif and trace it again, erasing those lines in the bottom figure that fall underneath the top figure (see Figure 9).

To utilize a repeat background, such as the bamboo pattern, trace the design on the workbook page onto tracing paper. Lay the tracing of the background under one corner of the master tracing and transfer it onto the master tracing with a dark marker. Move the traced bamboo to a contiguous part of the master tracing so that its lines abut and match the already traced bamboo, then transfer the background a second time (see Figure 10). Continue this process until the entire outline has been filled with the background. Wherever the background falls on an already traced design motif, omit tracing that part of the background, as if it actually continued behind the motif (see Figure 11).

As you can see, a limited number of motifs or components can proliferate into a virtually unlimited number of designs. To make it easier for you to create your own needlepoint compositions, the motifs are scaled compatibly; that scale, of course, is appropriate to large-size canvas. And all the designs and motifs share the same color key, which immediately precedes the design pages.

Figure 11

Like the project designs in Part II, these motifs are all project-size in that they can be traced right off the book page onto canvas (or tracing paper), or they can be enlarged. If you want to refresh your technical skills, refer to Part I where tracing, extending, enlarging, cropping, and graphed designs are explained in detail.

LETTERS AND NUMBERS

At the end of the Design Workbook you will find two alphabets and a set of numbers. With these you can sign, initial, and/or date your needlework. The lowercase script alphabet is particularly nice for creating a "signature," the uppercase letters for a monogram, and the block letters for a contemporary look.

All the letters and numbers are presented in 10-to-the-inch size—that is, their page size duplicates their dimensions when used on No. 10 canvas. They can, of course, be used on No. 5 and No. 7 (or any other size) canvas, but the size of each figure increases as the canvas mesh gets larger (and decreases with a smaller-mesh canvas).

When using letters and numbers, it is essential to count out each stitch, following the graphs in the Design Workbook; they should not be traced from the book if you want to be sure of uniform figures. As you can see, each letter and number contains within its outline a certain number of boxes; each box of the graph designates one stitch, that is, one intersection of canvas. To make the relationship between graph boxes and canvas grid uniform, arbitrarily assign the upper right corner of each box as the intersection for the stitch (see Figure 12). And plan all arrangements of letters or numbérs on graph paper to keep the spacing between them balanced.

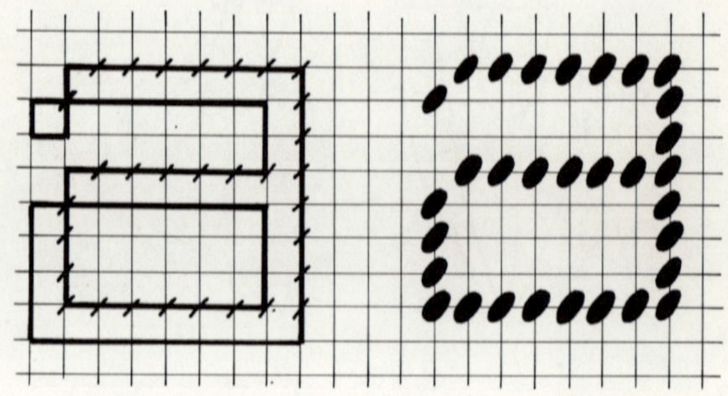

Figure 12

Color Key

- gold
- pink
- red-orange
- orange
- rust
- olive-green
- yellow-green
- royal blue
- gray
- black
- white
- 1 pale yellow
- 2 lemon yellow
- 3 golden yellow
- 4 brass
- 5 flesh
- 6 burnt orange
- 7 pale pink
- 8 hot pink
- 9 red
- 10 light green
- 11 kelly green
- 12 blue-green
- 13 dark green
- 14 gray-green
- 15 light blue
- 16 medium blue
- 17 navy blue
- 18 lavender
- 19 purple
- 20 fuchsia
- 21 aqua
- 22 turquoise
- 23 taupe
- 24 terra cotta
- 25 beige
- 26 medium brown
- 27 brown
- 28 cream

20
20
8
6
8
18
18
19
19
18
19
18
18
15
2
8
16
21
22
21
22
21
22
22
21
21
21
21
22
22
21
21
21

27
11
11
10
10
13
18
18
18
19
18
18
19
18
19
19
11
13
11
11
20
20
8
20
20
8
7
7
8
20
7
4
7
20
13
20
8
7
7
8
8
20
20
20
11
13

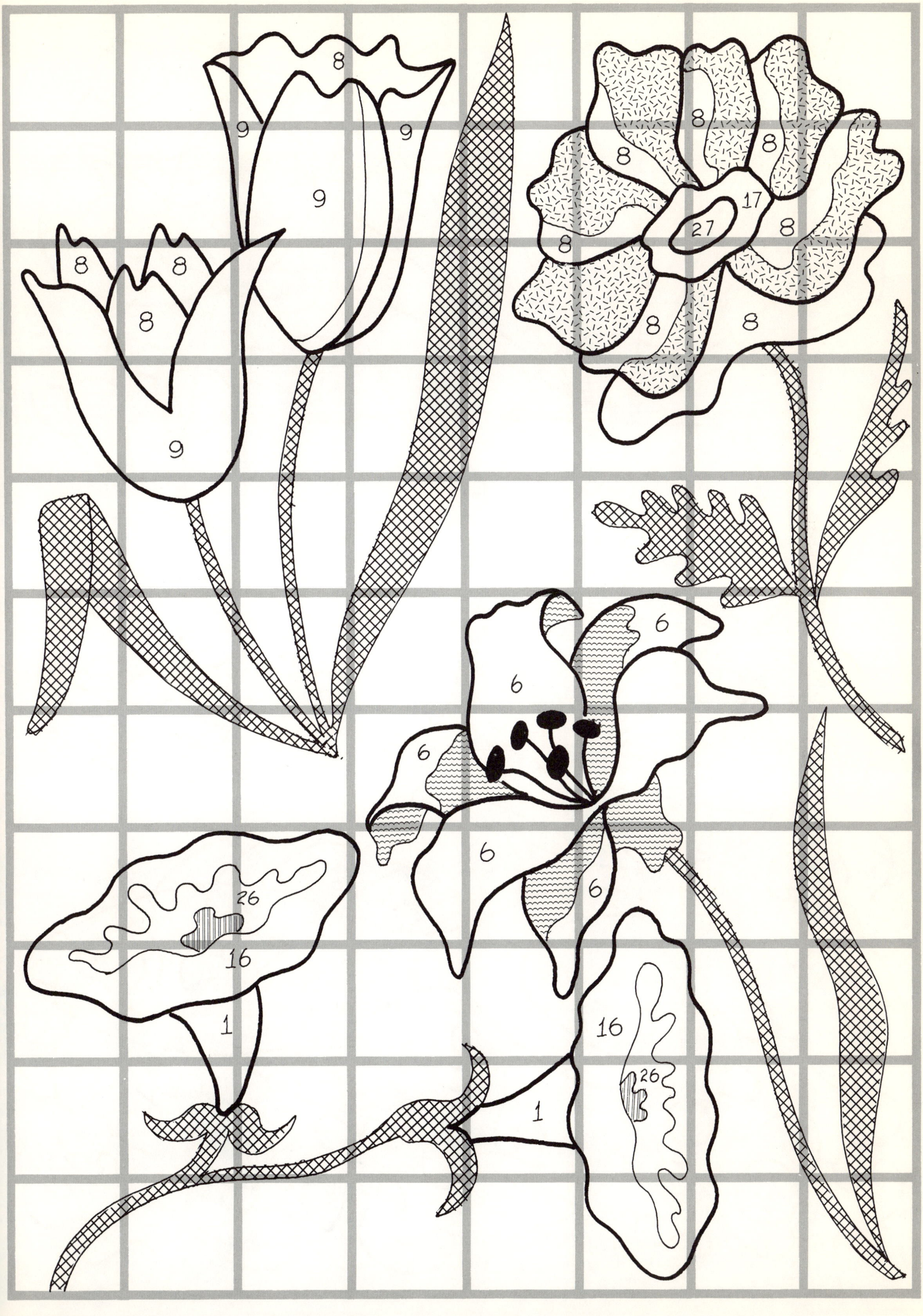
8
9
9
9
8
8
8
9
8
8
8
17
27
8
8
8
8
6
6
6
6
6
26
16
1
16
26
1

27
25
27
25
6
25
6
25
6
25
6
25
6
26
27
25
25
25
15
2
2
15
2
27
8
8
2
2
1
2
1
2
15
27
2
15
2
15
26
6
26
6
26
6
6
1
26
15
6
12
12

3
3
3
3
3
27
27
27
27
27
3
3
1
3
1
3
8
8
6
6
6
6
6
27
12
12
12
3
3

1
28
10
3
27
3
27
6
6
10
27
1
1
27
1
1
3
26
3
10
26

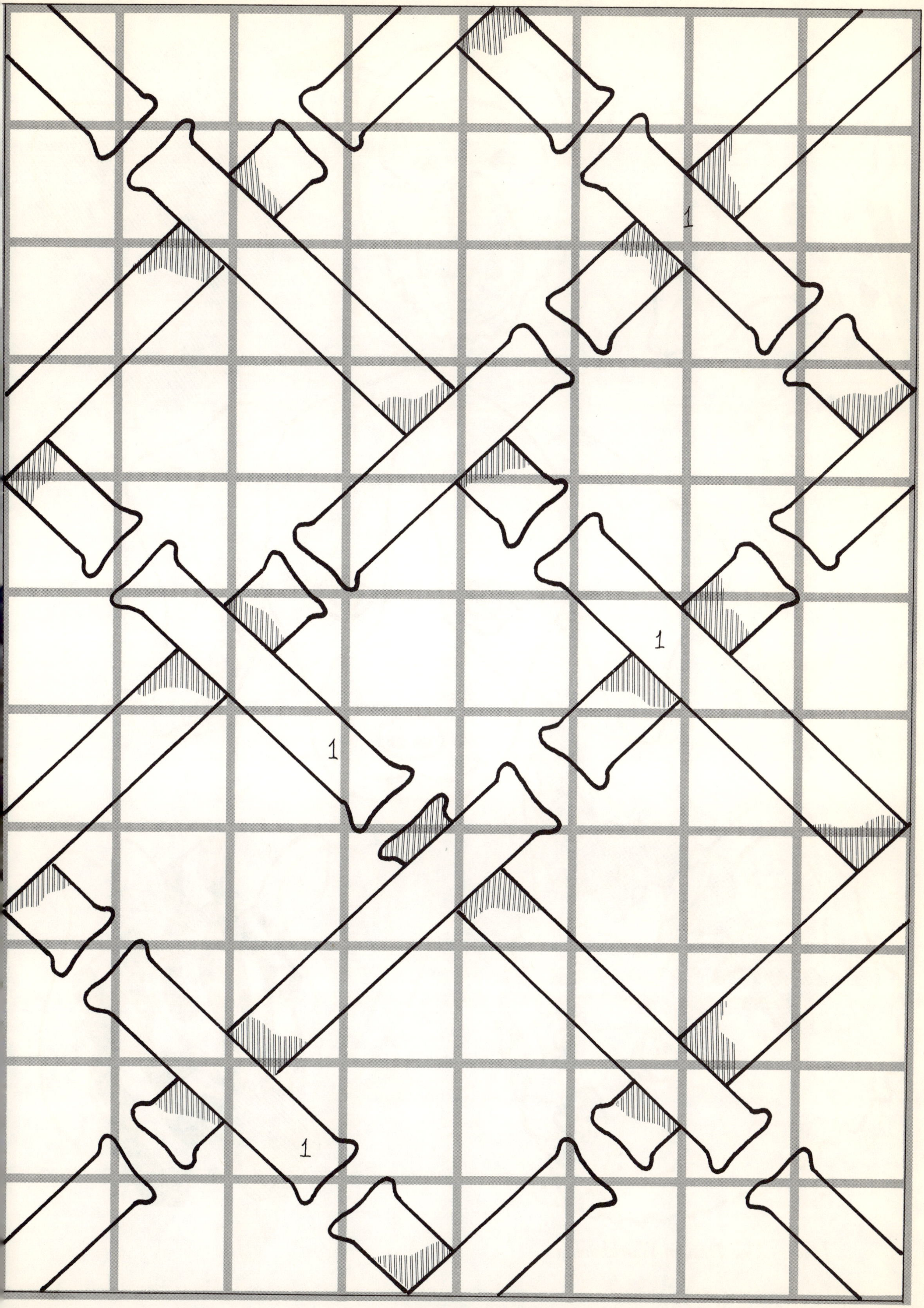
1
1
1
1

3
3
1
1
1
27
27
23
23
12
12
23
27
16
16
24
27
24

ORIENTAL DESIGNS

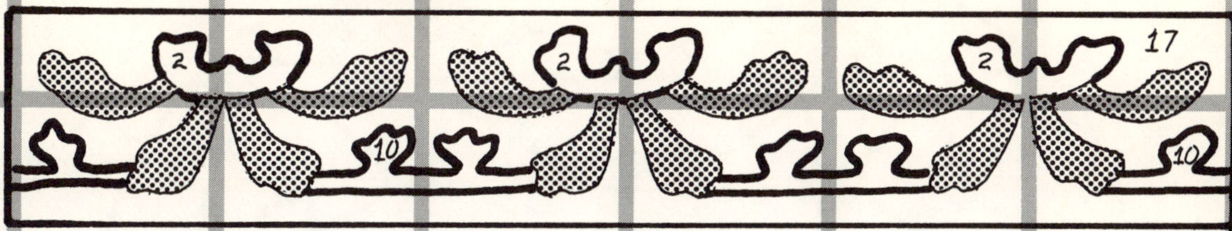

Lotus Border

Longevity

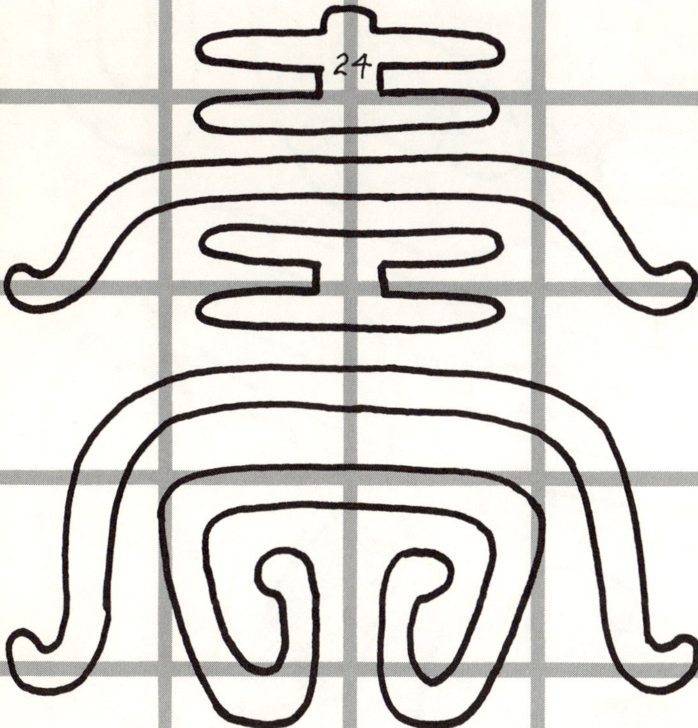

Double Joy

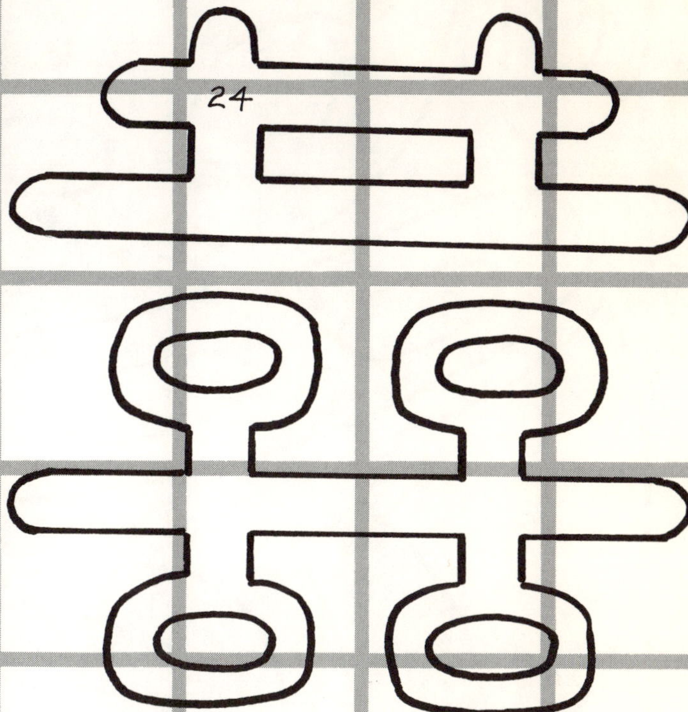

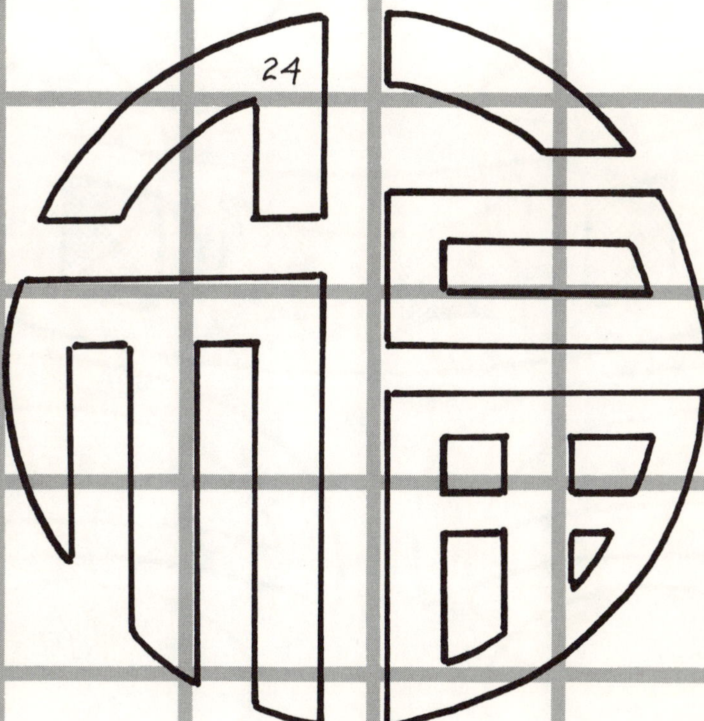

Prosperity

PRE-COLUMBIAN DESIGN

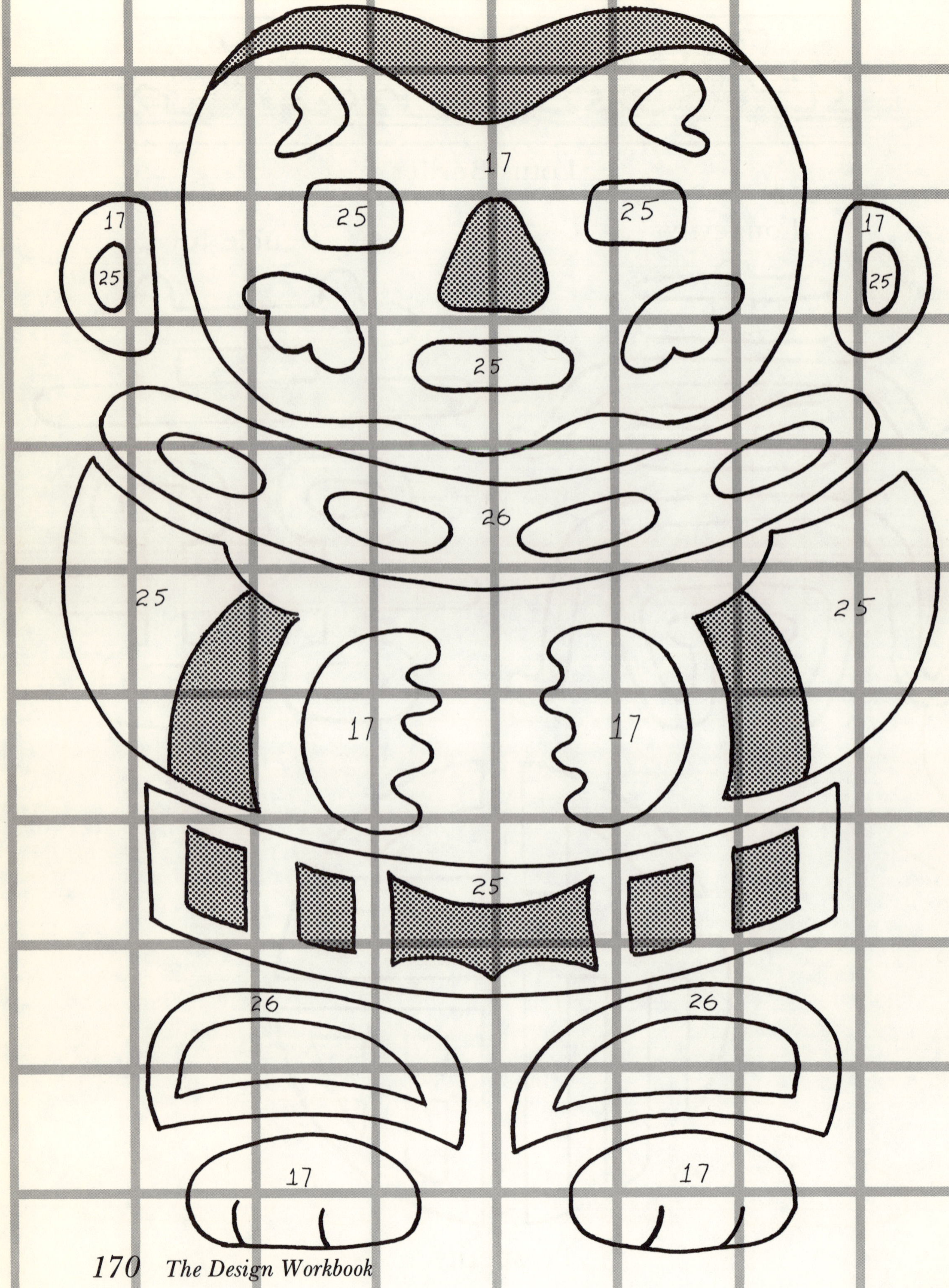

PRE-COLUMBIAN DESIGN

Aquarius

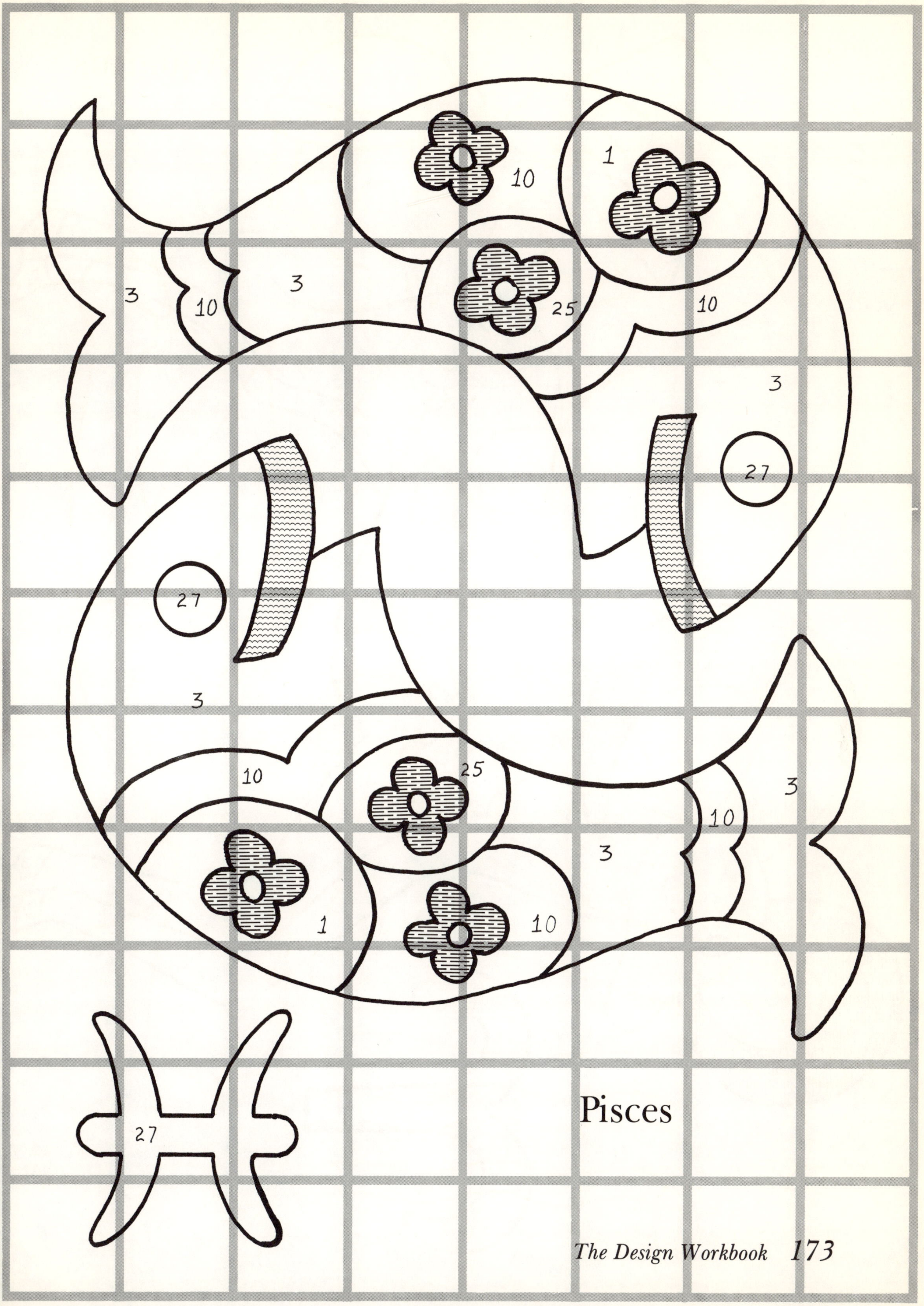

Pisces

Aries

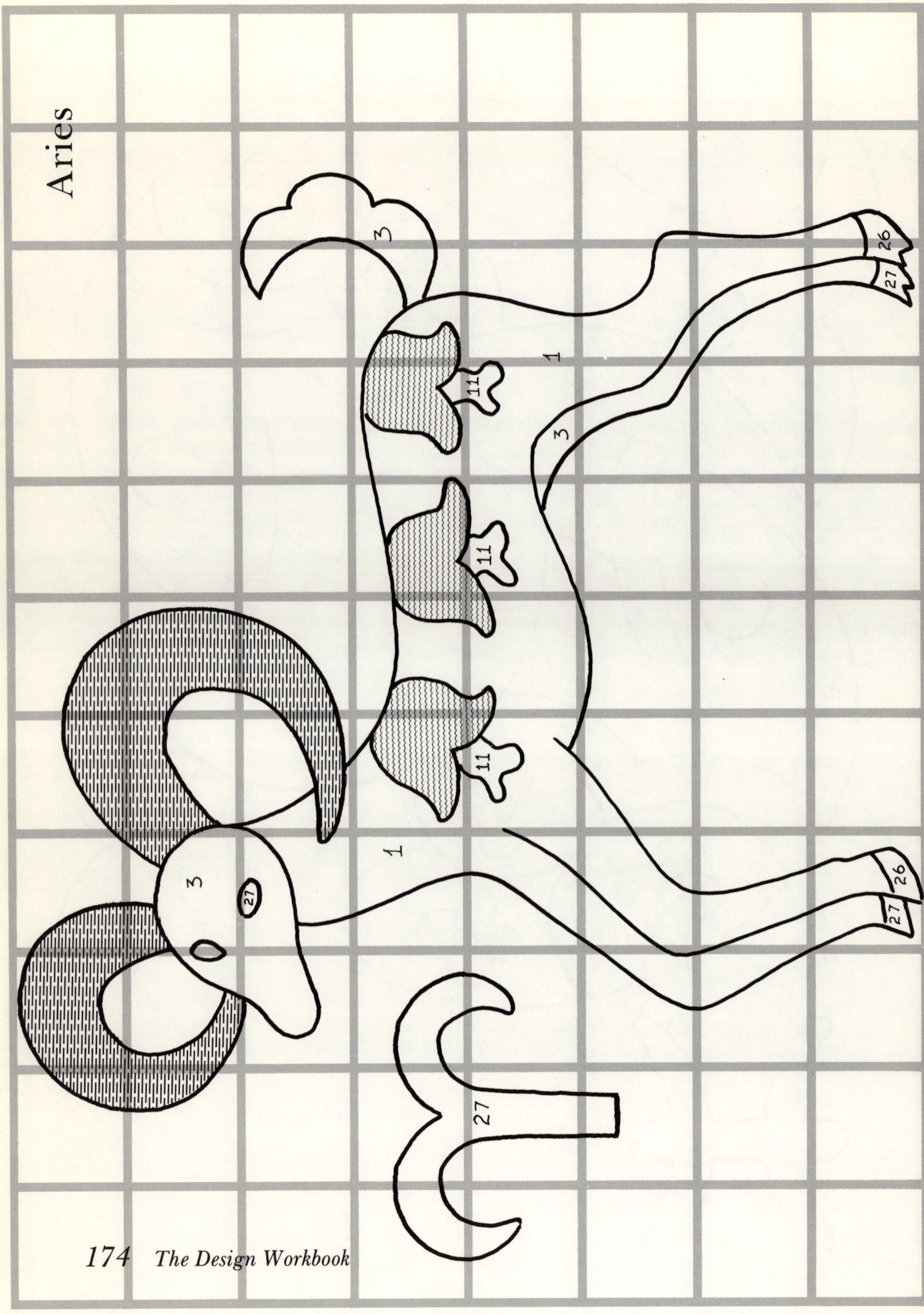

Taurus

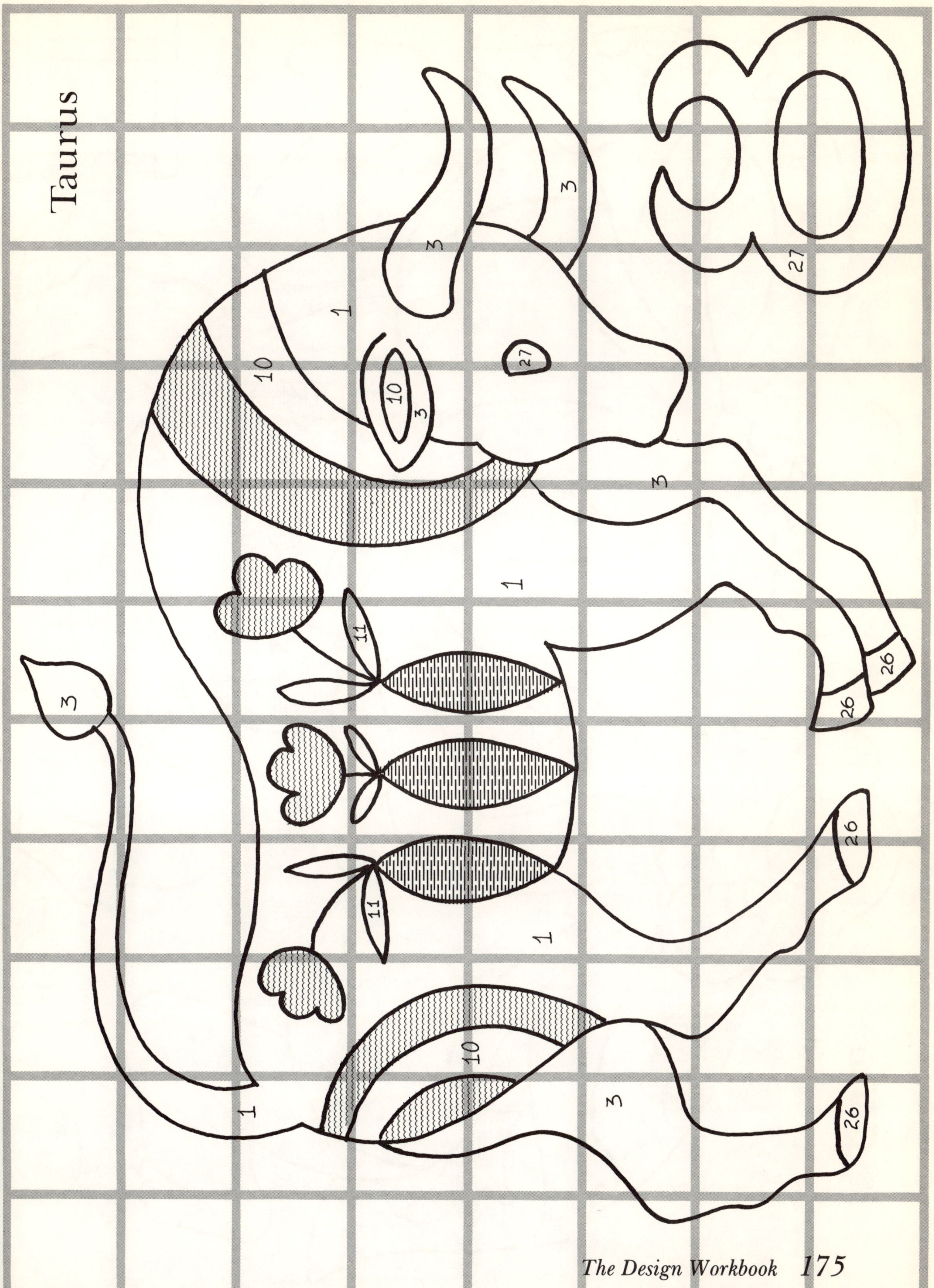

Gemini

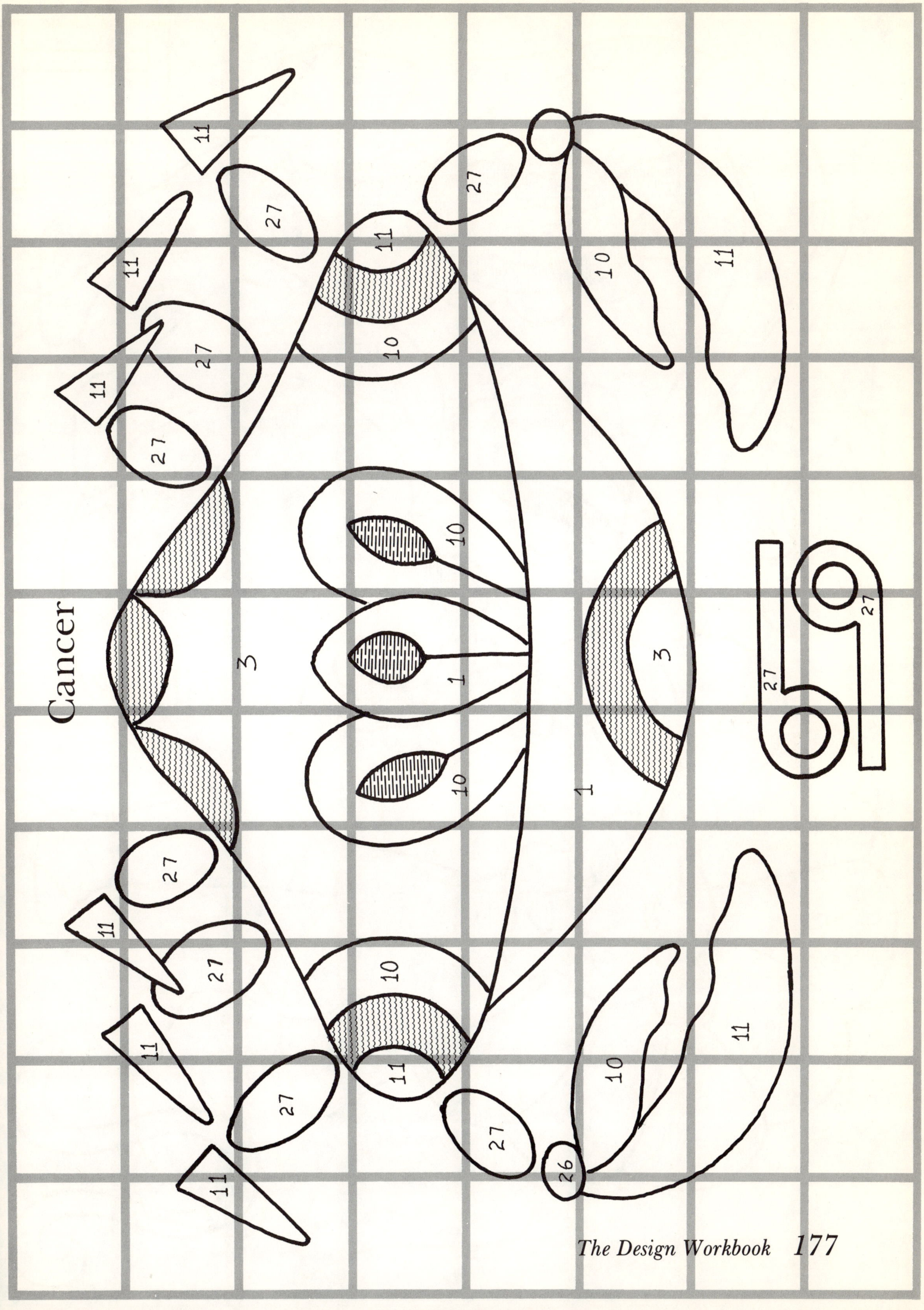
Cancer

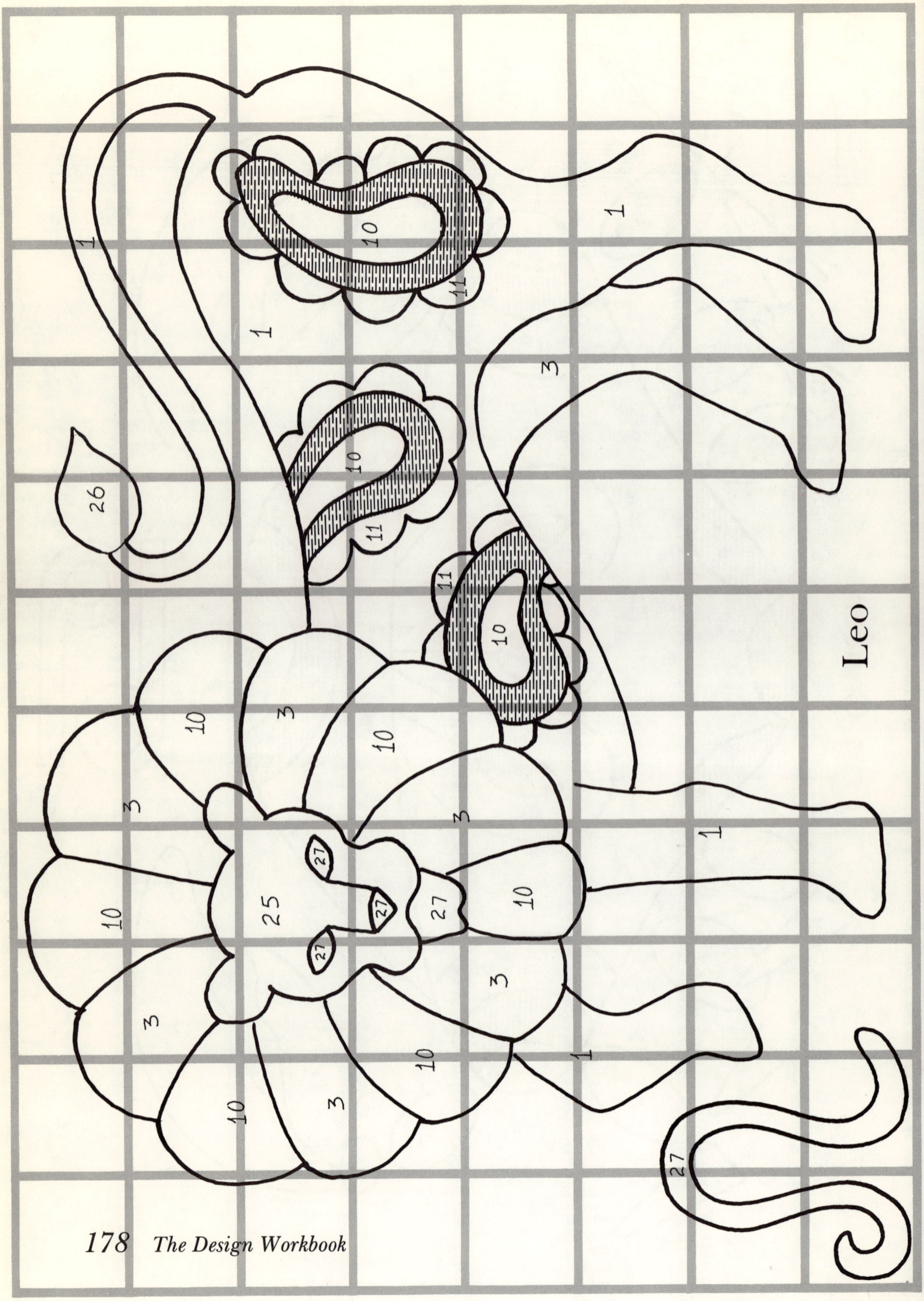

Leo

Virgo

Libra

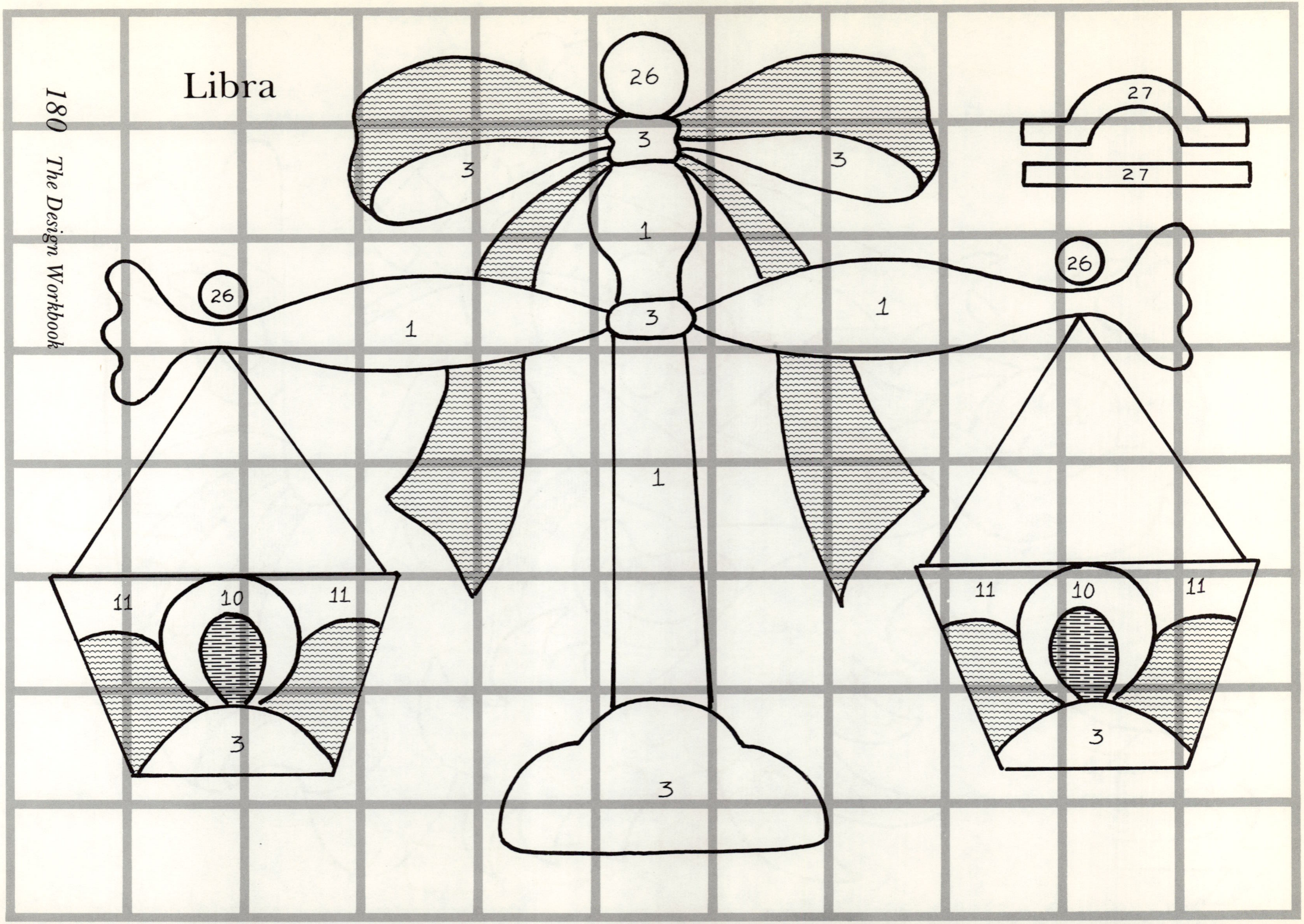

Scorpio

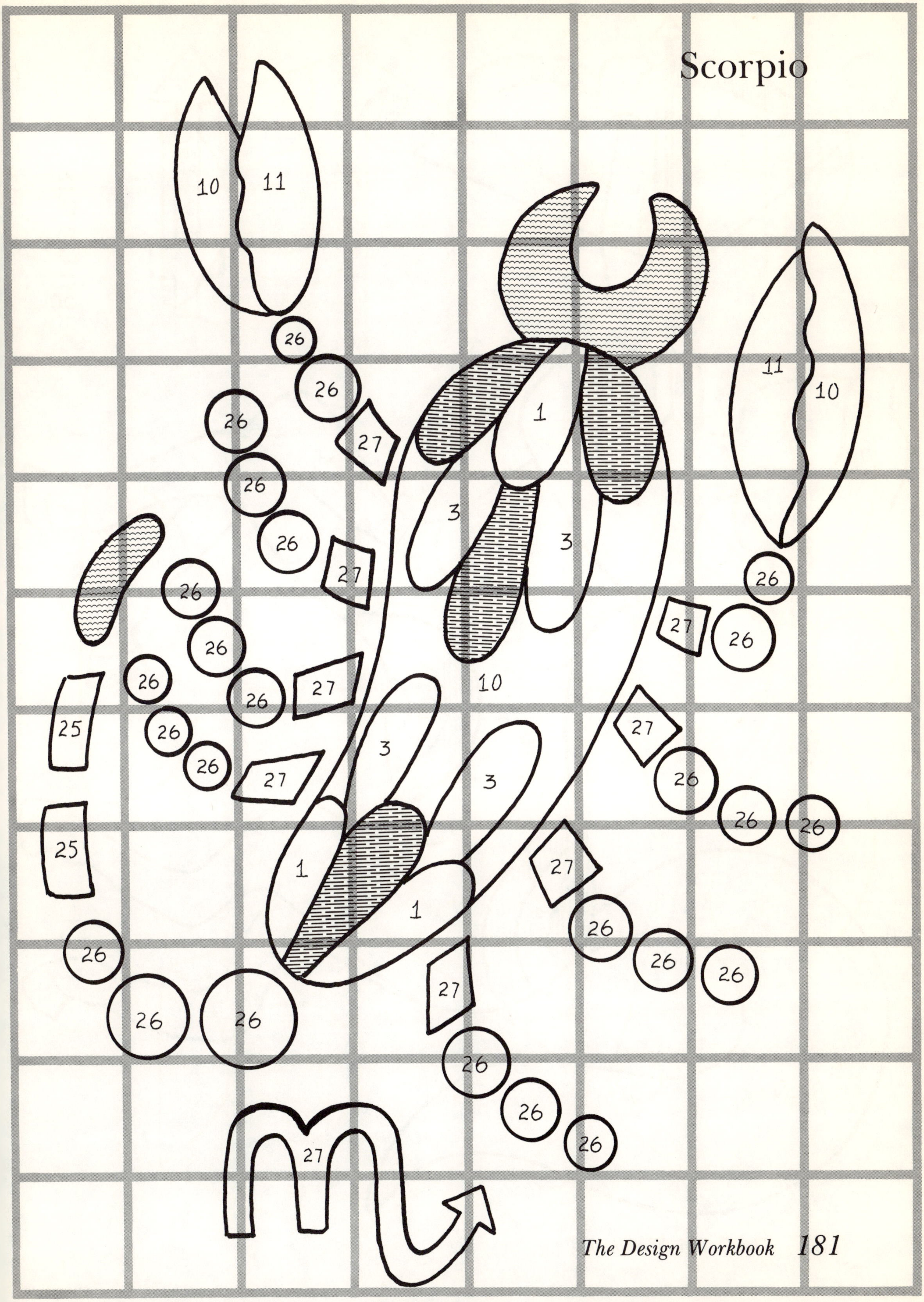

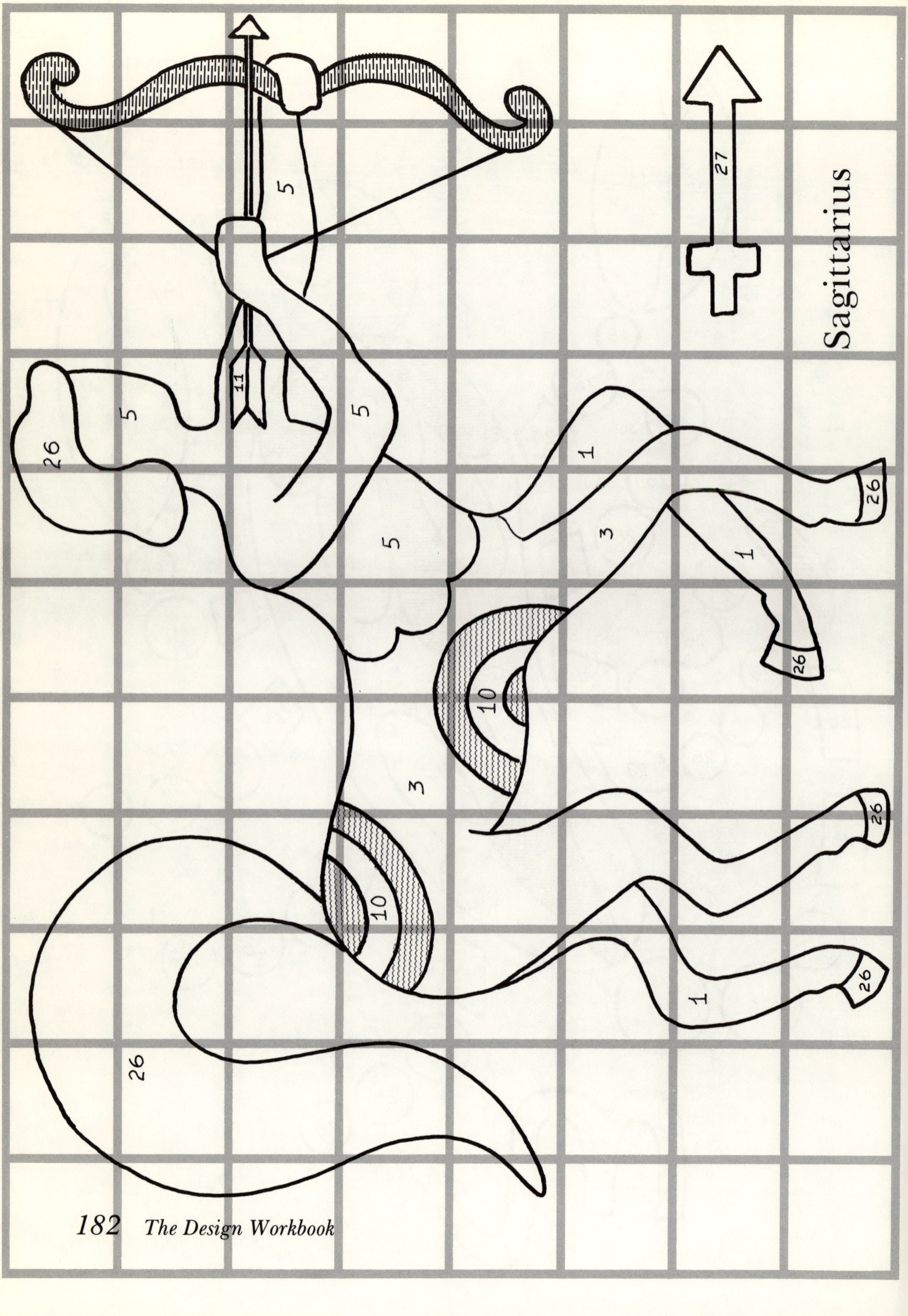
Sagittarius

Capricorn

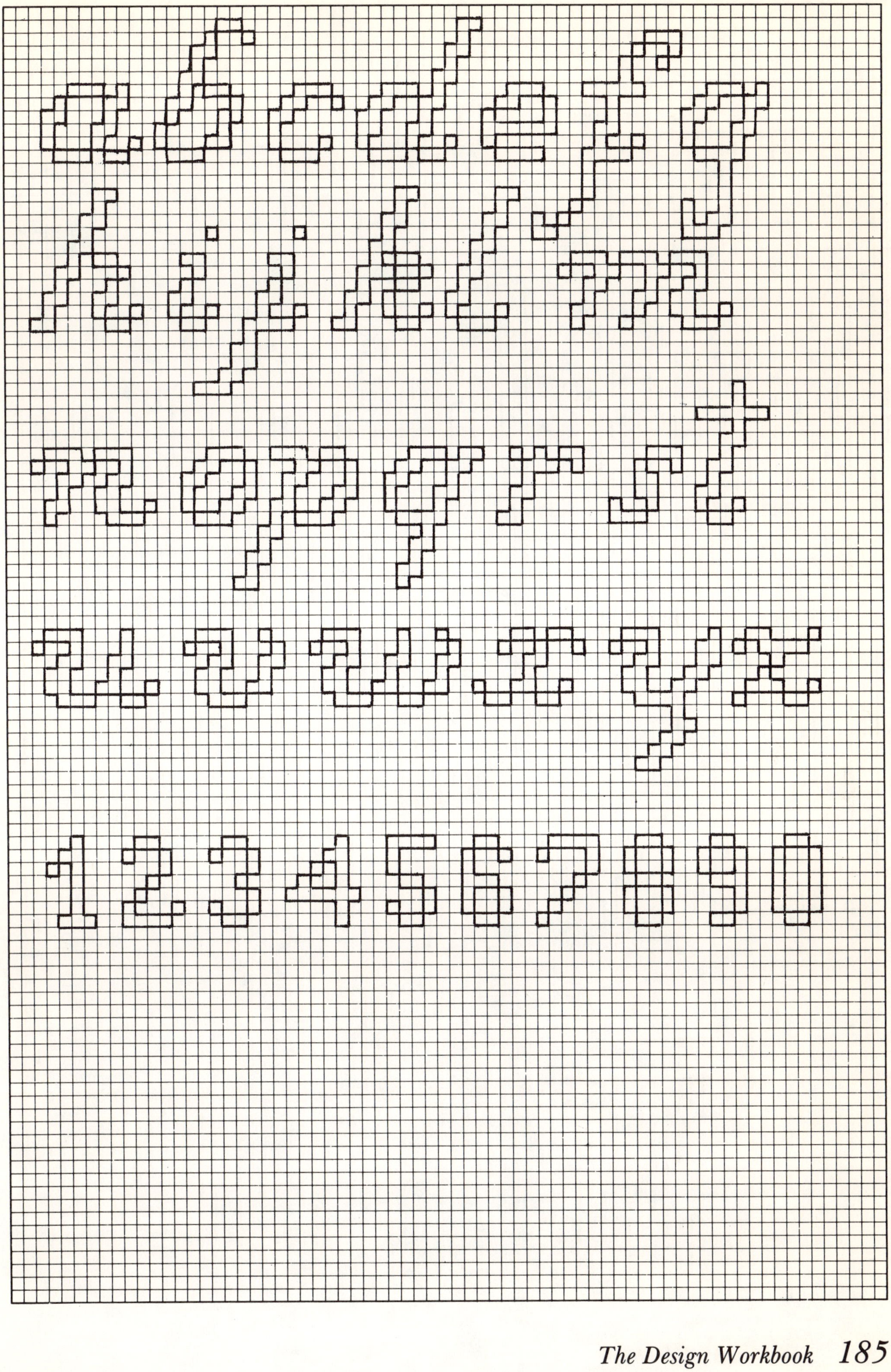
abcdefg
hijklm
nopqrst
uvwxyz
1234567890

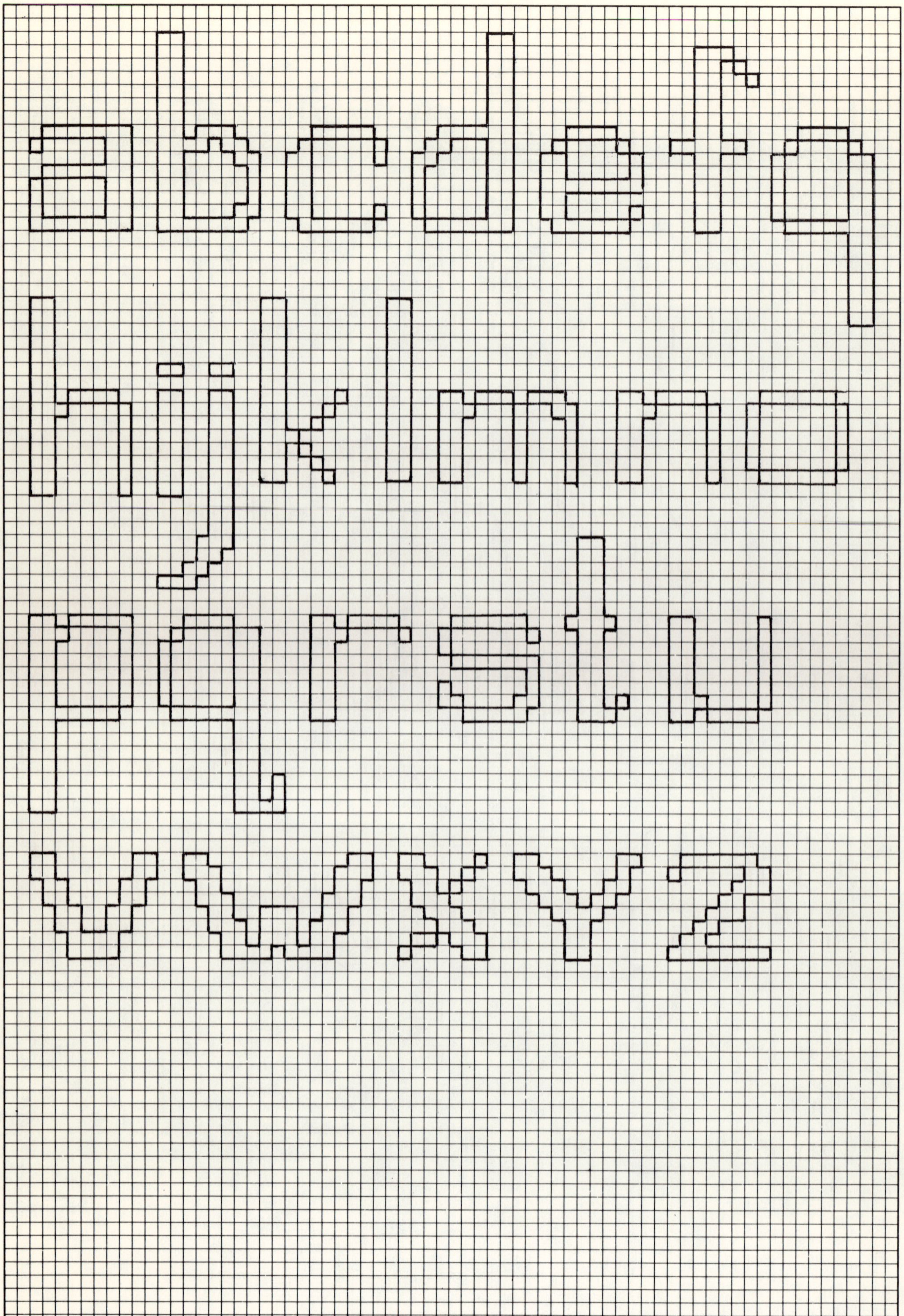
abcdefg
hijklmno
pqrstu
vwxyz

Sources of Supplies

Needlepoint supplies are carried by many shops, which will be listed in the classified pages of your local telephone book, usually under "Art Needlework." Department stores are also good sources, as are the mail order houses like Sears, Roebuck. Here are some retail sources listed alphabetically by state and by locality within states:

The Needleworks, 2906 Linden Ave., Birmingham, Ala. 35209

The Needlepoint Nook, 5037 North Seventh Ave., Phoenix, Ariz. 85013

Busy Work Needlepoint Studios, Inc., P.O. Box 609, Scottsdale, Ariz. 85252

Haystack, Ltd., Inc., 240 South Beverly Dr., Beverly Hills, Calif. 90212

The Nimble Thimble, 911 Capitola Ave. East, Capitola, Calif. 95010

Petit Point Junction, 373 North Robertson Blvd., Los Angeles, Calif. 90048

Lazy Daisy Needlecraft Shop, 602 East Walnut St., Pasadena, Calif. 91101

Nimble Needle, 2645 San Diego Ave., San Diego, Calif. 92110

The Knittery, 2040 Union St., San Francisco, Calif. 94123

The Yarn Depot, 545 Sutter St., San Francisco, Calif. 94102

The Needlecraft Shop, 4501 Van Nuys Blvd., Sherman Oaks, Calif. 91403

The Yarn Garden, Williams Village Shopping Center, 30th St. and Baseline Rd., Boulder, Colo. 80302

Golden Needle, 2356 East Third Ave., Denver, Colo. 80226

The Point, 755 South Colorado Blvd., Denver, Colo. 80222

The Designing Woman, Lakeville, Conn. 06039

The Yarnbee, 413 Main St., Ridgefield, Conn. 06877

The Daisy, 998 Farmington Ave., West Hartford, Conn. 06107

Colonial Yarn Shop, Inc., 3830 Kennett Pike, Wilmington, Del. 19807

Yarns Galore, Ponce de Leon Blvd., Coral Gables, Fla. 33134

Needlepoint Design by Lou Gartner, 312 Worth Ave., Palm Beach, Fla. 33480

Needle Nook, 6488 Central Ave., St. Petersburg, Fla. 33707

Papillon, Cates Plaza, 375 Pharr Rd., N.E., Atlanta, Ga. 30305

Needlepoint Works, Inc., 1660 North La Salle St., Chicago, Ill. 60614

Nimble Needles, 340 W. Armitage Ave., Chicago, Ill. 60614

Nina Needlepoint, 120 E. Delaware Pl., Chicago, Ill. 60611

Wild & Woolly, Inc., 5210 South Harper Ave., Chicago, Ill. 60615

LeeWards, Elgin, Ill. 60120

Magic Needle, 44 Green Bay Rd., Winnetka, Ill. 60093

Constance Ann's Needlepoint, 6502 East Westfield Blvd., Indianapolis, Ind. 46220

Craft Kaleidoscope, 6551 Fergeson St., Indianapolis, Ind. 46220

Town Stitchery, 6516 Cornell Ave., Indianapolis, Ind. 46220

The Little Needlepoint Shop, 223 Forest Rd., Davenport, Ia. 52803

Needle Nook, 7135 West 80th St., Kansas City, Kans.

Duquesa, 1901 Brookwood Rd., Shawnee Mission, Kans. 66208

The Crewel Cupboard, 15 East 8th St., Lawrence, Kans. 66044

The Quarter Stitch, 532 St. Peter St., New Orleans, La. 70130

Needlecraft Shop, Yorktowne Plaza Shopping Ctr., Baltimore, Md. 21030

Craft Kit & Caboodle, 10400 Old Georgetown Rd., Bethesda, Md. 20314

The Needlecraft Center, 1079 Rockville Pike, Rockville, Md. 20852

Nimble Fingers, Inc., 37 Newbury St., Boston, Mass. 02116

Nantucket Needleworks, Nantucket Island, Mass. 02554

The Stitchery, 204 Worcester Tpk., Wellesley, Mass. 02181

Needlecraft House, West Townsend, Mass. 01474

Needlepoint a la Carte, 325 South Woodward, Birmingham, Mich. 48011

Needle Arts, Inc., 2211 Monroe St., Dearborn, Mich. 48124

Peacock Alley, 650 Croswell St., S.E., Grand Rapids, Mich. 49506

The Needling Woman, 14421 Oak Park Rd., Oak Park, Mich. 48237.

The Jeweled Needle, 1009 Nicollet Ave., Minneapolis, Minn. 55403

Needlework Unlimited, Inc., 5028 France Ave. S., Minneapolis, Minn. 55410

The Picket Fence, Inc., 3924 Upton Ave. S., Minneapolis, Minn. 55410

Stitch Niche, France Ave. S., Minneapolis, Minn. 55408

In Stitches, 421 Nichols Rd., Kansas City, Mo. 64112

The Studio, 316 West 63 St., Kansas City, Mo. 64113

Krick Kits, 31 North Brentwood Blvd., St. Louis, Mo. 63105

Needlepoint Etc., 9841 Clayton Rd., St. Louis, Mo. 63124

Sign of the Arrow, 9740 Clayton Rd., St. Louis, Mo. 63124

Needlepoint Studio, 8707 Shamrock Rd., Omaha, Neb. 68114

The Knitting Needle, 2A McDonald Ave., Armonk, N.Y. 10504

T. E. Doelger, Box 126, Blauvelt, N.Y. 10913

Niddy Noddy, 416 Albany Post Rd., Croton-on-Hudson, N.Y. 10520

Hilde's Knit Shop, 305 White Plains Post Rd., Eastchester, N.Y. 10709

The Pot Holder, 525 Warburton Ave., Hastings-on-Hudson, N.Y. 10706

Eye of the Needle, 157 Larchmont Ave., Larchmont, N.Y. 10538

Art Needlework Treasure Trove, P.O. Box 2440, Grand Central Sta., New York, N.Y. 10017

Boutique Margot, 26 West 54 St., New York, N.Y. 10019

Coulter Studios, Inc., 118 East 59 St., New York, N.Y. 10022

Alice Maynard, 724 Fifth Ave., New York, N.Y. 10019

Mazaltov's, Inc., 61 West 23 St., New York, N.Y. 10010

Nina Needlepoint, 860 Madison Ave., New York, N.Y. 10021

Selma's Art Needlework, 1645 Second Ave., New York, N.Y. 10028

Erica Wilson, Inc., 717 Madison Ave., New York, N.Y. 10021

Black Sheep, 48 Purchase St., Rye, N.Y. 10580

Handy Lady, 72 Garth Rd., Scarsdale, N.Y. 10583

Wild & Wooly, 57 Willow Pond Rd., Staten Island, N.Y. 10304

The Needleworks, 90 East Post Rd., White Plains, N.Y. 10606

The Stitching Post, Inc., 131 East Post Rd., White Plains, N.Y. 10606

Needlepoint Only, 12801 Larchmere Blvd., Cleveland, Ohio 44120

Contemporary Stitchery, 2905 North High St., Columbus, Ohio 43202

Needlepoint Designs, 5210 E. Main St., Columbus, Ohio 43213

Elizabeth Lamprey Studio, 5940 S. Lewis Ave., Tulsa, Okla. 74105

Creative Hands, 515 S.W. Broadway, Portland, Ore. 97205.

Flying Colours, 1016 S.W. Morrison, Portland, Ore. 97205.

The Needlepoint Garden, 7518 Haverford Ave., Philadelphia, Pa. 19151

The Needle's Eye, 1724 Sansom St., Philadelphia, Pa. 19103

Sophisti-Kits, P.O. Box 5020, Pittsburgh, Pa. 15206

The Thread Shed, Inc., 307 Freeport Rd., Pittsburgh, Pa. 15215

Sinkler Needlepoint Studio, 223 Iven Ave., Radnor, Pa. 19087

Needlepointer, 793 Hope St., Providence, R.I. 02906

Indie, 618 South Semmes St., Memphis, Tenn. 38111

Canvas Patch Originals, P.O. Box 3072, Oak Ridge, Tenn. 37830

Needle Art Boutique, 2800 Routh St., Dallas, Tex. 75201

Needlework Patio, 6925 Snider Plaza, Dallas, Tex. 75205

The Knit Shop, 3516 South Shepherd Dr., Houston, Tex. 77006

Knit-Wits, 1379 East 3205 St. South, Salt Lake City, Utah 84106

Needlecraft, Ltd., 1615 Foothill Dr., Salt Lake City, Utah 84108

Three Bags Full, Manchester Ctr., Vt. 05255

Yarn Bazaar, 421 South Washington St., Alexandria, Va. 22314

Yarns Etcetera, 215 King St., Alexandria, Va. 22314

Needlework Nook, 431 Forest Ave., Richmond, Va. 23223

Corner Stitch, Ltd., 25th & Pacific Ave., Virginia Beach, Va. 23451

The Needlepoint Studio, 1501 Fifth Ave., Seattle, Wash. 98115

The Needle Works, 4518 39th Place N.E., Seattle, Wash., 98105

The Needleworks, 116 West Silver Spring Dr., Milwaukee, Wis. 53217

Ruhama's Yarn & Fabrics, 420 Silver Spring Dr., Milwaukee, Wis. 53217

Frederick Herrschner Co., Hoover Rd., Stevens Point, Wis. 54481

CANADIAN SOURCES

The Added Touch, 3026 Granville St., Vancouver, B.C.

Woolcraft (B.C.) Ltd., 512 West Hastings St., Vancouver, B.C.

Needleworks, 156 Spence St., Winnipeg, Man.

Martha Borbas Needlepoint Gallery, 1613 Bayview Ave., Toronto, Ont.

In Stitches Gallery, 102 Yorkville St., Toronto, Ont.

Brickpoint Studios, 2195 Crescent St., Montreal, Que.

Jeannette's Needlecraft Shoppe, 5322 Queen Mary St., Montreal, Que.

ACCESSORIES FOR NEEDLEPOINT

Giftiques Unlimited, P.O. Box 412, Little Neck, N.Y. 11363, for simulated leather desk accessories, such as picture frames, photo album covers, desk sets, paperweights, jewel boxes, and address- and engagement-book covers.

Sudberry House, Box 421, Old Lyme, Conn. 06371 for wood products for needlepoint, such as chairs, footstools, serving and desk trays, game boards for backgammon and chess, coasters, and Bermuda bags.

Toni Totes of Vermont, Inc., Rte. 100, South Londonderry, Vt. 05155 for prefinished handbags, totes, racquet covers, pillows, and belts for needlepoint as well as Lucite accessories, such as desk pads, bookends, coasters, eyeglass caddies, magazine racks, and backgammon sets.

Index

Boldface type indicates design page for project